FREDERICK ALBERT BEEDIE was born in May 1925 in Portsmouth, Hampshire, where he lived with his parents and siblings, until moving to Wallisdown, Dorset to escape the blitz of Portsmouth, during World War Two. He left school aged fourteen and joined the Royal Navy when he was seventeen.

On leaving the Royal Navy he served with the Mercantile Marine (more commonly known as the Merchant Navy). After that he worked as an aircraft fitter at Hurn Airport, near Bournemouth, and in various engineering jobs thereafter.

Fred has always been a keen historian, particularly of WW2, and reader of factual books. He also follows sport, particularly cricket, tennis and golf. He played cricket as a young man, being named Mr. Persil by his fellow cricketers, because his 'whites were always the whitest!'

His wife Joy and he were married for over seventy years – sadly Joy passed away in August 2019 she was a great help to Fred during the writing of his memoir. They have two daughters, two sons, six grandchildren, nine great-grandchildren and four great-great-grandchildren.

Fred now lives in a care home in Bridport, Dorset, where he is visited often by his family.

His memoir has taken two years to write and publish. His daughter Jackie typed the story from his own handwritten notes. Not a bad feat to have written 93,000 odd words at the age of ninety-four!

Fred's story is written from memory of events that happened seventy-five years ago. Consequently some of the detail may have been different, but the whole story is true. There may be some terminology which, if writing a memoir about the age we live in now, would not be used, but we have decided not to change it, as to do so would not reflect how things we have been changed to ensure the privacy of the people involved.

We hope that you enjoy reading this story of an ordinary acting able seaman, H.O., living in an extraordinary time in our history.

Acting Able Seaman – Hostilities Only

A Memoir

ACTING ABLE SEAMAN – HOSTILITIES ONLY

A Memoir

F A BEEDIE

SilverWood

Published in 2019 by SilverWood Books

SilverWood Books Ltd
14 Small Street, Bristol, BS1 1DE, United Kingdom
www.silverwoodbooks.co.uk

Front cover image: Winton, during leave,
having finished the course at Whale Island.

ISBN 978-1-78132-931-3 (paperback)
ISBN 978-1-78132-960-3 (ebook)

British Library Cataloguing in Publication Data
A CIP catalogue record for this book is
available from the British Library

Page design and typesetting by SilverWood Books
Printed on responsibly sourced paper

For my dear wife Joy

Contents

Acknowledgements

Special thanks to my daughter Jackie for the many hours she has put in, to make this book possible, and her husband John for his help with research.

Thank you also to my daughter Sandra and my sons Richard and David for their encouragement during the writing of my memoir.

Chapter One

Portsmouth before the War

I left school in August of 1939 aged fourteen. War was declared a month later in September, which meant that I was too old to be evacuated. My two younger brothers, Reg, aged twelve, and Ron, aged ten, were told to get ready for evacuation. My mother was very upset but realised that they had to go, and so off they went to Broughton in Hampshire. This left my father, mother, older sister Jean, aged eighteen, older brother John, or Jock as he was often called, aged sixteen, and myself at home. Jock was an apprentice in an engineering company. We all realised that we were in for a hard time.

A year or so before the outbreak of war, everybody was given a gas mask which was issued in a small cardboard box with a looped string to carry over the shoulder (we were all convinced that the German Airforce would drop gas bombs on us). At school, we would be doing lessons, a whistle would blow, 'Air Raid!' shouted, and we would all quietly stand up and file outside to the air-raid shelter and sit down. The shout 'Gas Masks On!' would fill the air and we would quickly comply. We would sit quietly until the 'all-clear' was given, at which point we would remove our gas masks, storing them safely away in the cardboard box and return quietly to our classrooms to resume lessons. This would happen about twice a week.

Portsmouth was very fortunate to have wise City Fathers, who knew that war was inevitable, despite the Prime Minister Neville Chamberlain coming back from Munich waving a piece of paper and stating, 'Peace in our time!' They started to prepare for war, Anderson shelters[1] were placed in every garden, Morrison shelters[2], named after the M.P. Herbert Morrison, were placed in houses with no gardens, static water tanks were built at the end of roads – made of very hard brick, then filled with hundreds of gallons of water ready for use if water mains were broken during air raids. Also built on the other end of roads, were splinter-proof shelters built with the same hard brick. These shelters would not withstand a direct hit, but hopefully would withstand a near miss.

As we feared, after hearing the news of imminent war, times were indeed hard, with unemployment being very high. I had a paper round at thirteen years of age – I used to get up at 04.30 wash, dress and have a cup of tea and piece of toast which my mother made for me. Then it was off to Marsden the newsagent by 05.00. The papers would soon be delivered by Owens the wholesalers van and I would be off on my paper round on a carrier bike, finishing around 07.30 when I would dash off home for my usual bowl of porridge before getting ready to go to school. There was no school uniform in those days. This was my routine all week.

At weekends I would be up at 04.30 as usual to do my paper round, back home for breakfast by 07.30 then off to Coopers the butcher's, whose shop was just around the corner from the road in which we lived. I would deliver meat all around the area on a carrier bike. At dinner time I'd have a quick sandwich, then the shop would be scrubbed from back to front, including the shop front and the pavement outside down to the kerb. Work would finish around 16.30, and the butcher would give me my 1/6 d, plus a piece of beef, a lump of dripping and a breast of mutton – this meant that Sunday dinner was safe and sound!

I also had a evening paper round, delivering the *Portsmouth Evening News*. Mr Marsden would pay me five shillings, this and the 1/6 d from the butcher's would go to my mother, who was a hard-working mum and housewife. I never had a ha-penny pocket money in my life – my mother would give me some money back, but I did not consider this to be pocket money!

One Sunday morning I was cleaning my brother's bike in the front garden when I saw a soldier coming up the road, his uniform torn and muddy. As he got closer I could see that he was unshaven, his eyes bloodshot. I said to him, 'Is that you Georgie French?' 'Yes,' he replied. 'You're a right mess!' I observed.

'I'm just back from Dunkirk,' he told me. 'I told the officer in charge of the returning soldiers, that I lived in Portsmouth, and I've been given fourteen days' leave, fourteen days' pay and fourteen days' ration tokens and told to be back in fourteen days. My mother is going to get a big surprise when I walk through the door!'

He was a great friend but I do not know if he survived the war, he deserved to – what's more, he gave me his tin helmet, which was painted in camouflage colours. That tin helmet became my constant companion – I took it everywhere with me!

Chapter Two

Portsmouth during the Blitz

The German air raids started in July of 1940. Some raids were made by up to three hundred aircraft. There were also 'hit and run' raids and lone nuisance raiders. After the first raid, which killed and injured many people, my mother and father decided to make the Anderson shelter as comfortable as possible. Every night they would fill the bath, pots and pans and kettle with water in case the water mains got hit. Candles and paraffin oil were almost impossible to buy. Thermos flasks became like gold dust. Luckily, 'wise' Mum managed to buy two and these would be filled with tea. Light was provided by Dad's torch.

At the sound of the air-raid siren, we would move down to the shelter. The noise of guns and bombs was terrible. One particular bomb exploded quite near. I remember saying to my dad, 'That was close Dad!' He replied, 'Don't worry about the ones we can hear, it will be the one we don't hear that will get us!'

At school we were told that if any of us were to be caught out in a day raid and could not make it to a shelter, we were to lie in the gutter and place our hands behind our heads and hope for the best!

Lone raiders would come from the captured French airfields. Flying just above the waves they would swoop up and over the land, machine-gunning and dropping bombs. This happened one Saturday morning when my mother was in Coopers the butcher's with other customers – all buying their weekly ration of meat. I was riding my butcher's bike back to the shop when a lone raider appeared from nowhere. The butcher quickly put all the women in the shop, including my mother, into the refrigerator, they were all really frightened. I dropped off the bike and lay in the gutter putting my hands behind my head as told to do in school. A terrific blast of hot air picked me and the bike up in the air and took us diagonally across the road some thirty feet before dropping me back to the ground. I was a little bruised and the bike was a little bent!

One of my classmates, Bertie, who came from a very poor family and suffered from rickets, was not so lucky. He got caught in the blast as he tried to run to the nearest shelter. The blast took him high in the air and dropped him hard back to the ground: he was killed instantly. I cried, 'What has Bertie done to be killed like that?' but no one answered.

Bertie and his family lived a few houses down the road from us, next to them lived the Middams. Johny Middam, who was about twenty years old, was lying in bed seriously ill with consumption. His mother would call on her neighbours, including my mother, to ask for clothes, which she would wash and place under Johny's chin to help him dribble his life away. Johny was unable to get to the Anderson shelter during raids, so his mother and father used to sit by his bed and stick it out with him.

After a night raid the 'all-clear' would sound and my father, next-door neighbour Mr. Stribley and myself would go outside to put out any incendiary bombs. Mr. Stribley had a wheelbarrow full of earth and a spade. Any incendiary bombs still burning would have two spadefuls of earth thrown over them.

On one occasion, we were out looking for incendiary bombs in a garden area surrounded by a high wall. My father and I were sitting astride the wall facing each other, my father had hurt his arm and was calling the Germans all the names under the sun. I started to laugh and he gave me a backhander that knocked me clean off the wall! I landed in the garden – that taught me not to laugh at my dad! Mr. Stribley handed Dad the spade, he threw it down to me and I got up and went and threw some earth on a couple more incendiary bombs – nothing more to say.

After leaving school I worked in a small sweet factory, where all types of confectionery were made and placed in glass jars, labelled on the front with the name of the sweets inside. It was my job to deliver these jars to the sweet shops in the area. I rode a very heavy tricycle which had a container-like box fitted on the front. The pay was about fifteen shillings a week for a five-day week.

Making my way to work one day, there had been a fairly heavy raid, houses had been on fire, hoses were all across the road, debris scattered everywhere, firemen working hard to dampen down the fires. I stopped by one burned house. Members of the Heavy Rescue service were bringing out the charred body of a woman, and fused to her breast was the body of a baby. Those heavy rescue men, eyes red rimmed with tiredness, lifted the body of that woman and her baby as if they were made of porcelain.

The raids continued in 1941. I remember one which seemed to last for ever. Three hundred planes dropped bombs, incendiary bombs and what we hated the most, land mines. These were about the size of a pillar box, carrying about a a ton of explosives; they drifted down to earth on parachutes. A ordinary bomb would enter the ground and explode upwards. Landmines would hit the ground flat and the explosion would go out horizontally, creating a vast amount of devastation. Over thirty of these were dropped on Portsmouth during the war. Planes would sometimes fly over the city to bomb Southampton, Exeter and Plymouth. Later, these would be intercepted by our night fighters.

Johny Middam was still clinging to life, tended by his devoted mother and father, night after night.

During the lull of one particularly heavy raid, Mr. Stribley climbed over the fence and looked into our shelter. He was worried about the old woman living next door to him. She was a recluse and did not want to know anybody (I can never remember seeing her). She had refused an Anderson shelter. Dad agreed that she should be in a shelter and went with Mr. Stribley to her house. They banged on the front door but she told them to 'Go away!' The raid started again and Dad shouted that he was going to break down the door, which he did. He and Mr. Stribley put the old woman, kicking and screaming, into Mr. Stribley's wheelbarrow and wheeled her to one of the splinterproof shelters, where A.R.P. Wardens took care of her, much to Dad's and Mr. Stribley's relief! After the raid, Mr. Stribley repaired the old woman's door. I don't think he ever received any thanks.

Chapter Three

The move to Wallisdown, Dorset, 1941

My father was born in Montrose, Scotland in 1878. His father and two brothers were Wild Salmon fishermen, fishing off the coast of Montrose and Aberdeen. They were hard, tough men. Dad finished his schooling aged thirteen and went to sea as a fisher boy. He wore a glengarry bonnet, a green jersey and a kilt. Nothing on his feet or his backside! He grew up as tough as his father and brothers.

Dad served in the Royal Naval Reserve. When the First World War was declared he was called up and drafted to Portsmouth where he met and married my mother. Throughout WWI he served on minesweepers. When the war was finally over, he joined the Mercantile Marine, as he called it (not the Merchant Navy).

He served aboard all types of ship in the Mercantile Marine, working in the engine room as an engineer. He finally left the sea in 1938 aged sixty. Meanwhile, my two younger brothers had moved from Broughton and were living in a village in Hampshire called Wallisdown. The road that ran through the middle of the village was rather unique as on one side was

Hampshire and the other Dorset.

My mother and father would visit them regularly and after one visit they decided to move from the dangers of Portsmouth to the relative quietness of Wallisdown.

My sister remained in service where she was settled in her work. My brother Jock was able to transfer to another engineering company. Dad and I had to find jobs, Reg and Ron were still at school. Mum remained a hard-working housewife.

Dad had picked out a three-bedroomed bungalow (of which there were many in the area) and arranged the rent conditions. Arrangements were made with a well-known Bournemouth furniture remover and a couple of days later the removal van arrived in Portsmouth to take our possessions to Wallisdown. The driver and his mate were two of the 'windiest' men I have ever come across, presumably because they were frightened that after five o'clock, the raids might start. All we got out of them was 'We must be out of Portsmouth by five o'clock!' repeated over and over again, although it was 'double' summertime and never got dark until about 2300 hours.

Five o'clock came and we had not quite finished. The two brave furniture removers said, 'That's it' and proceeded to close the doors of the van. How my dad stopped himself from laying his hands on them I'll never know! Jock, myself and Dad got in the back of the lorry. Mum sat in the front between our two heroes, she never even had time to take her apron off! Sadly, we didn't have time to say goodbye to our neighbours and friends.

Luckily we had an uncle, John, who lived further up the road on the right-hand side. Uncle John was a very nice man, he had served in the army in the First World War. His left arm had been badly slashed by a bayonet and he was also badly beaten and taken as a Prisoner of War.

I also had another uncle, Wilfred, who lived in the next road. He also served in the army; he had only been on the front line for four hours when a shell burst in the trenches and he was buried. When they dug him out, he was found with his leg hanging off and thirteen other body wounds. How he survived I'll never know! He was always grumpy and I put that down to his wounds.

Between them, the two uncles managed to finish clearing the house.

It did not take very long to get to Wallisdown. The attitude of the two 'warriors' changed dramatically when it came to a 'tip' – whether they expected one or not I don't know, but they never got one!

We soon settled in, what a difference! So peaceful, so clean, so quiet, we could hear birds singing. We all slept peacefully that night. Apart from Jean, the family was all together again.

Chapter Four

Life in Wallisdown

The road through Wallisdown ran from east to west, the road eastwards ran from the centre of the village towards Bournemouth; there were a few shops, and a pub, The Kings Arms. Four or five hundred yards further on was a church, opposite the church was Purchase and Vines Farm, whose fields ran back along the road and finished opposite the pub. There was also a post office, and few shops and houses going out of the village.

To the east was the Lodge Gates where one of the village lads lived with his parents. The road was quite long, almost a mile. Either side of the road was common ground and gorse which extended quite a long way either side of the road. In a hollow on the left side was a gypsy encampment, with their caravans and horses. Nobody ventured down there – the locals called it Heavenly Bottom.

The same road going eastwards reached a T-junction. Turning left went to Poole, turning right towards Ringwood. On the right-hand side was an engineering firm, a subsidiary of Whitehead Torpedoes Portland, they made underwater weaponry. The firm was supervised by a Commander Royal Navy, a White

Ensign flew at the head of a flag pole. My dad was fortunate to get a job there, looking after the boiler room. This suited dad down to the ground.

I found a job in Sharp Jones Pottery in Poole, who made glazed pipes for water mains and all types of drainage. It was hard work, but a good happy workforce; some of them were waiting for their call-up. I had to buy a bike to get to work. The road from Wallisdown going south to the factory was locally called the Alps for there was one long steep hill, then another, then a length of flat road, then another steep hill. I used to go pell-mell down the hills to try to get to the top without getting off the bike but I never succeeded, coming or going!

One of the workers, who must have been in his fifties and a very nice man, occasionally had fits of coughing. He had been gassed in the First World War. He would sit on the ground with his back to a wall and cough and gasp, his face would turn purple and tears would run down his face. It was terrible to see him suffer. There was nothing we could do for him. God knows what a ward full of gassed soldiers must have been like. After a while, his colour would return to normal, he would get up and carry on working. He never asked for anything from anyone. He did not want sympathy, he just wanted to do a day's work like everyone else. What a wonderful man – or hero?

I would cycle home over the Alps, tired and hungry. I never expected a large meal due to rationing. How my mother managed to feed us all, I'll never know – she was a marvel!

Mum decided to keep a few hens. Dad fenced off a piece of garden, made a coop and Mum bought six hens off the farmer. We hoped to get some fresh eggs. Mum used to save the potato and other vegetable peelings, put them in a pot, bring them to the boil and then add some powder she bought from the greengrocer, then the whole lot would be mixed together. It didn't smell too good but the hens liked it!

Mum was beginning to get attached to the hens and treated them like pets, but Christmas was coming and one of them had to become Christmas dinner – but which one, and by whom? We were all townies and never had a clue how to kill, pluck and clean a chicken; the butcher used to do that for us each year. Dad had joined the Conservative Club, and he soon found a countryman who said he would come to the house before Christmas and find the right one for Christmas dinner, take it away and bring it back ready for cooking. Problem solved and Dad would pay.

Dad decided to start a vegetable garden but he was no gardener, so we boys took over. Reg was a good gardener and planted cabbage, carrots, potatoes, everything for the kitchen – he seemed to have green fingers. He started to work in a market garden and seemed to enjoy getting his hands dirty.

Ron was still at school. John was still in his apprenticeship. I was still working in the pottery, Dad was getting on very well in his boiler room. Mum was still a marvel. The year was getting on, it seemed a long one, good news, bad news as the war went on. Jean seemed quite happy to stay in Portsmouth; she was courting a sailor, Bill Calton, who she eventually married.

Christmas 1941 was upon us and it was time for the countryman to come and choose the hen for Christmas dinner. He made his choice and took the hen away. Mum was quite sad. There wasn't much Christmas spirit about because of the war but everyone made the most of it. The Christmas dinner went down very well, though I don't think Mum ate much chicken!

I changed my job, the pottery work was very hard, the bike ride didn't help either! I found a job at Purchase and Vines farm. The farm had its own dairy and supplied dairy products around the area. I helped the milkman deliver milk. I had to get to the farm at 06.30 to help harness the horse and back him into the shafts and load the milk cart. The horse knew the round well. Bob, my boss, would deliver to one side of the road and I would deliver to the other. The horse would amble down to the next house and wait, he had a habit of mounting the pavement to bite a lump out of the house-owners' hedges!

Bob knew which house to stop at for a cup of tea and cake. The woman who lived there was very nice. Her husband had been in the army and fought at Passchendaele. Bob suffered from asthma but still smoked, he would sit there and cough and cough as he drank his tea and smoked. I never could understand it! I would sit there quietly and eat cake.

I would not have to work on Sunday as the orders would be doubled up on a Saturday. The horse had a day off. He knew when we were nearing the end of the round on a Saturday and would shift into another gear. By the time we got to the end of the round he was ready to go – it was about two miles to the farm and it was all Bob could do to hold him! When we took him to the Blacksmith for new shoes, if Bob let him he would break into a gallop – good job there was not much traffic in those days!

Sometimes after finishing the round I would help in the bottle-washing room. The used bottles would be put on a moving steel belt, washed and air dried, ready to be filled with lovely fresh milk, and then crated and put into a cold room. In the morning there would be an inch of lovely cream on top of the milk in every bottle. I really enjoyed the job, all the workers were a happy lot and being a dairy farm, included a cowman and two Land Army girls.

Some customers complained that there were holes in the cardboard milk tops. We found out it was birds that would stand on the bottle top and peck to get to the cream. We had to tell customers to provide some cover for their milk!

I had now turned seventeen, food was still short, I think the country was getting leaner, except the wealthy who could afford everything on the Black Market.

Christmas 1942 was coming and the dilemma of which hen should meet its maker and provide Christmas dinner raised its ugly head again. The veg garden was flourishing. We could still get good old English apples, but not fruits grown abroad, like oranges and bananas. Even rabbits were in short supply – poachers must have been doing well!

Christmas arrived. The countryman and Dad were now good friends so there was no problem as far as the hen for Christmas dinner was concerned. They just had to get past Mum, but she had been putting the odd one or two ration tokens aside, hoping there would be enough for a chicken. Mum was not going to give up one of her hens, they were all such good egg layers! She went to the butcher and he said, 'You just about have enough Mrs. Beedie' with a twinkle in his eye; he might even put a piece of dripping in! He was a pretty fair butcher to all his customers.

Christmas was a quiet affair. Dad, being an ex-merchant seaman, was worried about how many of our ships were being sunk. They were being sunk quicker that the U.S. and U.K. could build them. The loss of sailors was terrible, Dad was in a very sombre mood: 1160 ships were sunk by U boats in 1942. Us boys just kept quiet.

I left my job. The farmer had bought a three-wheel van and it just wasn't the same, what with having to jump in and out of the van, Bob coughing and smoking. I missed the old horse who did the work for us, knowing exactly where to go and when to stop, and being out in the fresh air. I don't know what the farmer was up to, using valuable petrol. I don't know what he did with the horse either; I hope he put him out to grass.

I got a job with Frederick Hotels, who had the licence to run the buffet cars on trains. The train I worked on left Bournemouth West about 7.45 in the morning and stopped at every station on its way to Waterloo. It would then be shunted back to Clapham Junction for about three hours, not the safest place to be! I had the choice of sitting in a carriage or walking about Clapham Junction until it was time to head back to Bournemouth West. I worked in the pantry mostly, making toast with cheese or jam, marmalade or scrambled egg, which was made with dried eggs. The passengers were only too pleased to have something with a cup of tea. The return trip would be similar with sandwiches, biscuits and cakes. We all knew though that it would only be a matter of time before the government stopped the buffet cars running.

When I had worked as a paper boy at Marsdens, sometimes due to bombing further up the line, the train would be late, which meant I'd be late delivering the papers and then had no time for breakfast and was late for school. One day when the train was late, I said to Mr. Marsden, 'I'll go and get the papers (the papers were only about four pages) on my bike.' The papers were very tightly bound, so made about a two-foot bundle. It was OK as long as I kept the back wheel down!

Mr. Marsden gave me ten Woodbine cigarettes and told me to find the person who handled our order and give him the ten Woodbines and he might serve me first. This I did, and it worked, so this I did every time the train was late, Mr. Marsden, having already been informed if that was the case. It was rather dangerous riding in the dark, the cycle lamp had been darkened, there was only about a half-inch gap across the lamp and until your eyes got used to the dark, you would be riding blind. After raids you never knew what you might run into; houses on fire helped you to see. Mr. Marsden's customers would clap when I got back to the shop, they were not aware that I was doing it for my own benefit, so that I got my breakfast and was not late for school!

One afternoon when working in the pantry of the buffet car, I glanced up the corridor and saw a sailor walking down towards me. I thought, 'I know you,' and I did – it was the chap I used to give the ten Woodbines to. I said, 'Hello, remember me?' He looked me up and down and said, 'Oh yes, I remember you, ten Woodbines!' I said, 'Yes, would you like a cup of tea?' 'Not half!' he said. I made him a cup of tea and he sat down, pushed his cap back, lit a fag and we had a good yarn. Then he said, 'I got to go'. He stood up, straightened his cap, we shook hands, I wished him well and he was gone. I hope he survived the war. The manager gave me a hard look but I never took any notice.

Chapter Five

The Home Guard

I had joined the Home Guard when I was sixteen years old, and was fully fitted out with full uniform, greatcoat, boots, gaiters, forage cap, a Canadian .303 Winchester rifle, thirty rounds of ammunition and a sword bayonet. People laugh at *Dad's Army* today but it was very different in 1940/4. Hitler had twenty divisions waiting to cross the channel, the British Army had lost almost all of its tanks, lorries, guns, etc. in France. The country had to prepare for invasion but thanks to the courage of the R.A.F. whose fighter pilots in the end destroyed the best part of the German Air Force, Operation Sea Lion was called off. It was a close thing.

I became a Private in 'C' Company, the 6th Battalion of the Hampshire Home Guard. We had to go to the firing ranges in Christchurch, Hampshire to learn how to fire a rifle. After a few lessons I became quite good at 200 yards but at 400 yards I could not hit a barn door!

One of the shops near the pub was a dairy shop, which belonged to the farmer. He let our Company use it as our H.Q. Our C.O. was the Post Master, Captain Pusey. There were woods by the church and in a clearing was our parade ground, where we would learn our foot and rifle drill. The first Great War had only ended twenty-one years earlier. Some of the Company were in their twenties when they were fighting in those terrible battles, so now they were in their forties and fifties; they were fully trained soldiers. They had fought on foreign soil, they would fight even harder on their home soil!

The farmer let us use one of his fields for training. On one evening exercise, we were using a hay stack as a German machine-gun post. Some of us were attackers and others defenders; I was an attacker. At the order, 'Charge' the youngest of us raced to the machine-gun post and were repelled not by defenders but by the wire the farmer put around the hay stack to stop the cows from eating it! We fell about laughing, much to the annoyance of Captain Pusey – there wasn't much to laugh about in those days.

In one training exercise we had to defend our HQ against the enemy, who were the Welsh Guards, we did our best but they roughed us up a bit. Anyone putting up a bit of resistance received a jab from the butt of a rifle. I didn't fancy any Germans chance with that lot!

On night guard, I was paid three and sixpence less a penny for a cup of tea. I and another private would go out on a two-hour foot patrol. It would be pitch black in the winter. The road east was very long, anybody missing the last trolley bus would have a long walk back to Wallisdown. We would challenge anybody about at night. It was an offence to be out without your identity card. Other pairs would be patrolling other parts of Wallisdown. One zealous pair stopped a girl, she had no ID so they escorted her home and one followed her right up to her bedroom where she produced her ID card. He then gave her irate parents a talking-to, telling them that they should make sure their daughter carried her

ID card when she was going out and that it was a criminal offence not to. Those two were quite proud of themselves!

If me and my partner challenged someone and they didn't have their ID card with them, we would remind them that it was an offence not to carry one. If it was someone we didn't know, we would take them back and hand them over to the Duty Sergeant. This did not happen very often. The people in Wallisdown were pretty good.

Getting back to our HQ I would sit down with a cup of tea and listen to any of those old soldiers who had fought in the last war. It was hard to believe how they survived such conditions. I felt proud to be in such company.

Our main armament was a Smith gun, a rope was attached to either side of the gun shield. One wheel was concave, the other convex. Three men on each rope would then pull the gun to its gun position, turn the gun on its side, concave down; the gun was then ready. The other was a spigot mortar, I can't remember how it fired, all I know is we only had one training mortar; after firing it, we would have to go and dig it up, clean it ready to be fired again. We were short of mortars, but then the whole army was short of all weaponry. We would carry out these exercises on the land to the right-hand side, past the lodge gates, where there was plenty of common land, and with a bit of luck we might hit a rabbit!

I was getting better at rifle shooting on the ranges at Christchurch. In fact we were getting to be quite an efficient unit. The soldiers from the WWI were now as good as they were all those years ago. They may have been a little slower but were much wiser; we others learned a lot from them.

A Sten gun had been given to us, the oldest man in the unit said he would like to have it and Captain Pusey said he could. I did not want the gun, some of them were known to have faulty safety catches: a Private in the next company to ours dropped his Sten gun and fired three or four bullets into his leg, which had to be amputated at the thigh. I thought they were cheap and nasty guns and that British soldiers ought to go to war with better weapons than that.

The war in the Atlantic was intensifying, and although we were still losing ships, the Navy was beginning to be given Asdics (underwater detection device) and radar. U-boats were being sunk with the valued help of the R.A.F., more than Admiral Doenitz could afford. Dad said that now the Navy had the new equipment they would not only be protecting the convoys, but would soon go on the hunt for U-boats. I said, 'I hope you're right Dad.'

Food was still short; Mum said that as long as we had the basics like vegetables and bread, it would not hurt us to go without luxuries. She still had her hens, Reg looked after the garden, Jock was still an apprentice – it was a very good trade he was learning. Ron was still at school. Jean's Bill was serving on the cruiser *Berwick*. My job with Frederick Hotels had ended and I decided that after Christmas I would join the Navy.

On Sunday mornings, the Home Guard would fall in, except for those who were working. We would be in full uniform and armed. After inspection, we would follow the Boys' Brigade Bugle Band and march up and down the main road with Captain Pusey in front – he was very proud, with his medals on his chest, he had every right to be.

Chapter Six

Joining up

I found a job in a big restaurant in Bournemouth, working in the pantry. The owner's name was De Havilland, it was said he was the father of Olivia De Havilland and Joan Fontaine, the film actors; whether that was true or not I do not know. The cook was a very lovely lady with a wonderful smile, her hair was tied back in a bun. It was a very happy pantry, but behind that lovely smile was sadness, as her husband had been killed serving with the British Army at Bethune in France. She was a marvel in the kitchen, the meals she cooked with the limited rations were amazing. Mr. De Havilland was lucky to have her.

As I had made up my mind to join the Navy, I wasn't too worried about work and perhaps I slackened off a bit. I think the manager had a word with Mr. De Havilland, as I was summoned to his office. He quietly told me off, saying that everybody had to pull their weight, then he showed me a photo of a young pilot: it was his son who had been killed in the Battle of Britain. I felt quite ashamed, what with Beth the cook losing her husband and Mr. De Havilland losing his son, they were both carrying on as strongly as they could.

The year 1942 was coming to an end, it had been a bad year for shipping. The 8th Army had successfully beaten Rommel at El Alamein and was pushing up the desert after the earlier success of General Auchinleck.

Christmas was a quiet affair – there didn't seem to be any problem with the chicken, vegetables were plentiful thanks to Reg. Mum's spotted dick with custard was lovely.

The threat of invasion was now over. Captain Pusey still held exercises and parades. We still marched up and down with the Boys' Brigade and I think the people of Wallisdown rather enjoyed it.

I quietly got on with my job, then one day in 1943 I went off to work as usual. When I arrived, I asked the manager if I could leave at 11 o'clock as I had an appointment. He said it was an unusual request, I told him it was rather important and he said, 'Alright, just this once.'

I went out, got on my bike and rode to Bournemouth Central Station. I had saved up my three and five pence guard money, so had enough to pay for a return ticket to Southampton. Arriving at Southampton I asked the way to Lamb Memorial Hall. After being directed here and there, I eventually stood outside the Naval Recruiting Office at the Hall. I opened the door and walked in. There in the centre of a large hall was a Chief Petty Officer sitting at a desk. He looked old enough to be my grandad. I walked over to the desk and stood there. He looked up and said, 'What do you want lad?' I said I wanted to join the Royal Navy for twenty-two years. He said, 'You want to join the Navy for twenty-two years?' I said, 'Yes.' He said, 'Sit down lad, I'm sorry but we are not taking on any regular sailors at the moment, we have enough. What we are taking on though are H.O.s, which stands for Hostilities Only. That means you serve for the war only, but if you survive the war and still wish to join the Royal Navy, you can then apply to become a regular sailor.'

I was rather disappointed. Then he said, 'You would do the same work as a sailor, get the same pay, dress the same, the only difference would be that you would be called an H.O. instead of a regular sailor.' So I agreed to join the Royal Navy as an H.O.

I filled in all the necessary forms, name, address, age, etc., and was then sent to sit and wait to be called. I was the only one there (not many H.O.s that day). My name was called, I went into a room and was told to undress and was given a good examination by two or three doctors – eyes, ears, teeth, height, weight, cough, say ahh!! They finally said I was fit enough to become an H.O. and to get dressed and return to the room and wait (they must have been bored stiff!). One of them brought out some forms, took them to the C.P.O., he called me over and said, 'Are you sure you want to be an H.O.?' I said, 'Yes.' He said, 'Sign this then', which I did. He then said, 'You are now an ordinary seaman H.O., your number is P/JX 516441, now go home and wait to be called.'

We shook hands and he wished me luck. I walked out of the building returned to the station, caught the train back to Bournemouth Central, jumped on my bike (it was still there) and rode home. I walked indoors and Mum said, 'Where have you been? Your tea is spoiled!' I said, 'I have joined the Navy.' She turned her face away. Dad said, 'About time too', which is what I expected from Dad, and that was that.

I went back to work and got on quietly with my job and waited. There were several older lads than me who had joined up and were waiting to be called up too. Three of them for the Navy. I wondered if they would be H.O.s as well.

There were several hit-and-run raids on Bournemouth and

Poole. Bournemouth gasworks were hit while the workers were at lunch in the canteen. There were quite a few casualties.

Major Butt, Commanding Officer of the 6th Battalion the Hampshire Home Guard, a regular soldier, visited us and told Captain Pusey that he thought we were doing too much marching on a Sunday and not enough exercising. He said that although there would be no sea invasion now, Hitler could still land Paratroopers in quiet parts of the country like Dorset and Devon and try to 'put the wind up us', so we still had to be alert. Captain Pusey was quite put out!

While I was with the Home Guard, we never fired the Smith gun but still carried on with our mortar.

At Christchurch ranges I was getting quite a marksman with the Canadian Winchester .303. At the shoot, we would put sixpence in the hat for the winner with the highest score at 200 yards. There were about twenty-four of us. I won with nine bulls and a inner. That was twelve shillings, I was a millionaire!

Eventually the buff envelope arrived telling me to report to H.M.S. *Collingwood* on the 29th April 1943. I was seventeen years old.

At the next guard duty I told Sergeant Waddilove that the next parade would be my last. He told me to bring all my uniform, my faithful Winchester, bayonet and thirty rounds of ammunition back at the next parade, but that I could keep my boots. This I did. The parade had had a whip round for me and the amount was quite considerable. I felt rather choked. I shook hands with all my happy band of brothers, walked to the corner of the road, turned and waved, then walked away. I never saw any of them again.

Chapter Seven

H.M.S. Collingwood

April 29th arrived and it was time to say goodbye. I had said goodbye to my brothers earlier as they had to go to work. Ron was still at school. I never saw Jean as she was still in Portsmouth. Mum gave me a big hug and a kiss. Dad shook my hand. There were tears in Mum's eyes and I'm not sure that Dad's were not a little damp, too. Then I picked up my suitcase, walked up the short hill, at the top turned, waved, and walked to the bus stop to catch a bus to Bournemouth Central Station. I caught the train to London, changed at Southampton for Fareham, then had a long walk to H.M.S. *Collingwood*.

I walked through the gate – there were quite a few new recruits standing around, I joined them and waited. More started to arrive 'til there were quite a few of us. Then a P.O. appeared with a clipboard. There was quite a babble going on, the P.O. shouted 'QUIET' and there was instant silence; he then said, 'I will call names, those whose names I call will answer, "Here" then move over to my right.' He started to call names, some were present, others hadn't arrived. When there were twenty-eight, of which I was one, he shouted, 'You twenty-eight, fall in over there, three deep.' He then called to a leading seaman to take charge 'of this bunch'!

The leading seaman slowly got us into three ranks, the P.O. then shouted to us, 'You twenty-eight are now Class 25Q. The leading seaman will march you to your hut, you will carry your suitcases in your left hand, you will swing your right arms. Take over, leading seaman.'

The leading seaman said, 'Suitcases into your left hands, attention, quick march.' Good job Hitler couldn't see us, what a bunch! The leading seaman said, 'We turn left at the next turning, I will give the order "left turn", you will keep formation as you turn.' When we finally reached our hut, the leading seaman shouted, 'Halt, right turn, stand at ease'. He then said, 'This is your hut, go in, choose a bunk, then between you, you will choose a class leader. Once he has been chosen, he will be in charge. If any of you have a complaint, tell him and he will see the Duty P.O. who will then see you.'

We started to file into the hut, there was a figure lying on a bunk, hands clasped behind his head. I looked then shouted, 'Colegate!' The figure stirred, looked up and shouted 'Beedie!' I grabbed the bunk next to him. He was a member of a family I knew in Bournemouth. I said, 'What are you doing here?' He said, 'I joined a week or so ago, went down with tonsillitis, I'm alright now, but been back classed. That's the first job of the chosen class leader, to report that the class is one too many.' Colegate and I had known each other for years, but had never called each other by our first names.

The class leader was chosen, I think he was from a public school. We were a right mixed lot. The leading seaman appeared and told us to fall in outside, three deep, and we would march to the mess hall to see if there was any food left. He locked the door of the hut, called us to attention then shouted, 'Right turn, quick march, swing your arms', and off we shambled.

I'm afraid I can't remember the Navy's menu for 1943 but there are two things I must mention. One was the Navy's pea soup, which was fabulous, no matter which Navy establishment you were sent to, it was always the same. I could live on it! The other was the yellow peril, square chunks of yellow haddock. When all the trays of the yellow peril were laid out in the mess hall, the steam and the smell threatened to lift the roof!

After having something to eat, we marched back to the hut. The leading seaman showed us where the ablutions and toilets (heads, as the Navy calls them) were. He told us that the rest of the day was our own. Some had come a long way and were tired out. He also told us that in the morning we would do the joining routine and have a medical which would include injections.

At about 21.30 a P.O. came in and said, 'Lights out at 2200 hours.' Most of us had been to the ablutions and washed etc. At 21.30, there was some embarrassing movement as we started undressing. Some were undressing and putting on pyjamas, the majority were staying in vest and pants, including Colegate and myself. One lad knelt down by his bunk to say his prayers, to a rather embarrassed silence. He finished his prayers, climbed into his bunk and buried his face in his pillow. We all then climbed into our bunks. Although it was double summertime (during the war, double British summertime was invented as an energy saving device, effectively putting the country on the same footing as mainland Europe e.g. GMT plus one in the Winter and GMT plus two in the Summer. In 1947, Britain reverted to normal), we had to 'darken ship' before 2200 hours. At 2200 hours the order came, 'Lights out, pipe down.' Later on there came some quiet sobbing from one or two of the bunks.

Hands (ships crew) were called at 0600 hours each morning. A P.O. would walk down the side of the hut rattling a stick on the corrugated sides, then come in bellowing, 'Come on, show a leg.' There would be muttering and moaning, not looking forward to the day ahead.

After breakfast we returned to the hut. There were two small lockers above each bunk, one for each occupant. We were all given a key. The lockers were for personal gear. The leading seaman appeared, told us to fall in outside three deep. He then locked the door and after shuffling us around managed to get us into three ranks and we marched off to do the joining routine, another medical and the injections. We got through the joining routine and medical. One of the injections was alright, the other was T.A.B. or something like that, it made some quite ill, as if they had the flu. They were taken to the sick bay. Another side effect for some was that our left arm swelled so much we could not take our shirts off. We all felt pretty rotten, so were confined to the hut and were glad to turn into our bunks that night. The lad never knelt outside his bunk to say his prayers again. I think he must have said them quietly to himself when he was in his bunk.

The following morning those of us who were not in the sick bay were told that after we fell in for parade at 0800 hours we would march to be kitted out; that brought some moans as our arms were still swollen and painful. However, at 0800 the leading seaman marched us to the stores, we were given a kitbag and two of everything: oilskin, greatcoat, black cap, white cap, black jersey for when we went into winter routine, boots, jumper, two collars and trousers, all stuffed into the kitbags. We were also given a wooden block with our name engraved on it, black ink was also supplied and we used this to mark our gear. We then lugged all our gear, which included gas masks, back to the hut.

The leading seaman showed us how to dress, there were more moans when we had to pull our jumpers over our heads. Once we were dressed to the leading seaman's satisfaction, brown paper was produced and we parcelled up all our civilian clothes – these were then addressed and sent to our homes.

There was no laundry but there was a washing room with deep basins and a small mangle. There was also a drying room. We had to do our own washing, or 'dobeing' as the Navy called washing. I had some idea because as children, when Dad was away at sea, we had to help Mum with the washing, using a copper filled with hot water and a scrubbing board, then the washing had to be well rinsed, then put through the mangle – that was hard work!

The only soap we had was the Navy's Pussers hard yellow soap, a block about six inches by two. I soon got used to it, some of the class had never washed a hankie, they were having difficulties. There was an ironing board but no iron – we had to have a collection to buy one, which the P.O. supplied.

When the class was fit enough we started foot drill, rifle drill and learned how to salute. It was rather different to the Home Guard. I made a mistake at foot drill and was made to double (run) around the parade ground, with a rifle held above my head. On the way around, I ran between an instructor and his class, he was some sixty yards away teaching his class Power Command (how to shout orders). I never saw him but he saw me – apparently I had committed a crime and was told to double around the parade ground again. When I got back to my own class the instructor said, 'Where have you been?'

I told him I had run between an instructor and his class. He said, 'That's a crime. You've missed some instruction already, it won't hurt you to miss some more, double around the parade ground again!' Three times around the parade ground with my rifle above my head or down by my chin by now, the double became a trot – it was going to be a hard day!

I think we were allowed to go ashore after three or four weeks. Colegate and I decided to go, I think we had to be back by 2200 hours. We walked into Fareham and made our way to the Salvation Army Hall. There were quite a few sailors in there enjoying the delicacy of the day, cottage pie and mash, we joined them. After eating we went outside and saw that opposite was a pub, Colegate and I went in and I had my first pint of beer, which I rather enjoyed. We then walked back to Collingwood.

I enjoyed the seamanship course: how to tie knots, splicing, boxing the compass, heaving the lead, learning the rules of the road (in Navy terms this means navigating safely) and boat drill. Drill finished on Fridays at 16.00. We still had to fall in on Saturday mornings and were detailed different jobs. I was detailed to cell sentry and was sent to the regulating office. There were a small number of cells at the back of the building. The longest a prisoner could be kept in cells was fourteen days. Any more than that would mean being sent to a naval detention centre.

I reported and did my best to keep out of sight. A P.O. spotted me and told me to take one of the prisoners his daily ration. The prisoner was a stoker who had gone 'absent without leave' (AWOL), had been caught and sentenced to fourteen days in the cells. First three days on low diet, which meant a half mug of cocoa, or kye as the Navy call it, and one pound of ship's biscuits, then half a mug of cocoa in the evening. I took the cocoa and two half-pound packets of ship's biscuits (I think you could have built a wall with them!) into the cell and placed them on the table. As I turned to walk out of the cell, there came an anguished cry and the two packets of biscuits came flying at me. I ducked and they hit the cell door with a thud. He shouted at me and pointed to his mouth – he never had a tooth in his head and had lost his false teeth! I dived out of the cell and told the P.O. that the prisoner had lost his false teeth. The P.O. sighed and said he would sort something out. I was glad when my four hours was up! That was the most exciting Saturday morning I had. Other Saturdays were spent sweeping and picking up fag ends.

My eighteenth birthday came and went, no celebration.

On the 23rd May 1943, a Sunday morning, a hit-and-run raider flying just above the wave tops and under the radar screen swooped over the cliffs at Bournemouth and dropped its bombs, which hit the Metropolitan Hotel. Some two hundred Canadian personnel were killed, seventy-seven were pilots. What a tragedy and terrible loss to Canada, to us and our allies.

The class had now finished its six weeks seamanship training, whether we were any good or not I don't know, the P.O. never praised us but was pretty severe if mistakes were made. I could vouch for that as could others! The class had a collection and we bought him a present – I think that was the norm.

My class mates were a pretty good bunch. Some felt hard done by, they had left good, well-paid jobs and comfortable homes to be conscripted as H.O.s into the Royal Navy for three shillings a day. The class leader had had few problems. We now moved to the Gunnery section.

The parade ground was in the middle of Collingwood, the north end facing the main gate; the huts there were called Forecastle division, the south-end huts were called Quarterdeck division, the east-side huts were Maintop division and the west-side huts were Gunnery section. We moved from the north side to the west side, opposite Maintop. I didn't think we were going to learn much gunnery in two weeks.

Thursday the 18th was no different to any other day at the office. The evening was the same as always – at 2200 hours the tannoy piped 'Out lights, pipe down.' Three or four hours later we were awakened by a line of very heavy explosions. The door blew off, the windows blew in, we were literally blown out of our bunks. There were shouts and cries, debris started to rain down on the roof. The AA guns started firing, the searchlights raked the sky.

The scene in the hut was bedlam. Pitch black. A voice from outside bellowed, 'On boots, oilskins and caps – file into the shelters as soon as you can!' There was broken glass around the bunks near the windows and the occupants were bare-footed, as we all were. All of us were trying to find our boots – they should be by our bunks – we were all groping around in the dark until we found them. We grabbed any oilskin, put our caps on then moved on out to the shelters.

I looked left, Maintop was well alight the fire and rescue squads were there, they were well trained for this type of incident. An incident that they had hoped would never happen but now it had come with a vengeance. Maintop had been bombed and thirty-three young sailors had been killed.

I sat in the shelter and said to myself, 'Welcome to Portsmouth!' The war had been on for three and a half years. Collingwood was a few miles from Portsmouth but had never been attacked. I had been there for just a few weeks and it was bombed!

The all-clear sounded, we filed back into our hut to try and sort things out, apart from the burning Maintop it was pitch black. The bedding from the bunks near the windows had to be shaken out. The glass had to be swept up. Lucky it was summer and quite warm. By the time we had sorted ourselves out it was about 0400 hours in the morning. We turned in our bunks. The tannoy stated

'Hands will be called at 06.00, hands will fall in for divisions at 08.00.' We could not believe our ears, some of the class had come from the North, Wales and Ireland; they had never heard a gun fire let alone a bomb and were still some what shocked.

At 06.00 hands were called. Colegate and I turned out and made our way to the wash house, as did others. There was a lot of moaning as we washed and dressed. After breakfast we all stood by the edge of the parade ground waiting to fall in, the Royal Marine band was tuning up – 'Hearts of oak are our ships.' The order 'Fall in for divisions' sounded. We all trotted to our allotted positions, then off we marched with the Royal Marine band playing 'Jolly tars are our men.'

The rescue squads were bringing out body parts from Maintop and were laying them on white sheets (there were no black body bags in those days) in the corner of a drill shed. We carried on marching, the C.O. taking the salute. When divisions were finished we were told to return to our huts.

Gunnery section was opposite Maintop, the first hut being ours – it was some what damaged, windows had to be boarded up, the door repaired and refitted. Debris had to be removed from the roof. The bedding was thoroughly shaken out again and bunks returned to their proper positions. Then the floor was swept and polished. We were not going to get any daylight until new windows had been fitted.

The class and everybody else had to carry on as if nothing had happened. I thought of those in Maintop – they had been just like us a few weeks ago, they had said goodbye to their mothers, fathers, brothers, sisters, aunts, uncles and sweethearts. Now they were going back home in coffins.

The last week of our eight weeks' training consisted of gun drills and weapon training.

Our last evening together came. Before the bombing we were quite a happy class but this last week had been very quiet. When we looked across at the ruin which was Maintop, we realised how lucky we had been. A few seconds either way and it could have been us.

The next morning began with the last rattle of a stick on the corrugated iron of the hut and the shout, 'Show a leg!' We washed, dressed had breakfast and were told to pack our kitbags and put them outside the hut. A navy lorry came to collect our kitbags and hammocks (which had been stowed in the stores). The Navy had given us a brown case for carrying our personal effects.

We were told to fall in on the parade ground, carrying our brown cases in our left hands. Then the order came: 'Attention! Right turn!' The Royal Marine band began to play and we marched a hundred yards or so with the band leading, the C.O. taking the salute. Out through the main gate the Royal Marine band marched, then turned left and continued up the road for about a hundred yards, and we followed. Then came the order to 'Halt!' followed by the order to climb aboard the lorries waiting there. The band then marched away and the lorries took us to the Royal Naval Barracks in Portsmouth. And so ended the first naval phase of twenty-eight H.O.s.

I wonder who had the iron!

Chapter Eight

Royal Naval Barracks – Portsmouth and Stockheath Camp, Havant

Once inside the barracks we were told we would have dinner, then be given leave warrants etc. We marched to the dining hall – Aagh, yellow peril! But the soup was good.

After dinner we marched to the parade ground, it was a fine sunny day. A table had been set out, at which a Pay Officer sat with an assistant. We fell in in alphabetical order. When my name was called, I marched up to the table, placing my cap on it. The Pay Officer put the pay due on top of my cap. As well as my pay, I was also given ration coupons for nine days, a rail warrant to take me to Bournemouth station and a return rail warrant for the trip back to Havant, at which point I would have to find my own way to Stockheath Camp. My kitbag and hammock would be forwarded. Whilst I was waiting for the officer's assistant to sort out my coupons I thought back to my first ever pay from the Navy. On that day the Pay Officer had put my pay on top of my cap, I had looked at it, the Pay Officer had said, 'Well?' I had replied, 'There's not enough, I am ten shillings short.' He had said, 'Is this your first payment?' 'Yes,' I had replied. He had looked through some papers, looked up at me and said, 'The Navy has been sending a five shillings a week allowance home to your mother.' I had told him, 'No one has asked me about sending a payment home?' He had replied, 'The Navy does not have to ask'!

I waited for Colgate to get his pay etc, we were then given permission to leave, so out of the main gate we marched, carrying our brown cases and gas masks.

The really heavy bombing had finished in 1941, it was mainly hit-and-run raiders now, but there were times when a raid would consist of more enemy aircraft. One large bomb had fallen near the barracks blowing one of the corners off – the public could now watch the sailors training!

Colegate decided he wanted to see more of Portsmouth and would catch a later train. He had been drafted to Coastal Forces at Lowestoft. We shook hands, I doubted if I would see him on leave, said goodbye and we parted.

I walked to the Central station, showed my railway warrant, bought a paper, walked to the end of the platform, sat down, pushed my cap back and settled down to read the paper. Suddenly a heavy hand fell on my shoulder. I looked up and saw a uniformed monster, it said, 'Stand up.' I stood up, he said, 'Do you know you are committing a crime?' I said, 'No sir.' 'Don't you sir me,' he replied. 'I am a Chief Regulating Petty Officer, put your cap on straight and come with me.' He then escorted me down the platform into his regulation office. 'You were committing a crime by wearing your cap flat-a-back,' he said. 'How long have you been in the Navy?' I replied, 'Eight weeks.' 'What is your name and number and where are you going?' he enquired. I told him I was going on nine days' leave to Poole. 'Where have you to report to after your leave?' he asked. I replied, 'Stockheath Camp, Havant.' 'Right,' he said, 'I will send them a full report, you can go now, enjoy your leave.'

I walked out of his office a little stunned and caught the next train home, changing at Southampton. Mum and Dad were very happy to see me. I gave Mum a big hug and kiss and shook hands with Dad. Mum gave me another hug and said, 'Thank you for the allowance.' I said, 'You are more than welcome Mum' and I meant it. We, the family, had been through some tough times. I never told Mum or Dad about the bombing. It was lovely to know that they were safe and sound.

I didn't do much during my leave, I was quite happy to lounge around reading – reading was my favourite hobby. I went to the cinema once and would go to the club with Dad, sit with his old mates and put the world to rights. The leave had been somewhat dampened for me by the cap incident!

Jock had a good job earning good wages, Mum said he worked long hours, so they never saw much of him. Reg still worked at the garden nursery. Ron would soon leave school, Jean was happily married. Everything seemed alright. I never had anything to worry about. It was a good thing when Mum and Dad had decided to move from Portsmouth.

The leave was soon over and it was time to say goodbye again. I and my brothers gave each other a friendly clout, I shook hands with Dad, gave Mum a big hug, picked up my brown case and gas mask, walked out the front door and up to the bus stop. Caught the bus to Bournemouth and then the train to Southampton, then changed trains at Havant. After making a few enquiries about directions, I found my way to Stockheath Camp.

I marched inside and made my way to the regulation office. The P.O. looked up and asked me what I wanted. 'I was told to report here,' I said. He asked me my name and looked through some papers. 'Oh Ordinary Seaman Beedie,' he said. 'Do you realise you have come back one day early?'

After going through the joining routine he made matters worse. 'All the huts are full,' he told me. 'I am afraid you will have to live in a bell tent, I will give you the number of the tent, we will leave your hammock stowed, you need to take your kitbag. You will share the tent with four others. There is a ground sheet already down.'

'Join the Navy and live in a tent!' I said – he didn't express any sympathy but did show me where to go.

I humped my kitbag up a road, past the huts then stopped to look. There was a front line made up of offices which linked up with offices and stores on the left- and right-hand sides. The parade ground was in the middle. There was no back to the camp, it ran away into open fields.

Behind the huts were the bell tents and I found my tent without difficulty. As I had come back one day early, I had the tent to myself. I humped my kitbag right to the back. Other tents were occupied and I made myself known to some of my neighbours. They were not happy about their accommodation. They showed me where the heads, ablutions and mess hall were. They were all waiting for their drafts.

There was nothing to do. It had been raining and the place was getting muddy. Mud and blue serge do not go together! My neighbours told me to 'just follow the pipes.' It started to rain again. I went back to my tent and sat down on the ground sheet, the ground felt hard.

The tannoy piped 'hands to dinner.' I followed the crowd. The Navy menu had not changed. After dinner I had to find the store to procure a blanket. When I found the store I was issued with one blanket and a hammock mattress, no pillow. That night I put my oilskin open on the ground, then the mattress, rolled my jersey to use as a pillow, undressed, wrapped myself up like a

51

cocoon in my blanket, laid down and spent a restless night.

The next morning I got up and went to the ablutions to wash; some of the others in the washroom were complaining about conditions. It was July 1943, quite warm but heavy showers were causing a problem. The paths between the huts and tents were getting very muddy. Later on in the morning my four tent mates turned up. They were not happy, in fact no one was happy! The complaining must have reached the 'top', as a senior officer came and inspected the conditions and decided that duck boards should be put down along the tent paths. We were also to be paid one shilling extra a day 'hard lying' money (this is paid if work is hard and dirty, also if conditions are bad).

Eventually the inevitable happened – 'Ordinary Seaman Beedie report to the regulation office.' I doubled to the office. A petty officer marched me in to another office where a Royal Navy Lieutenant was sitting behind a desk. I stood to attention in front. The P.O. said, 'Off cap.' I swung my right arm around my face, gripped the side of the cap, then swung it down to my right side. The officer then asked about the offence. The P.O. answered saying, 'On such and such day at such and such time on platform nine of Portsmouth railway station Ordinary Seaman Beedie was sitting on the platform waiting for a train and was inappropriately dressed as he was wearing his cap flat-a-back. He was seen by a regulation officer who told him he was committing a crime and took him to the regulation office where he was charged. As he was about to go on leave, he was told that the offence would be dealt with once he reported to Stockheath Camp.'

The officer said, 'Is it a first offence?' The P.O. replied, 'Yes.' 'Three days 10A' said the officer. 'On cap,' said the P.O. I swung my right arm across my face, gripping my cap on the left side, and placed it on my head. 'About turn,' barked the P.O. 'Quick march.' Off we marched out of the office. When outside I asked the P.O., 'What happens now?' He simply said, 'Follow the pipes.'

I walked back to my tent and joined the other four disgruntled H.O.s. I thought I had been treated rather harshly. Three days 10A meant three days' stoppage of leave, three days' stoppage of pay, if I had been over twenty years old they would have stopped my grog for three days too. I also had to muster four times a day, plus I would lose my hard-lying pay for three days.

At noon the tannoy piped 'hands to dinner, men under punishment to muster.' I and quite a few other criminals raced to the regulation office, were mustered, names called and then dismissed. We then had to race to the dining hall before all the dinner was gone. The pea soup was lovely, as was the cottage pie and pussers (peas).

As those in the huts were slowly drafted, so those in the tents took their places, losing their shilling a day hard-lying pay.

At 1600 hours, all hands were dismissed but men under punishment had to muster on the parade ground. All the criminals, there were a good few, including me, fell in. Our names were called. The P.O. then shouted for us to collect our rifles. There was a mad rush to the drill shed. There were not many rifles but there were a lot of pikes – a length of pipe with a bayonet welded on the end. I collected a pike and we all fell in on the parade ground.

The order came: 'High port arms!' I moved the pike diagonally, my left hand just above the left side of my face, my right hand down by my right hip. The others did the same.

The order was given to double march. We then started to double around the parade ground, which we did for the next hour. It seemed like a very long hour! At 1700 hours the order was given to return rifles and pikes to the drill shed and fall in. A galley party then had to be picked to go and clean pots and pans and clean the galley itself. In due course the galley party was chosen and off they went. They seemed very happy to be cleaning pots and pans – I soon found out why!

The P.O. then shouted, 'The rest of you – over there you can see a pile of lumps of concrete, you will double over there, you will pick up a lump of concrete and carry it across to the other side of the parade ground. You will place in on the ground, you are not to throw it, you will then double back and get another lump of concrete, carry it across and place it on the pile. Once you have moved all the concrete from that side, you will carry the lumps back again. You will do this until 1800 hours, when men under punishment will finish. You will muster again 2100 hours tonight. Men under punishment living in bell tents are excused the 0600 hours' muster tomorrow morning. Carry on!'

I doubled across to where the pile of concrete lumps were, picked one up, not too big, and grunting carried it over to the other side of the parade ground, placed it on the ground, turned and doubled back to pick up another lump. Others were doing the same, and so we carried all the lumps over to one side and then started to carry them back. At 1800 hours, the P.O. called us to a halt, then dismissed us. I was too tired to go to tea, so walked back to the tent and sank down on to the ground sheet.

We arranged the tent with a kitbag just inside, then a hammock mattress, then another kitbag, then another hammock mattress, until all five kitbags and mattresses were in a circle. A blanket had been loaned to each of us. At night we undressed, placed our clothes on our kitbags, pulled the mattress from between the kitbags and with a makeshift pillow attempted to get some sleep. It was quite light with double summertime. We all had to sleep on our sides and hoped nobody wanted to go to the heads. When we arose we stuffed the mattress between the kitbags, which gave us a little more room.

I was still thinking that the three days 10A were a bit tough. The loss of three days' pay plus a shilling hard lying was bad enough, the parade ground punishment I thought was disgraceful. I would be glad to leave this place.

At last my name was called to report to the drafting office. I doubled over to the office, wondering what ship I would be drafted to. I reported in and was told 'Ordinary Seaman Beedie, you are drafted to H.M.S. *Excellent* for a three-month gunnery course.' H.M.S. *Excellent* was reputed to be the finest gunnery school in the world. My heart sank down into my boots, I had hoped to be drafted to a ship. The drafting officer said, 'Report back here at 1400 hours with all your kit, return your mattress and blanket.' I trudged back to my tent, we had dinner, my tent mates all sympathised with me, hoping they would not get the same.

I packed my kitbag, brown case and gas mask, and said goodbye to my tent mates; our time together had been short but not sweet. The place was a pit. I carried my kitbag and case to the drafting office, then returned my mattress and blanket and fetched my hammock from the baggage store.

I returned to the drafting office and waited. Eventually a small canvas-topped Royal Navy van arrived and I put my kit in the back. The driver went into the office and returned with some paperwork. We both got into the van and off we went. Good riddance to Stockheath Camp!

Chapter Nine

H.M.S. Excellent – Gunnery School, Whale Island Portsmouth

The driver was not talkative and nor was I. We soon reached H.M.S. *Excellent* and drove in through the main gates, passing the main gate sentry. The driver stopped in front of the regulation office and we both got out of the van and went in. The driver handed over the paperwork to a clerk who took them to an officer. I expected that my criminal offence would be in them. The clerk came back and told the driver to report me to the chief of mess decks. Off we went, soon stopping outside a building block. The driver went into an office and came out with a C.P.O. I took my kitbag out of the van being told to leave my hammock for the driver to take to the baggage store and stow away.

The C.P.O. was in charge of the large block of mess decks. He told me to pick up my kitbag and case and follow him. We entered the building and walked up a broad set of stairs that led to several flights of mess decks. He stopped at the first one, a long room with bunks either side then signalled for me to enter. There were some sailors standing around. The chief told me to select a bunk, which I did. He then told me to wait and off he went. I looked at the sailors, they seemed different, they certainly were not H.O.s.

A. P.O. Gunnery Instructor signalled me and another green-looking H.O. called Bunce over. He then turned to the other sailors and called their attention. They were New Zealanders who were from the cruiser H.M.S. *Achilles*, which was in Portsmouth dockyard having a refit. She had distinguished herself in the Battle of the River Plate against the German pocket battleship *Graf Spee* on 12th December 1939.

'There are twenty of you' he said. 'I am splitting you into two classes of ten.' He looked at his clipboard, called out ten names including myself and Bunce and said, 'You ten are now 38th of QRIII, you others are 39th of QRIII. You will each now choose a class leader, any problems – see him, he will then see me. You now come under Royal Naval discipline. Everybody here between the hours of 08.00 and 16.00 will double everywhere. All of you over the age of twenty will be entitled to a tot of rum. I will be your P.O.G.I (Petty Officer Gunnery Instructor) for the entire course. Next you will report to the regulation office to receive your station cards. You will need your station card when you go ashore. You will need to hand it in to the regulation officer when you go ashore, and collect it when you return. Ten of you will be the first part of port, the other ten first part of starboard. You can go now – don't forget to double. I and another P.O.G.I. will see you at the edge of the parade ground at 08.00 tomorrow morning.'

After collecting our station cards, Bunce and I returned to the mess deck, sat on our bunks in a kind of a daze. The New Zealanders were not unfriendly, but kept themselves to themselves. We never joined in any of their conversations. They selected a Kiwi called Hornton as class leader. A name I will never forget. He was a tall rangy kind of chap, who later on, if I made a mistake, would delight in kicking my backside!

The following morning after a not very good breakfast, Bunce and I, in our number three uniforms, belts and gaiters, stood by the parade ground along with eighteen somewhat disgruntled Kiwis. The P.O.G.I. was there with another P.O.G.I. who took over the other ten Kiwis. The order 'fall in parade' was shouted and we all fell in. The other class was marched away and we had nothing more to do with them. The 38th of QRIII fell in two ranks of five. The G.I. called us to attention and said, 'Let's see how we get on, quick march, left right, left right, swing those arms, left right.' After a few minutes he called, 'Halt, I see I am going to have trouble with you lot!'

The 38th QRIII had a problem, his name was Digger. He would start off swinging his arms correctly then would suddenly start swinging his right arm with his right leg and the G.I. went nuts! Digger gave a little half smile and said, 'Sorry I just can't help it, it just happens!'

'I am going to keep you lot marching until he learns to swing his arms properly,' shouted the G.I. and so we marched and marched and marched. Digger did not wear any socks, his feet must have been sore. 1600 hours came. The tannoy sounded 'Parade Dismissed, standfast 38th of QRIII.' The G.I. glared at us and said, 'I should be sitting down with a nice cup of tea!' We carried on marching and marching and marching. Digger slowly got better. The G.I. told him in no uncertain terms to concentrate on his marching and forget about his sheep farm back in NZ. 1700 hours came and we were dismissed. It was suggested that the man behind Digger should try and give him a kick when he started to swing the wrong way.

We went to see if there was any tea left. Shore leave was not granted. The Kiwis were not very happy and Hornton was not in a very good mood. Bunce and I kept clear of him, he was too free with his backside kicking! I don't know what he expected of us.

The following morning after falling in on parade we doubled to a store where we were issued with a length of rope about six feet long, a splice on one end, a hook on the other. We were told to wrap it bandolier fashion over our shoulder. We then doubled to Shanghai Beach where we were to do the assault course. Shanghai Beach was a backwater, the beach was stony and not very wide. There was a wooden wall about ten feet high with holes cut in it for hand and foot holds. If the tide was out a better run could be made to the wall. The backwater that morning was still, there was barely a ripple.

We fell in two ranks, six in the front, four in the rear. The tide was full, so there was not much of a run to the wall. The backwater was lapping over the rear rank's boots. The G.I. said, 'You are in a landing craft, when I shout "craft grounded, ramp down GO," Bunce will run to the left side of the wall. Beedie will run to the right – then both will climb to the top and begin giving covering file whilst you other eight race over and climb the wall. You will then drop down to the ground, I repeat DROP DOWN. Bunce and Beedie will do the same. Then follow your nose.'

He shouted the order 'craft grounded, ramp down, GO.' I shot off to the right-hand side and started to climb, balancing myself on the top. I pretended to give covering fire. Bunce was doing the same. The other eight were up and over and down. Bunce and I dropped down then ran through some bushes and into a clearing where a wooden construction had been built. It was about thirty-foot high with a platform at the top; a bar had been fitted to the backside of the platform. At the top of the bar, a wire had been attached. The wire ran diagonally down to where it was attached to a stout post fixed into the ground. On the frontside a ramp ran up to the platform diagonally from the ground – slats had been fitted across the ramp.

Taking off my hook rope I ran up the ramp and hooked it on to the wire, then hanging on tightly I slid down the wire to land in a heap at the bottom. Unhooking the rope I ran on to a structure shaped like a pyramid only longer. It was about thirty-foot high or more and made of lengths of round pieces of timber attached horizontally and vertically to each other with gaps of about three feet between them.

I started to climb, we were all doing the same, hauling ourselves across the gaps to the top. Very carefully I transferred myself to the other side and climbed down. Hitting the ground I ran to a wall about eight feet high. The others had already reached it. Two of the strongest Kiwis leaned against the wall, cupping their hands and humping the others over – they could have thrown me clear over if they wished! Then they had to get themselves over.

We carried on running for about fifty yards, turning left and running another sixty or seventy yards, coming to a six-foot water jump (sometimes I made it, sometimes I didn't and got wet feet!).

We were to do this assault course once a week.

The following morning the class was in a far corner of the parade ground learning bayonet drill – how to take a bayonet out of a scabbard and fix to the rifle, then return it to the scabbard. After a few times the G.I. told us to fix bayonets and charge bags of straw hanging on a crossbar. Suddenly the orders became louder and crisper; on the edge of the parade ground, standing as stiff as a ramrod was the imposing figure of Warrant Gunner Pantlin, mechanical man – one of the finest, if not the finest warrant gunner in the Navy. He was surveying his domain, his eyes missing nothing. Anything amiss would be sorted out later.

He was absolutely immaculate, from his polished boots to his cap, not a hair out of place.

Eventually he marched off across the parade ground to where the Royal Navy Lieutenant's Long Course Gunnery Officers were training. He was pretty rough on them. Should any Royal Navy lieutenant wishing to be a gunnery officer fail to make it, it would not be the fault of Warrant Gunner Windy Pantlin!

Looking across the parade ground I said to Buncie, 'Look at that poor devil.' There was a rating trying to double but he was tottering about all over the place. Buncie said, 'What is that he's carrying?' I said, 'It looks like a dummy four-inch projectile, we will have to be very careful Buncie not to make a mistake, because if we do, that will be the punishment!'

In full, the punishment was to double to the ammunition section where a G.I. would place a four-inch dummy projectile weighing sixty to seventy pounds, if not more, in your arms. He would then tell you to double to Fire Control and report to the G.I. who would tell you to report to the G.I. at the Armoury. Reaching the Armoury, you would be told to double and report to the G.I. in Hydraulics who would tell you to return to Ammunition.

I said to Buncie, 'I don't think I could do that punishment, Collingwood and Stockheath were bad enough!' Buncie said, 'I don't think I could either! I don't think he is going to make it!' I replied. 'He will have to even if it takes him all day!'

The G.I. turned to us and said, 'What are you two talking about, get in line!' We carried on stabbing bags of straw.

Every two weeks the Kiwis would go down to the dockyard and draw their pay from the *Achilles*. They could then go and have a good time if they could find one!

One evening, Buncie was asleep and I was lying on my bunk when one of the Kiwis staggered into the mess deck. Somebody must have helped him into the block, how he got through the main gate I do not know. He had lost his cap and he didn't know whether it was Christmas or Easter! I got out of my bunk and carefully approached him, aware that he might start swinging! I gently took him by the arm and led him to his bunk, where he promptly fell down – his was a lower bunk and with a little bit of help from him I managed to get him up onto the bunk. I straightened him out and took off his shoes. His cigarettes and wallet had fallen out of his jumper pocket so I picked them up and looked in the wallet. There was ten pounds or more, I had never seen so much money! I didn't know what to do with the wallet but finally decided to put it between a pillow case and pillow and sleep on it.

In the morning, after we had all washed, shaved and dressed I went over to him and said, 'This wallet fell out of your jumper last night.' He said, 'Did you put me in my bunk?' 'Yes,' I said, 'with a bit of help from you.' 'Thanks,' he said. 'I thought my wallet had gone for good.' From then on, I and Buncie were one of them and they told Hornton to stop kicking our backsides, which he did.

Saturday, after dinner, I said to Buncie that I was going into town to post some letters and have a walk around and did he want to come with me. He said no because there was nowhere to go, Aggie Weston's had been burned down, the Sailor's Home Club had been bombed as had most of the cinemas. What few pubs had survived were closed. I said, 'There must be a Salvation Army somewhere', but no, he did not want to come, so slinging my gas mask over my shoulder I went on my own.

Passing the parade ground I saw a squad of sailors, they had gaiters and belts on, small packs on their backs plus a rifle. I said to a sailor who was watching as well, 'What's going on?' He replied,

'They've been naughty boys, there is about fifty pounds of sand in the packs.' The squad then raised their rifles above their heads and started to double. 'This place is like a military prison,' I observed. 'Yes,' he replied the Navy can get quite nasty when it wants to!'

I handed in my station card and walked out of the main gate. It was a free gate, which meant that I could walk out any time. It was situated at the bottom of an ordinary road with houses either side. I walked to the corner turned right, to walk to the centre of town.

There was a pub called the Air Balloon still standing but it was closed. It was quite a walk, I passed the burned-out Hippodrome, the Royal Sailor's Rest, the Lamport Drapery Bazaar, C & As and many more. Walking around a corner I remembered there used to be an Italian ice cream parlour run by a lovely Italian family, and as children we used to queue up for their lovely home made ice cream. 'Where are they now?' I wondered, 'interned I suppose.'

Next I passed the burned-out shell of the magnificent Guildhall. I walked into Victoria Park – where were all the mums and dads and children? Where was the lovely big aviary with every kind of bird from all over the world? I looked up, all I could see was barrage balloons.

I walked down through the War Memorial, passed walls engraved with hundreds of names of those killed in the First World War. I came to row B, looked up and down the names until I came to J Brehaut, my mother's first husband. He was killed when H.M.S. *Bulwark* blew up in Sheerness Harbour in early 1914, making my mother one of the Royal Navy's first war widows. I have his Ditty Box, it was found floating in Sheerness Harbour. The Ditty Box is a very strongly built box, 12 x 8 x 6 inches; it was given to every sailor in those days. It had a lock and was used to keep personal items and correspondence secure. I took that box everywhere, it was part of my kit and I still have it now.

I stood and looked at the burnt-out ruins of Aggie Weston's. Agnus Weston was a wealthy lady, who opened rest rooms for sailors of the Royal Navy in 1876. Over the years, her work for sailors progressed, to the point where a multi-storey sailor's rest was built, enabling sailors to get a good night's sleep when needed. She was looked upon as the mother of the Royal Navy. She was born in 1840 and died in 1918, she was made a Dame by Queen Victoria. When she died, she was buried with full Naval honours, the first women to receive this honour.

I looked for the Sailor's Home Club but that had been burned down, too. I could not find a Salvation Army Hall. I can't remember if I found a place for a cup of tea. I walked back to *Excellent*, picked up my station card and walked to the mess deck. Buncie said, 'Are you alright?' 'Yes,' I replied, 'I think I will go and see if there is any tea left.'

We were now learning about hydraulics. It was a nice change to be able to sit down and listen to a different P.O.G.I. Hydraulics was a strange course for Buncie and me, we would both have to concentrate if we were to pass our exams. At least we didn't have the other G.I. shouting at us, what a lovely change!

After Hydraulics came Fire Control. We had to learn how to put out fires, including running through one door and out another, the room being full of tear gas. We'd come out coughing and spluttering, eyes streaming – the Kiwis thought it was bloody stupid. Our G.I. said it was necessary!

Ammunition and Director Sighting were interesting and helped by the fact that the class could sit down and take notes if we wished.

After Fire Control, Ammunition, and Director and Sighting, came the most important of all – Gun Drill. Every man had to know every position on the gun. The class were training on the breach of a four-inch gun. The Kiwis made it look easy. Buncie and I found it hard when it came to our turn to be 'loaders'. We had a leather pad strapped on to our right knuckles to help push the projectile up into the breach.

One of the most important drills was to learn the misfire drill. At the order 'STILL, MISFIRE – GUN'S CREW IN FRONT OF THE GUN', we would rush around in front of the gun, in case the breach exploded.

There were seven crew members in a four-inch gun crew: the breach worker, three gun loaders, the communicating number, a gun layer, and a gun trainer. The layer making the gun barrel rise and fall, the trainer making the gun barrel move to the left and right. Other men, for example cooks and stewards, would feed the loaders from the magazine.

There were four tests left and the course would be over – the Gunnery test, the Hydraulics test, the Director and Sighting test and lastly the Assault course. Before these last tests, Buncie and I decided to walk into Portsmouth. Buncie couldn't believe the devastation. The air raids were reducing and the barrage balloons had stopped the hit-and-run raiders, but Hitler would send over two or three bombers now and again to let us know he was still around. There was a pub called The Golden Fleece, so we went in and had a pint of beer. It was very nice to sit down in a very different atmosphere.

It was time for the Gunnery test. There was a custom-built room for the test. The gun breach was on a specially made platform raised off the ground by large heavy springs to make the platform rock and roll. Above was a large tarpaulin filled with gallons of water.

Seven of us were picked: Buncie was to be layer and I was

to be trainer (making the gun move from left to right), then there was the breach worker and three loaders, each holding a four-inch dummy projectile. The communicating number was sitting down by the gun, then came the layer and then me, the trainer. As the breach contacts were not in communication with the transmitting station, the breach worker would shout 'READY.' the communicating number would act as the gunnery officer in the Transmitting Station (T.S.), and would shout 'FIRE.'

Either side of the breach was a small seat for the layer to sit on, in front of him was a dial with 360 degrees on it. There was a top ring on it with an arrow pointing downwards, and a ring underneath with an arrow pointing upwards. These arrows were to be pointing at each other. The layer and trainer had handles that had a similar action to bicycle pedals and were made of brass. They could be turned backwards or forwards following the top arrow, which would be coming from the transmitting station. The trainer would have a small seat as well.

Dressed in anti-flash gear, oilskins and tin helmets but no ear protectors, we were ready for the gunnery test. It is some seventy-four years since I heard these orders – I will do my best to explain how the test went.

The platform started to rock and roll, the rain started to come down, thunder flashes were thrown in, it was pitch black. Large bulbs started flashing as if enemy fire was coming our way. The Communicating Number shouted, 'ALARM, STARBOARD, ENEMY DESTROYER, ONE MAST, TWO FUNNELS, ALL GUNS FOLLOW DIRECTOR.' The layer, Buncie, and trainer, me, started the bottom arrow to follow the top arrow. The order 'LOAD, LOAD, LOAD' came. The first loader pushed the dummy projectile up into the breach and then stood back. The top arrows stopped and Buncie and I lined our arrows up.

Buncie shouted, 'LAYER ON.' I shouted, 'TRAINER ON.' The communicating number acting as the gunnery officer in the T.S. shouted, 'FIRE.' The breach worker opened the breach and the number-one loader caught the dummy projectile and quickly got out of the way. This process was repeated until twelve rounds were fired. The test was then over.

We came out of the test room, deafened and soaking wet. The Kiwis were incredible and I think they really enjoyed it. After dinner we had the Hydraulics oral and written exams – these were completed without any problems.

The following morning the class assembled at Shanghai beach for the last time. It was going to be very noisy with thunder flashes and Bakelite grenades being thrown and making very loud bangs. The grenades had to be thrown at least forty yards away from the assault course as there was a lead ball in the bottom of the grenade.

The class lined up, six in the front rank, four in the rear. It was half tide so we had a decent run to the wooden wall. The G.I. shouted, 'LANDING CRAFT COMING IN, LANDING CRAFT GROUNDED, RAMP DOWN, GO.' Buncie ran to the left, I ran to the right and scrambled up the wall. We sat across the corners giving covering fire, while the rest climbed over and down. There was a loud bang and I felt something ping off my tin helmet. I dropped to the ground and ran through the bushes, across and up the ramp – hooked on and slid down the wire, landing alright, and ran on to the wooden hill. We all scrambled over and ran to the wall, over we went running fifty yards, turning left and running another fifty yards to the water jump, over that and we'd finished. We stood there panting. One of the Kiwis shouted, 'Where's Buncie?'

The G.I. shouted back, 'He fell at the wall, go back and get him.' We all turned and ran back to the wall. There was Buncie, face down and unconscious, snorting bloody froth out of nose and mouth. A Kiwi and I carefully turned him over. I said, 'Oh Buncie!' The lead ball from a grenade thrown too close to the course had gone through his right jaw then through his left jaw, taking his teeth and tongue. Through his left jaw he was snorting blood and pieces of teeth, laying in a pool of blood.

I turned to the G.I. and said to him angrily, 'Why didn't you tell us?!' The P.O.G.I. thrust his face into mine and snarled 'THERE IS A WAR ON, take him to the sick bay, the rest of you back to the finish line.' Four Kiwis picked up Buncie, one on each limb and slowly carried him face down to the sick bay. The rest of us slowly walked back to the finish line. I guess we forgot to double. The Kiwis opinion of the Royal Navy was already rather low. I expected it would be even lower now. One remarked that if Buncie had landed on his back, he would have choked on his own blood.

Nobody wanted any tea. The Kiwis, instead of being happy to have finished the course were quiet and somewhat sad. They were going out to celebrate the end of the course and their return to their ship the next day. I knew it would be a quiet celebration. One or two of the other mess mates from further up the mess wanted to know what had happened to Buncie. I told them. The question was who threw the grenade, it was thrown forty yards too close. I had felt bits of Bakelite hit my helmet, the lead ball must have passed me and hit Buncie. We would never know who threw it.

It took me a long time to go to sleep that night. All I could see was Buncie's broken face. In the morning, after breakfast, the Kiwis started to pack their kitbags and get ready to leave. They all came over and shook my hand and said goodbye. I would never forget them, especially Digger Green, and I certainly wouldn't forget Hornton!

The chief of the block came and told us that at the sick bay they had quickly done what they could for Buncie and then he had been taken to the Royal Navy hospital at Haslar, Gosport. He then said to me that I could go to the regulating office and collect a return railway warrant to Bournemouth, the pay I was due and seven days' ration coupons. I could go anytime. The Kiwis would have their exam results sent to the ship. I would have mine when I came back from leave.

A lorry and coach arrived and the Kiwis loaded their kitbags onto the lorry and boarded the coach and were gone. Only too glad to see the back of H.M.S. *Excellent*. We never saw any sign of our P.O.G.I.

I packed my brown case, secured my kitbag, slung my gas mask over my shoulder, then looked around the mess. No Kiwis, no Buncie. It was a sad week when I left Collingwood, now a sad day, leaving *Excellent* without Buncie. I made my way over to the regulating office, picked up my railway warrant, pay and ration coupons and walked out of the main gate. The Royal Navy had gone into winter routine, so instead of wearing a white front and white cap, I wore a black jersey and black cap. I always think that a black jersey looks more seaman-like.

With my black cap fitted fair and square I walked to Portsmouth station, thinking it had been a hard three months. I'd met and made some good ship mates but the injuries to Buncie knocked away any joy I would have felt at finishing the course. I would have to wait to see if I had passed my exams to become a third-class gunnery rating, plus sixpence a day more pay.

I walked into Portsmouth railway station bought a paper, went to the ticket office, handed in my warrant and was given a ticket. I walked up the platform keeping an eye out for the uniformed gorilla, sat down on a seat and opened the paper. The train arrived and I boarded it, changing to another train at Southampton for Bournemouth Central Station. On arrival in Bournemouth, I caught two buses and then made the fairly long walk home.

Mum gave me a big hug and kiss and told me I looked thinner. It was nice to be home. I sat down in an armchair and Mum brought me a cup of tea and asked me how I was getting on in the Navy. I said, 'It's been a little harder than I thought it would be Mum, but I've made some good friends. The New Zealanders were a good crowd and I made friends with a lad called Buncie, but sadly he got injured in training and will be spending a long time in hospital, I think. It's sad because I was hoping we would be drafted together.'

I asked how she was coping and she said, 'Reg keeps the veg garden in good order and the hens are very good layers. A few more things are slowly being put on the shelves off-ration, which is a good sign.'

Well, if anyone could make a silk purse out of a sow's ear it would be Mum. Dad was still working a ten-hour day. A bus would pick him up at the top of the road, along with others, at seven thirty in the morning and bring them home at six thirty in the afternoon. He was now sixty-five years old.

Jock was working for Airspeed Oxford at Hurn Airport near Bournemouth. Reg still worked at his market garden. Ron was still at school but would leave at Christmas. Jean was happily married to Bill Calton. Everything seemed alright, no worries.

The bungalow next door to ours was the last one in the row. Beyond it was a large field. Apparently a few weeks earlier a battery of Canadian artillery appeared and tents were erected in the field along with three 5.5 Howitzers. They had made themselves quite comfortable. This had caused some excitement in the village.

On Saturday night I decided to go to the local pub. I didn't really expect to see any of my friends, as when I'd been in the pub on previous leave, there had just been a few locals in the bar. On this evening, though, there were a lot of new faces both male and female plus some Canadians. I went up to the bar and placed an order, the barman brought my drink and I paid him. When I checked I noticed he'd given me the wrong change. I said, 'Hey! I gave you a pound note and you've given me the change of a ten-shilling note.' I gave him a dark look and continued, 'I live in this village, I'm a local!' He muttered something about being confused and gave me the correct change. I thought, I expect he gets confused with the Canadians quite often!

On Sunday morning while in the garden I heard the sound of a bugle band, which meant that Captain Pusey and his troops were marching up and down the Wallisdown Road. It seemed as if Captain Pusey had taken little notice of Major Butt!

I was quite happy to sit at home, listen to the radio and read the daily paper. I went up to the club with Dad a couple of times. I enjoyed talking to his friends, especially Mr. Habgood who seemed to have such a wise head on his shoulders. When I walked in with Dad he would always stand up and shake my hand and say, 'Hello son.'

It was soon time to go back. I got up early to say goodbye to my brothers and give them a friendly clout. Shook hands and said goodbye to Dad. Sat down and had breakfast with Mum, then packed my case, slung my gas mask over my shoulder, gave Mum a big hug and a kiss – then out the door and off to Bournemouth Central Station.

I arrived back at HMS *Excellent* in time for dinner. I collected my station card and made my way to the mess deck. The bunks were now occupied, although the occupants were currently out on the parade ground. I wondered if they had the misfortune to have the same P.O.G.I. as our class had had.

After dinner I sat at the mess table with the others and they asked if Buncie was OK. I said I didn't know, said I only knew he had been taken to Haslar Hospital. One said, 'I don't suppose we'll ever know who threw the grenade.' I replied, 'No, I don't think we will.' Someone else enquired if I'd had a good leave. I replied, 'Yes, but there is not a lot to do in a small village. I was going to go to the Odeon in Bournemouth, but it's a long bus ride then a long walk and in the end I didn't think the film was worth it.'

Another shipmate said, 'Do you live in Bournemouth?' I said, 'No I live in Poole but I have to catch the train from Bournemouth to get back here.' He replied, 'You don't want to let the old pensioners who have been called back in hear you mention Bournemouth.' 'Why?' I asked. 'Because they reckon that between the wars, in the 20s and 30s, in the parks in Bournemouth there were signs saying Dogs and Sailors not admitted!' I said, 'I can't believe that!' but he replied, 'Well, they are still pretty wound up about it, so don't mention Bournemouth!'

They started to get up and make their way down to the parade ground to await the order to fall in for another couple of hours of punishment. I was sitting alone in the mess deck when the chief of the block walked in. 'Concerned about your mate?' he asked. 'Yes,' I said. 'Have you heard how he is and who threw the grenade?' 'Sorry,' he replied, 'but no I haven't and we never will know who threw the grenade.'

He then said, 'I have the results of your exams here, also would you like a cushy little draft? You don't want to hang about here waiting for one. It wouldn't be for long, about three weeks.

The place is called Frazer Battery and it's down at Fort Cumberland near Eastney, where the ferry goes across to Hayling Island.'

I said, 'Yes I would Chief.' He said, 'I thought you would. Have your gear outside the regulating office in an hour's time.' I said, 'Thanks very much Chief.' There were some decent chiefs and P.O.s around but in my opinion they were few and far between.

I opened the letter containing my results. I didn't do bad, I didn't do good! I received 350 out of 500, my best score was for oral Fire Control where I scored 45 out of 50. My worst was oral Director and Sighting, where I scored 44 out of 80. I know these results are correct, as I have my naval papers and results in front of me now, after all these years. I was now a fully fledged QRIII gunnery rating with sixpence a day more pay, taking me up to three and sixpence a day.

My kitbag was already packed and I humped it with my small case and gas mask to the regulating office. I then went to the hammock baggage store and drew my hammock and waited.

As I waited, it crossed my mind that there would be one good thing that H.M.S. *Excellent* would remember our class for – in the entrance of the Gunnery section there was an Honours Board, at the top was listed the 38 QRIIIs for the fastest time in the Gunnery test, beating even the instructors. I wondered if the Kiwis would ever know!

Up rolled the little canvas-topped van. I put my gear inside and then the chief of the block came out and gave the driver some paperwork. We shook hands and he wished me good luck. I said, 'Thank you Chief', and got into the van and off we went. I thought that would be the last I saw of H.M.S. *Excellent* but I was wrong.

Chapter Ten

Frazer Battery

We drove through Portsmouth and Eastney, and then at a corner with a large pub on it, we turned right, down the road which led to Frazer Battery, the road straight ahead going to the Hayling Island Ferry.

The driver drove in and stopped at what seemed to be the regulating office. There didn't seem to be much activity. The driver handed in the paperwork then off he went. The rating in the Regulating office said, 'Take your kit down those steps to the hut on the right-hand side, here's the key, go in and make yourself comfortable.' He pointed me in the right direction and off I went.

Humping my gear, I went down the steps and unlocked the door to the hut and went in. There were about twelve bunks down each side, eighteen of them were occupied. I found a free bunk and dumped my gear on it. Sat down and thought, 'What's going on?' I had no idea what the time was but guessed it must be mid-afternoon. I sorted myself out, made up my bunk, laid on it and waited for something to happen.

After what must have been an hour or so I heard the tannoy

sound 'All hands dismiss.' I then knew it must be 1600 hours. A quarter of an hour or so later hands started to come in to the hut, they were all Leading Seamen AAIIIs. One of them, who I could see by his badges was the senior rating, came over and asked who I was and what I was doing in the hut. I said, 'I've been drafted here and was told to come to this hut and make myself comfortable, which I've done. I don't know anything else.' He said, 'Nor do I but I'll try to find out what is happening.'

The tannoy piped 'hands to tea' and everyone got off their bunk and made their way to the mess hall. I followed suit. After tea the senior rating came to me and said, 'I'm going now to try to find out what is going on.' I said, 'Thanks', and off he went. I made myself comfortable. The other hands were either playing cards, writing letters, reading or swotting up. They never took any notice of me. After a while the senior rating came back, sat down and told me that I had been sent here to await a draft, that I would not become a member of the permanent staff, but he would find me something to do until such draft chit arrived. He told me that shore leave was available, but I told him that I wasn't interested in going ashore.

The hut was very cold but there was a big coke stove in the middle of the room and two of the leading seaman were cleaning it out and soon had it alight and glowing red hot. Some of the hands set to, making toast. Where they got the bread and butter from, I don't know.

The senior rating said, 'In the morning after we've washed, dressed and had breakfast, we make up our bunks and make our way up on to the ranges for 0800 hours. I want you to get the stove alight and make sure it's glowing red, so when we come back in, it is ready to make toast. You can sweep up the floor, tidy any bunks that need it and the rest of the day is your own.

The regulating staff know you are here but they don't seem very interested in you. I will see you in the morning.' I went and had a wash, came back and turned in.

We were all awakened at 0600 hours, got up, part dressed and trooped over to the wash house. Returning to the hut, we finished dressing and awaited the call 'Hands to breakfast.' On hearing the call we all made our way over to the mess hall. I had porridge, jam on toast and a cup of tea then returned to the hut sat down and waited.

The senior rating came over and said, 'We're now off to the ranges, we'll go straight to the mess hall for dinner at 12.00 midday, then will come back to the hut until we go back up on to the ranges at 1300 hours. We'll be back at about 16.15. Don't forget to lock the door if you go out and about.' With that he and the others were gone, leaving me sitting on my bunk and wondering if the Chief of the block back at *Excellent* had anything to do with this strange business.

I set to, cleaning the stove and raking out all the ashes. Once I'd finished, I locked up and went off to find some firewood. I thought the obvious place would be behind the galley and I was right. There were empty boxes stacked up that had contained deliveries. There was no one about so I helped myself to one of them, which I broke into pieces. I also spotted a pile of coal behind the galley, so I helped myself to a bucket of that as well. Back at the hut I also helped myself to a bucketful of coke from piles stacked up behind our hut. Armed with my pieces of wooden box, my buckets of coal and coke and some old newspaper, I went inside and soon had the stove burning nicely.

It was strange, I was in no man's land. I never saw a P.O. or officer all the time I was there, yet there was a railway warrant ready each weekend for me to go home. The only ratings I saw were at mealtimes. I swept the hut out, tidied some bunks, cleaned around the stove and that was it, finished.

I ventured out to see if I could find any activity. I crossed over and went up the steps. The regulating offices were about thirty feet away to my left. I went right to see what was behind them. There were huts, probably the Wrens quarters and the permanent staff quarters. On the right-hand side was a heavily barb wired beach, a road passed me to the right, it had to be a turning off the long road that led to the ferry. Also down the road about a hundred yards was a five-barred gate, standing by it was an armed sentry who appeared to be frozen. It was bitterly cold. He was the only person I saw.

I made my way back to the warmth of the hut, still seeing no one. There were papers around so I sat down and read one until the tannoy piped 'hands to dinner.' I grabbed my cap, locked up and ran to the mess hall. After dinner I ran quickly back to the hut, unlocked and made sure the stove was still burning. Soon the hut was filled up with leading seamen.

I said to the senior rating 'I haven't seen anybody all day, I can't understand what is going on!' He said, 'All I've been told is that you are here to await your draft, how long that will be I don't know. Just carry on as you are until you hear something.'

I think the leading hand was getting a bit fed up with me! None of the others spoke, they were not a very friendly lot. I suppose I was an ordinary seaman H.O. whilst they were seasoned leading seamen.

The hands had sorted themselves out in the hut. There was a sink and draining board and a kettle. A shelf had been put up on which there was Camp coffee, Nestlé condensed milk, tea and a variety of mugs. The senior rating said I could help myself to a cup of Camp coffee every morning.

That evening two leading seamen went over to the galley. The galley fires had to be kept burning all night – it was the job of the duty stoker to keep them fired up. The leading seaman put two large mess kettles full of water onto the galley fires, whilst two others went out to the sea wall which was about six feet high and four feet wide, jumped up on it and made their way across and dropped down on to the stony beach below. They then made their way through the barbed wire, which they must have been through before. The tide was out and they made their way on to the rocks and started to poke around with a steel bar. Soon they had poked out a couple of lobsters. They threw the lobsters up to a couple of their friends who took them to the galley and popped them into the galley kettles. A little while later the leading seamen were cracking and eating lobsters. They didn't offer me any. The New Zealanders certainly showed them up as far as hospitality was concerned!

I decided to do just what I had been told to do and nothing more, no more questions, just carry on until the three weeks were up or I was drafted. A couple of the leading seamen had papers delivered and I could read them as long as I left them looking untouched, so I had plenty to read.

One afternoon while scrounging for firewood, I decided to pluck up enough courage to go into the galley – it was bitterly cold – to see if I could scrounge a cup of tea. I carefully opened the door, put my head around and a voice said, 'Come in.' I entered to be faced by a large Chief Wren cook. I expected to be told to go away, instead she asked if I was cold. I said yes I was and she turned to a young wren and told her to make me a cup of tea, which she did.

The chief wren seemed to take a bit of a shine to me and said that they were busy in the mornings but I could come to the galley in the afternoons, which I did. The young wren was the same age as me. Her name was Leigh, we struck up a friendship – I would go to the galley in the afternoons, sometimes she was there, sometimes not, but I always had a cup of tea. It was nice to talk to somebody if only for the time it takes to drink a cup of tea. The chief cook didn't seem to mind. One Friday afternoon she said, 'Are you going home this weekend?' I said, 'Yes I am.' She replied, 'Come and see me before you leave.' I said, 'Alright, thank you.'

That Friday night the senior rating told me that as there was no training on Saturdays and Sundays, there would be someone in the hut all the time, but that I should do my usual work in the morning, and then when finished I could get ready to go home, collect my railway warrant from the regulating office and go, but to be back on Sunday night.

In the morning I got on and did my work and was soon ready to leave, dressed in my number ones with my little brown case and gas mask. I made my way over to the galley where the chief cook gave me a little parcel, saying, 'Give this to your mother.' I thanked her, putting the parcel in my case. I said goodbye to her and Leigh and headed for the regulating office where I received my railway warrant and two days' ration coupons.

I walked out of Frazer Battery to the bus stop to wait for the bus to take me to Portsmouth station. The bus finally came and we drove through Eastney and Southsea, passing the burned-out Town Hall which was opposite the railway station. Air raids seemed to be happening much less. No one at Frazer Battery took any notice when the siren sounded. There was no shelter near our hut, in fact I didn't know where there was one! I suppose that Frazer Battery was a long way from Portsmouth Dockyard.

I walked into Portsmouth station, produced my railway

warrant, received a ticket and, again keeping an eye open for the uniformed gorilla, walked down the platform, found a seat and sat down to wait for the train. The train came in on time and I was soon on my way. I changed at Southampton for Bournemouth, caught two buses then made the long walk home.

Mum was pleased to see me, as always, and I gave her a big hug and kiss. Dad was at work, Ron was out with his chums, Reg was out on his bike – apparently since Reg had bought his bike he rode it for miles. Jock was out with his friends, he was earning very good money. I had missed dinner so Mum boiled a precious egg which I had with some soldiers. I opened the little parcel the chief cook gave me: inside were rashers of bacon and some butter for which Mum was very grateful and she told me to tell the chief cook that it was much appreciated.

Sweets were rationed in 1942. The week's rations for one person in 1943 were: 2 oz tea, 8 oz sugar, 4 oz jam, 3 oz sweets, 2 oz lard, 2 oz butter, 2 oz margarine, 4 oz cheese, 4 oz bacon, ¾ lb meat, one egg. I said to Mum, 'I don't know how you are going to use just two days' ration vouchers.' Mum said, 'The grocer and butcher know you are in the Navy, so I should not worry.'

Dad came in from work, Mum fried him some bacon and another precious egg as a treat. It must be very hard work for him in the boiler room as they were coke boilers. After he had his treat, he got up and went and sat on his old armchair and said, 'We'll go up the club later.' He wasn't going to miss his Saturday night out with his mates. Then he nodded off. Saturday night was the only night of the week he went out.

At 20.00, Dad was ready, it was only a ten-minute walk to the club. Saying, 'cheerio' to Mum, off we went. As usual I got the same greeting from Mr. Habgood – when we entered the club he stood up, shook my hand, said, 'Hello son.' Sat at the table was another of Dad's mates, Paddy Daley who had been pulled out of the wreckage when Bournemouth gasworks was bombed. Two of his sons were in the services, Harry was serving in the eighth army, Jim was in the Navy. Paddy was one great guy. His daughter Josie was being courted by a chum of mine, Jammy James, who was serving in the marines. At 22.00, after a couple of beers and a good yarn with Paddy and Mr. Habgood, Dad and I left the club and walked home.

When we got back I settled down with a cup of cocoa. I told Dad about the strange goings-on at Frazer Battery, that I had not seen a petty officer or Naval Officer all the time I had been there. I told him what little I had to do, He said, 'That doesn't sound like the Navy to me.' I said, 'I know Dad, I keep taking the subject up with the senior rating but he tells me to shut up, do as I'm told and wait.' Dad said, 'If that is what he said then that is what you should do.' I said, 'Alright that's what I thought I should do, too, but there must be a reason why I've been sent to Frazer Battery even though there is nothing for me to do!'

Saying goodnight to Dad, and giving a hug to Mum, I went off to a nice comfortable bed. In the morning I had nice long soak in a hot bath. It was nice to sit at the dinner table with all the family, except Jean, whose husband Bill had applied to be transferred to the Indian Navy as an instructor. He had been successful. He and Jean had talked it over and she knew Bill would be away for some time – until the end of the war. She was now expecting a baby. Jean said she would have some lovely company while Bill was away. He would become a petty officer and then later a chief petty officer. More pay to save, which was behind the idea to apply for the Indian Navy.

Mum had prepared a lovely dinner; she was very shrewd at saving ration vouchers. After dinner we had a cup of tea which

Mum made and then my brothers all went out and Dad sat down for a doze. I prepared to go back, I wanted to be back before tea. I packed my case, gave Dad a gentle shake, shook hands and told him I was off. Gave Mum a big hug and kiss, said I'd see them next weekend, then I was off out of the bungalow and on my way to the bus stop. Next stop the train station. There were not many people around. The train was on time, I changed at Southampton and got off at Portsmouth. I had just missed a bus to Frazer Battery, so had a long wait and by the time I got back I had missed tea. I wasn't worried, I'd had a lovely dinner followed by Mum's spotted dick and custard!

There were a few leading seamen in the hut. Surprisingly, a few of them asked me if I'd had a nice weekend and I replied that I had and it had made a nice change. I reached my bunk and sat down. The stove was burning red hot for toast. A couple of leading seamen were getting ready to make toast. I could have done with a slice, but I knew there was no chance of that so I undressed, went for a wash and then turned in on my bunk and read my book. I must have fallen asleep as the next thing I knew the tannoy was calling 'All hands rise and shine,' it was 0600 hours. I rose, half dressed and went across to the ablutions, washed (I hadn't started to shave yet), went back to the hut and finished dressing. I sat on my bunk and waited for breakfast call. One or two of the leading seamen had started talking to me, but only to tell me what a soft job I had! I replied that I never asked for it!

So, it was the same routine – about 07.45 they would be gone up to the ranges. I would clean out the stove, light it, sweep the hut, tidy the bunks and then make myself a cup of Camp coffee, and read the papers – it was too cold to wander around outside. It was then a case of waiting for the dinner call, when I'd lock up the hut, race to the mess hall, quickly eat my dinner then race back to unlock the hut – mustn't keep any of them waiting!

After a short kip in the afternoon I would go over to the galley where Leigh or another wren would make me a cup of tea. I gave the chief cook Mum's thanks for the rations. She said that was alright and that if I was going home at the weekend to call into the galley before I left.

And so the week went by. It was a mere 'hello' to the senior rating. Nobody came to see me. I saw a few wrens up on the perimeter. The leading seamen carried on making toast and lobster fishing. The weekend came and I got ready to go home. I went over to the galley where the chief cook had a small parcel for me, I thanked her and said goodbye to her and Leigh. Then off I went to the regulating office, where a rail warrant plus two days' ration tokens were waiting for me.

I walked out of Frazer Battery and went to the bus stop, waited for the bus; it soon came and I boarded. We soon arrived at the ruined Guildhall, where I got off the bus and crossed to the train station, handed in my warrant and received my ticket, keeping an eye out for the uniformed gorilla (of course). I had seen no sign of him but I bet if I were to sit down and tip my cap back, he would soon appear! My train came and I was soon in Southampton, changing for Bournemouth; then the two buses and a long walk home.

I greeted Mum with a hug and kiss. I had missed dinner again, so had some scrambled egg on toast, which was thoroughly enjoyable. In the evening I went up to the club with Dad, met Mr. Habgood and Paddy. Paddy said that his son Harry had been wounded serving in the 8th Army but he hoped not too seriously. Dad said that the Navy and Air Force were getting the upper hand in the Atlantic although still losing too many ships.

I asked Dad if the job was getting too much – ten hours a day.

He said, 'No, there's a good canteen, where we can have a decent lunch' – perhaps the canteen was allowed more rations. Dad seemed to get on alright with the Commander, two old sea dogs together I guess.

After a couple of beers I said goodnight to Mr. Habgood and Paddy and Dad and I walked home. I told Dad that nothing had changed at Frazer Battery. I had seen no one, no one came to see me. Nothing had changed with the leading seamen, toast and lobsters. Dad said there must be a reason. I said yes, I had a feeling I would not be at Frazer Battery much longer.

The next day I had a nice lie-in and a hot bath. Mum opened the parcel that the chief cook had sent for her. This time it was cheese and butter. The butcher was quite generous with the two days' ration coupons and Mum was able to cook a nice Sunday dinner. After dinner, I got ready to go back, hoping I'd be back in time for tea. Packed my case, said goodbye to my brothers – I had already said goodbye to Dad, the night before – gave Mum a big hug and kiss and off I went, the long walk, the two buses, train to Southampton, changing for Portsmouth. Made the bus this time and got off at Frazer Battery in time for tea.

After tea I settled down to read a book. The senior rating came over and said that he had enquired about me, he said that I was to wait for a draft and in the meantime to carry on as normal. I replied, 'Alright', and that was that. I went and had a wash, came back and turned in to my bunk. Nothing had changed!

At 0600 hours the next morning, I turned out of my bunk and the same routine was had. Dressed, breakfast, clean the stove out and soon had it burning – there was plenty of firewood and newspapers. The leading seamen seemed to be unusually cheerful. It turned out it was the last week of their course, it would end on Friday – strangely the same time as my three weeks would come to an end.

I carried on as usual. Dinner time would lock the hut, run across for dinner, run back to unlock the hut and make sure the stove was still burning bright. After the leading seamen had gone back to the ranges I'd get my head down for an hour or so then go over to the galley for a cup of tea. I would have liked to have asked Leigh out, but Frazer Battery was miles away from anywhere. There was nowhere to go. Places were burned out – there was only the pub and I wasn't used to drinking and neither was Leigh.

The week soon went by. The senior rating carried on as normal – told me that my warrant and ration token would be ready at the regulating office – he never told me that this would be their last week of training.

On Saturday morning I turned out of my bunk as usual, washed, dressed, had some breakfast came back and cleaned out the stove, set it alight, made sure it was burning brightly then changed into my number ones. Packed my case and went over to the galley where the chief cook gave me a small parcel. I thanked her and said goodbye. I went across to Leigh and told her that this would be my last week – I think she was a little sad – said goodbye to her and made my way to the regulating office and picked up my railway warrant and ration tokens, then walked out of Frazer Battery, walked to the bus stop, caught the bus and was soon on my way to Portsmouth station. On arrival I made my way to the ticket office and exchanged my warrant for a ticket. I made my way to the platform, looking out for the uniformed gorilla – where does he hide? – I must have been unlucky to have been caught. I bought a paper, walked up the platform and sat down, making sure my cap was straight, and read the paper until the train came.

The train was on time and I boarded, thinking that this would be the last time I would make the trip home. As usual I changed at

Southampton for Bournemouth, then two buses and a long walk home. Walking indoors I gave Mum the usual big hug and kiss. Dad was at work.

I said to Mum, 'Dad didn't ought to be working all these hours – he should be sitting in his armchair, smoking his pipe!' Mum replied, 'Dad has made up his mind to work until the end of the war', but how long would that be? Dad was confident that this country would come out on top, but we were still losing too many ships.

Mum made me a nice meal. My brothers were out and about. I sat in Dad's armchair and fell asleep. Reg and Ron came in, Jock was out with his friends, he was earning good money so could afford to. Mum made us tea. There was more food about now. More tinned food, cereals, washing powder. More of the essential stuff. Mum said things were getting better.

Dad came in from work. Mum cooked him bacon and egg thanks to the chief cook's parcel of bacon, butter and cheese. I told Mum and Dad that this would be the last weekend I would be coming home and had an idea that I would be drafted on Monday. I'd been lucky to have been able to come home this last three weekends. Dad sat down in his old armchair, said he would have a nap for an hour and then we would go up the club.

The Kings Arms was now a popular pub with the Canadians, they certainly livened up the village night life! My one pound nineteen shillings a week could not compete with the Canadian's earnings. Money seemed no problem with them.

Dad woke up, got himself ready, said goodbye to Mum and we walked up to the club for the last time in a while. Entering the club with Dad, I shook hands with Mr. Habgood and Paddy. Dad said that the Americans were building a new cargo ship called Liberty ships. It was hoped that they would be able to build them fast enough that they could compete with the losses in the Atlantic. Paddy's son was wounded at the battle of the Mareth Line, but was getting better.

We carried on yarning until about 22.00 and I then told them that I expected to be drafted on Monday and did not know when I would see them again. I thanked them for their company over the last three weekends and Dad and I walked home. Mum made me a cup of cocoa, and said to thank the chief cook for the rations. We talked for a while, Dad said that work in the boiler house was not too hard, he'd had one or two altercations with a couple of the younger men who were exempt, otherwise everything was fine.

I said, 'I'm off to bed', gave Mum a goodnight kiss, said goodnight to Dad, was soon in a warm bed. In the morning I had a lie-in and a hot bath. The butcher had sold mum a nice piece of beef plus a piece of dripping, so with some of the vegetables that Reg was growing (it was November so I think we had Brussel sprouts or cabbage) Mum was able to cook a good Sunday dinner, followed by apple pie and custard.

After dinner I sat talking with my brothers. After a little while I said, 'I better get ready to go back.' Packed my case, gave my brothers a friendly clout, shook hands with Dad, gave Mum a kiss and then an extra kiss. Told them I would write as soon as I knew what was happening. Then I was out the door to start the long walk to the bus stop – I turned around and gave Mum a wave, didn't know when I would see her again.

The journey back was the same as ever, two buses, two trains and I was back at Frazer Battery in time for tea. When I got back, the senior rating told me that on Saturday night all the leading seamen had gone up to the Cumberland pub to celebrate the end of the course, they caught the bus up to the pub but had to walk back. It was a very long road, along which the Portsmouth bus service used to park quite a few of its double-decker buses; they were quite safe there.

The eighteen tipsy sailors had turned down the side road that ran in front of the ranges and were making merry when they were challenged, 'Who Goes There?' by the sentry. In return he got eighteen different names, some apparently quite rude! Some of the leading hands had brought their beer mugs with them – at the start of the journey the mugs were full up, by the time they got back most of the beer had slopped out! The leading hands took the sentry's rifle from him, sat him down then let him drink as much beer as he liked. They placed the empty beer mugs around the sentry box – and walked away, leaving a very happy sentry!

There was quite a different atmosphere after tea in the hut, some were still talking about the previous night. Apparently nothing had been said about the sentry or the beer mugs – what a place! A few made themselves some toast for the last time. They were quite a different lot now, I wonder how many survived the war? I read a book until time to turn in.

In the morning, I washed, dressed and went for breakfast, came back, cleaned the stove, said to the senior rating, 'Shall I light the stove?' 'No, leave it,' he said. 'You need to report to the regulating office, you are on draft!' What a surprise!! I made my way to the regulating office, where I was told I was drafted to H.M.S. *Alresford*, which was lying in Portsmouth Naval dockyard, and I should get my kitbag and hammock and be outside the regulating office at 10.30.

I went to the galley and told the chief cook that I had been drafted, thanked her for the rations she had given me for Mum and for all the cups of tea. I think she was a little sorry to see me go. I went over to Leigh and thanked her for her friendship, said goodbye, shook hands, turned and walked out of the galley, across to the regulating office to wait for the little canvas-topped RN van for the last time.

I had had plenty of time to think about why I had been drafted to Frazer Battery. Buncie had been injured on the Friday afternoon. The P.O.G.I. never came to see us to tell us what was happening. The Chief of the Block told us that he had been sent straight to the Naval hospital at Hasler, Gosport. On the Saturday morning the New Zealanders had left and I was given seven days' leave. Buncie's parents would have been devastated, broken hearted, and only the disgraceful P.O.G.I. would have been there to answer any questions – and judging by his behaviour on the day, he may not necessarily have answered honestly. There should have been an enquiry into such a terrible injury. Perhaps there had been. If I had still been at *Excellent* I would have told them exactly what had happened but within a few hours of being back from leave, I was on my way to Frazer Battery, and now after three weeks I was to be drafted. I will always wonder who threw the grenade that injured Buncie, but I and the New Zealanders would never know.

The little van finally turned up – I put all my kit in the back and climbed into the front seat. The driver went into the regulating office and came out with some paperwork. He jumped in the van and off we went. I left Frazer Battery still not having seen a P.O. or Naval Officer.

Chapter Eleven

H.M.S. Alresford –
November 1943-January 1944

The driver made his way through the traffic and into Portsmouth naval dockyard. He spoke to a dockyard policeman, who showed him where H.M.S. *Alresford*[3] was lying. Soon the van stopped alongside an old-looking ship. I got out of the van, walked around to the back. The driver must have read my mind, as grinning he said, 'And she's a coal burner!' He gave me a hand with my kit up the gang plank and on to the quarter deck, where a quartermaster and bosun's mate were standing. The driver gave the quartermaster the paperwork and then with a cheery 'good luck mate' he turned and walked back down the gang plank and was soon gone.

The quartermaster came over to me and took me to a desk, opened what was a day book and wrote: *11.00 hours, 24th November 1943, Ordinary Seaman Frederick Beedie H.O. drafted to ship.* He then told the bosun's mate to give me a hand with my kit. We made our way forward, where a covered ladder on the forecastle lead down into a large mess deck. Humping my kitbag, case and gas mask down the ladder, the bosun's mate followed me with my hammock. I looked at my surroundings, there were three or four sailors working. The bosun's mate told me the nearest sailor was

Charlie Fox. Charlie came over to me and was about to speak when there was the clatter of someone coming down the ladder; it was a leading seaman, whose name I cannot remember (so I will refer to him as leading seaman X), he introduced himself, gave me a station card, telling me I was in the 1st part of port watch. He told Charlie Fox to show me where to stow my gear.

The mess deck was split into two parts, separated by the ladder coming down from the upper deck. The right-hand side was the stokers' mess. On the left-hand side was the seamans' mess. These were also split in two, so you would have the 1st port separated by about four feet from the 2nd part of port. Likewise on the stokers' mess.

The bosun's mate vanished up the ladder, followed by leading seaman X. Charlie Fox showed me a locker in which to stow my gear, also where I could sling my hammock at night. He explained that in the morning after lashing the hammock and taking it down, I should stow it in the hammock 'flat' (why it is called a 'flat' I do not know). About four feet from the foot of the ladder was an open hatch about four feet square, halfway along the front of the hatch was a steel support post, which went from the deck to the deckhead; this would also help prevent anyone from tumbling down into the hammock flat. Beneath the support post, running either side, was a bulkhead to the ship's side; a ladder went straight down into the hammock flat.

I struggled down with my hammock. On the left side of the ladder was a partition about four feet high, running along to a forward bulkhead, forming a compartment on the left side where the hammocks were stowed. I stowed my hammock.

Going back up to the mess deck, Charlie Fox asked me where I had come from. I told him, 'Whale Island.' He said, 'It's a bit tough there!' I said, 'Yes, it is!' 'Is this your first ship,' he asked.

'Yes,' I replied. 'You will find it pretty hard on here too,' he told me. 'I and the other three here are all setting up the tables for dinner. Every week a fresh hand from each mess becomes cook of the mess. I am this week's cook of the mess, it's nearly dinner time now, when the hands are all down, I and another hand, usually Steve Conner, will go to the galley to fetch the dinner. All hands help to prepare the meals, they are then taken to the galley where the cook cooks them. He does not do any preparation. The duty cook is expected to make seconds, to make pastry and dumplings. We have stew today (called pot mess) with dumplings (dough boys), then rice pudding (what, back then, we called Chinese wedding cake). There are three or four hands who apparently are very good, and they prefer to do the mess cook job between themselves. The rest of the mess, which includes me, they reckon are all rubbish!'

There was a clattering of feet as the hands came down to the messes. There were eight in the 1st part of port. I can remember every one of them. I am not so good at remembering all in the 2nd part of port. Charlie introduced me, they all greeted me and asked me where I had come from. I told them that I was an ordinary seaman H.O. and had been drafted from Whale Island. In the mess they were all able seamen, all seasoned sailors, I was treated as if I had been on board for months. For the first time I was happy to be in the Navy.

Charlie and Steve Conner went to the galley and brought back the pot mess, boiled potatoes and peas (pussers). The stew was wonderful, dough boys as big as tennis balls and light as a feather. It was the best meal I had had since joining the Navy. For afters there was rice, with a lovely brown skin across the dish. Charlie then brewed an urn of tea.

After we'd eaten, one of the hands went to the galley and

92

fetched a mess kettle of hot water. A hand full of soda was thrown in and then Charlie and a couple of others did the washing up. That done, most sat back with a mug of tea and lit a cigarette.

Suddenly came the shrill sound of a bosun's call from the top of the ladder. 'Hands detailed pump fresh water!' Behind the ladder was a large wheel about four foot across, with a large handle one side and on the other side, hanging on the bulkhead, was another handle, which fitted onto a shaft on the other side of the wheel.

Four seamen, two each side, would start turning the wheel; they were pumping fresh water from the water tanks, below deck, up to the water tank on the boat deck. It looked like back-breaking work – and it was! Only seamen were called on to pump fresh water. To fill the tank on the boat deck, could take up to twenty minutes; to the stronger seamen it wasn't too bad, but for the likes of me, it was sheer hard work!

In the summer time, more water was used, which meant more pumping! Add the fact that the ship was a coal burner, with coal having to be shipped quite regularly, and I soon realised that Charlie Fox wasn't far wrong when he said it was going to be pretty hard work! We were all paid an extra shilling a day, hard lying money, taking me to four and sixpence a day.

When all the hands had gone back to work, I was talking to Charlie Fox. He said to me that the main armament on board was a 1912 12-pounder. I said to him, 'I have just finished a three-month course on 4-inch, 4.5-inch, 5-inch and 6-inch guns and I am sent to a ship whose main armament is a 1912 12-pounder! To make it worse, my leading seaman, seaman X, is the breech worker. He has not done a gunnery course, I have. Now I, an Ordinary Seaman H.O., will have to take that gun position from him as I have completed a gunnery course and he has not. It also means that I will have to ask him the workings of a 1912 12-pounder!

Charlie Fox said he was a good leading hand and not to worry.

Charlie then went up on deck. I followed, he showed me the heads (toilets) which were on the port side on the upper deck, the wash room was also on the upper deck a little further on. I opened a door (the light inside went out when the door was opened and came on again when the door was shut) and stepped into the washroom, which was a little larger than the average living room; on three sides were four fixed enamel wash basins which emptied when tipped. Above each basin was a cold-water tap. On the fourth wall was a copper boiler with a cold-water tap above to fill it. A small wheel on the bottom controlled the steam. There was a small tap on the side – I would hold a large metal jug under the tap, one jug would be enough for two ratings to wash and shave. I didn't need to shave, so it was no problem for me. Ratings had to supply their own mirrors. We stood in line to fill the jug.

H.M.S. *Alresford* was the tender for H.M.S. *Dryad*, the Royal Navy's Navigational School. Her job was to teach navigating officers pilotage out in the Solent or Spithead; this happened once or twice a week. Four or five nights a week she would go out and anchor in the Nab Channel to spot if any German aircraft were dropping parachute mines. If any were spotted, bearings had to be taken. The 12-pounder's gun crews plus the 2-pounder pom-pom gun that was aft on the boat deck, were closed up around their guns. Bombing had started to be a little more active in 1943.

Leading seaman X was in no way worried about me taking over as breech worker. There was nothing complicated about the operation of the 12-pounder. I soon learned it in a couple of hours. He was quite happy to be No. 1 loader. A few gun-crew exercises, taken by the forecastle Petty Officer May, made us quite an efficient gun crew.

The ship was not fitted with radar, Asdics nor echo sounder, she only had degaussing gear, which consisted of four heavy cables running round the entire ship's side , occasionally passing through heavy electrical boxes also attached to the ship's side. This gear was fitted to prevent the ship being blown up by a magnetic mine.

The ship was commanded by a Royal Naval commander, F. G. Chevallier D.S.O., a first lieutenant R.N.V.R. (Royal Naval Volunteer Reserve), a sub-lieutenant R.N.V.R., a divisional paymaster officer, two navigating officers, a coxswain, one petty officer and four leading seamen. Also there were, of course, the stokers – a chief stoker, P.O.s, leading stokers and stokers – how many I do not know.

One of the two navigators was rather elderly, he had been called back up having retired some years before. He was a Royal Naval lieutenant. The other navigator was a lieutenant R.N.R. (Royal Naval Reserve). The Captain and the R.N. lieutenant navigator turned out to be the best two naval officers I served under in my short naval career, not only to me but to the rest of the crew also. It was a hard ship but a happy ship.

It was now getting towards Christmas 1943 and we were told there was no Christmas leave but ordinary shore leave would be granted.

I had now been out to the Nab Channel several times, it proved to be rather cold and uncomfortable. Some of the gun crews had duffel coats, I had just an oilskin; most had towels around their necks and leather sea boots. I had a lot to learn!

One night the sirens sounded and we heard the sound of German aircraft, their engines sounding completely different to ours. The searchlights lit the sky, however the sound of the aircraft slowly died away, they were heading towards Southampton or Plymouth. Eventually, the same aircraft would return in dribs and drabs. Once again the sirens sounded 'red alert' – out in the Nab Channel, we could do nothing but watch.

At dawn, the ship returned and on reaching Portsmouth Harbour, hands lined the ship, saluting the Commander In Chief in the signal tower. We passed two mine sweepers which were going out to sweep the main channel irrespective of the fact that the ship had not spotted anything. The sirens were wailing the 'all-clear'. The ship entered the tidal basin and tied up to the south-west wall.

The gun crews went below to have a wash, a mug of tea and a fag, then a couple of hours' sleep, with the rest of the crew to carry on doing normal ships' duties. We were told that we were to 'coal ship' the next day and with that cheerful news I turned in to my hammock and was soon asleep but woke in time for dinner.

The following morning we turned to at 0700 hours, the ship left the basin, steamed right up Portsmouth Harbour and tied up to a coaling lighter (a flat bottomed barge); the ship's crew turned out, looking like pirates, bandanas around their heads, old clothes, leather sea boots – over the top they had overall trousers pulled over their sea boots. Steve Conner told me to go down in the hammock flat and look for some sea boots. On the right-hand side of the hammock flat, there were two cabins. In one was a pile of leather sea boots and kitbags. I rummaged around until I found two boots that fitted me. I put on my oldest boiler suit and pulled the legs down over my sea boots. I wrapped an old towel around my neck and tucked it into my boiler suit and put my cap on. The idea was not to show much skin.

On the quarterdeck was a skylight that allowed light down into the ward room, this was protected by a large wooden cover.

P.O. May signalled me, Jock Towney, Piggy Grant and Steve Conner down in the lighter. I worked with Piggy Grant. I held a sack which would hold about two-hundred-weight of coal, it had very strong rope handles. There was no way a shovel could be used until we reached the steel deck bottom of the lighter.

The coal was in fairly large lumps of best Welsh steam coal. When four sacks had been filled, all by hand, a sling would be passed through the handles. The sling had an eye splice on each end. The lighter had a crane, which would lower a hook, the sling handles were hooked on to the crane's hook, the sacks were then hoisted up and over and down on to the quarterdeck.

Halfway up the port and starboard decks was what looked like a manhole cover, this was taken up. Below were the ship's coal bunkers. Inside, below, was a stoker armed with a small shovel and an old oil lamp. Back on the quarterdeck, several of the hands each had a porter's truck, on which was put a sack of coal; the hand would then push the truck up to the hole and tip the sack of coal into the bunker. The stoker would then distribute the coal evenly around the bunker. The hand would then push the truck around the ship and get behind the queue ready for another sack.

1000 hours came and the call came 'stand easy'. Mug of tea and a fag. Ten minutes later 'out' pipes. Steve Conner, Piggy Grant and Jock Towney changed with Charlie Fox, Jock McDonald and Jock Brown. I stayed in the lighter, I could not push a truck, I was not strong enough. I teamed up with Charlie Fox and we took turns to hold and fill the sacks.

We were told that coaling had to be finished by 1800 hours. My hands started to blister, there were no gloves to wear and I was glad when the lighter bottom was reached and I could use the shovel. There were white streaks of sweat running down our coal-dust covered faces.

1200 hours, hands to dinner, corned-beef sandwiches and coal dust, washed down with a mug of tea! At 12.30 we resumed coaling, the first three men that had changed, changed back. I had

Piggy Grant again. Now we had reached the steel bottom of the lighter, shovels could be used. We had to keep going if we were to finish by 1800 hours. At 1500 hours the call came 'stand easy' and we could have a mug of tea and a smoke. At ten past three, pipes sounded and we carried on. I asked Piggy, 'How much coal have we got to shift?' He said, 'Between eighty and a hundred tons!'

At 1600 hours, Charlie Fox, 1st part of port, and Jock Towney, 2nd part of port, were told to get cleaned up and prepare a meal. I thought, 'Lucky them, they will have the washrooms to themselves.' The stokers did the same.

My back was aching, I could hardly straighten up to hold the sack open. We finally finished coaling before 1800 hours and the trucks were handed back to the lighter. The Captain gave the order to leave the lighter, and lines were let go. The ship turned and started down Portsmouth Harbour. P.O. May shouted, 'Out hoses, stiff brooms and squeegees.' Soon the decks and bulkheads were being hosed down and the decks scrubbed. I was glad I had my sea boots on. The decks were soon awash.

The ship turned into the basin and was soon 'tied to' bollards on shore. Cleaning ship continued, I could hardly stand up. The ship had to be coaled every eight to ten days. I would never last! When the ship was cleaned to P.O. May's satisfaction, he dismissed us.

The stokers had had the chance of washing themselves whilst the seamen cleaned ship, and had used most of the water. The two seamen Fox and Towney had to leave getting the meal ready to two stokers who had been detailed. They then pumped more fresh water.

The rest of us then made our way to the washroom, stripped off, looking like coal miners just up from the coal face. I soon realised that a bucket is one of the most cherished items a sailor on a small ship can have. I must try and get one when I next go on leave, I thought. I will write home and ask Mum if she could buy one from Timothy Whites.

I watched the experienced hands. We were all naked. They washed their black faces with cold water in the basins, getting most of the coal dust off their faces and hair. They then filled their buckets with hot water and got the water as soapy as possible with Pussers hard yellow soap. They then washed themselves from top to bottom, giving themselves a jolly good scrub. There was a cold-water tap fitted alongside the boiler. They then filled their buckets with a mixture of hot and cold water and poured it over each other.

Steve Conner lent me his bucket and I did the same – having washed my face and hair in the basin, I filled the bucket with hot water and got it as soapy as possible and had a good scrub down, then poured warm water over myself to rinse. I towelled myself down as quickly as possible, then with the towel wrapped around my waist, ran along the upper deck and down the ladder into the mess deck. There, I dried myself properly and got dressed. Those with buckets put their overalls in hot water to soak with pieces of Pussers soap. I would have to wait until I could borrow a bucket.

I knew that soon fresh water would have to be pumped. I hoped that I would not be detailed. Charlie Fox had made a lovely cottage pie, the meat was as tender as it could be. In the refrigerator room there were stacks of Argentinian beef, frozen in sacks. That's one thing we were not short of.

To me, this had been a nerve-wracking day. To the others it was just another day's work.

The locals were doing their best to catch the last 'liberty' boat at 1900 hours. All I wanted to do was sling my hammock and turn in. Fresh water had to be pumped, but luckily I wasn't detailed, so I climbed into my hammock and soon fell asleep.

At breakfast next morning, I was told that there was a room, or caboose as it was called, next to the washroom, where all the clean clothes were kept – so there was no need to run to the mess deck to dress after washing. I had wondered why there was nobody in the messes the day before!

I was also told that I should mark my overalls, so I borrowed some Milton from Steve Conner, and getting my overalls, I dipped a matchstick in the Milton and etched my initials on the top pocket – the Milton took the dye out of the cloth, leaving the initials F.A.B. At 0800 hours the next morning both watches fell in on the quarterdeck. P.O. May called everybody's name and we each answered, 'Aye aye P.O.' He looked at me and saw my initials – F.A.B. – and from then on I was known as Ordinary Seaman FAB, H.O.

P.O. May detailed the two cooks of the mess to their messes. The rest of us were detailed to clean ship again. Hoses, deck brooms, squeegees, the boat deck had to be scrubbed, the bulkheads washed with a mixture of soft soap and hot water, this was the usual routine.

It was bitterly cold, we were off to the Nab Channel that evening. On arrival we dropped anchor and the gun crews closed up. It was going to be a long cold night. I put on a pair of leather sea boots, an extra jersey and an oilskin. I wrapped a towel around my neck and pulled a sock onto each hand.

We were told that there was quite a lot of activity going on in the channel. E-boats were trying to lay mines around the Isle of Wight and Dorset's Lyme Bay. They were being interrupted by our destroyers. We couldn't hear or see anything. There were no air raids. Perhaps it was because it would be Christmas in two days' time.

At dawn we upped anchor and steamed down the swept channel, passing the two mine sweepers who were on their way out to sweep the main channel. We lined the ship and saluted the C in C (Commander in Chief) in the signal tower. On entering the basin we tied up alongside H.M.S. *Plover*, which was a minelayer, full of mines! The ship was to be tied up for a few days. I don't think another ship took our place in the Nab Channel.

The gun crews had a cup of tea, some had a light breakfast of a cup of tea and a piece of bread and jam. I went and had a wash, came back and turned into my hammock and was soon asleep.

The Captain left the ship in the hands of the First Lieutenant. It was believed that the Captain had something to do with D-Day. Apparently he frequently attended meetings, it was said, in Newcastle. What was a full Commander D.S.O. doing captaining and old ship like this?

The next day was Christmas Eve. Leave was given from noon on Christmas Eve until 0800 hours in the morning on Christmas Day, which meant the locals would be home for Christmas Eve but had to be back on board by 0800 hours Christmas morning. All the officers had left the ship except the RN Navigating Officer, he never went ashore.

P.O. May was the scruffiest P.O. I had ever seen. His jacket and trousers were stained and grubby, his cap all out of shape, he wore a scruffy pair of wellington boots turned down at the tops. He scuffed along, not lifting his feet. He would have given the P.O.G.I. in Whale Island hysterics! He had a caboose on the portside upper deck filled with everything a seaman P.O. might need. It had a wonderful smell of old rope.

The ship had a coxswain but we hardly ever saw him, he seemed to leave the running of the ship to P.O. May. The ship also had P.O. yeoman of signals, one leading signalman and two signalmen. One was named Bob Jay; he and I made friends, we would go ashore together.

On Christmas morning those who had been on shore leave started to drift back. It was freezing cold, I was turned in my hammock! All hands turned to at 0800 hours and worked chipping rust until 'stand easy' at 1000 hours, at 10.10 'out pipes' was shouted and we carried on working until noon. Shore leave was granted from noon to 0800 hours the next morning.

Steve Connor had prepared a lovely roast dinner and made a large jam tart covered in custard – he called it a Manchester tart. Most of the crew who had had their tots of rum and a big dinner like that just wanted to get their heads down in the afternoon.

Steve Connor, Charlie Fox, Piggy Grant and Mick Johnson decided that they would do 'cooks of the mess' in future. I don't think they trusted the rest of us, which suited me down to the ground!

There was one problem when we were all sat down for a meal: Mick Johnson and a South African didn't get on. They hated one another, an argument would start between the two of them and before you knew it they were at each other's throats. I kept out of the way until they had been separated by Jock McDonald, Piggy Grant, Charlie Fox and Steve Connor. I think that Mick Johnson had been to South Africa on another ship and did not like what he saw. The South African believed in apartheid. I never ever saw two people who hated each other so much as those two! Mick Johnson had to be careful, he was on course for Leading Hand.

Some went ashore in the evening, there were some pubs that were still open if you were prepared to go and find them. All-night leave had been granted, which suited those from the local area. Others who had been out on leave were now drifting back. It was still bitterly cold (was there a place as cold as Pompey Dockyard on a Christmas Day?!).

Fresh water had to be pumped, I was one of the four who had to work the pump. It was hard work, took about twenty minutes to fill the tanks. When finished, I went and had a wash, fetched my hammock, slung it and turned in (Merry Christmas!). Boxing Day was the same, turned to at 0800 hours, had to scrub the decks – on leather boots, out deck scrubbers, squeegees and hosepipes – still freezing cold. At 1000 hours, stand easy, at 10.10, out pipes, put away deck cleaning gear, carry on chipping rust on the deck, forward of the breakwater and red lead.

At 1200 hours, hands to dinner. Those over twenty had their tots of rum to look forward to, I would have to wait another seventeen months. Steve Connor was still the cook of the mess. He had made a stew, or pot mess. Steve was renowned for his dumplings (dough boys), using plain flour, baking powder, butter and salt. They used to go into the pot the size of golf balls and come out the size of oranges! Steve prepared plenty of boiled potatoes as well. I would have two or three platefuls. Some of the mess would flap their arms and squawk and call me a gannet. I said I was a growing lad!

There was a 12.30 and 13.30 liberty boat. Not many went ashore. I and others were writing letters or playing cards. One or two were doing their dobeing (washing clothes).

There were three breweries in Portsmouth, two had been bombed, leaving one in operation – Youngs. Leading Seaman Burns was living the sailor's dream. He had married the daughter of a landlord, who owned a pub in Portsmouth, which had survived so far. If you were on shore leave and in the same watch as Leading Seaman Burns, and happened to be passing the pub and decided to go in for a drink, you would probably be served by him.

Tea time came, and we had the usual tea, bread, butter, cheese and Daddies Sauce. Then we peeled the potatoes for tomorrow's dinner. I was learning to play cribbage, it seems to be the favourite game, or ludo (or uckers, as it was called).

The Captain and officers had returned to the ship, as had the shore goers, and they were busy slinging their hammocks. I had already slung mine, so I went for a wash and then turned in. 'Out' pipes sounded at 2200 hours in the evening.

At 0800 hours, P.O. May detailed some of us to do chipping and wire brushing. Scraping and painting the foredeck before the breakwater seemed to be the main work. The motor boat crews had to clean the inside of the boat. I was hoping to get a job on the motor boat. Mike Johnson was the coxswain. The engine-room stoker was another of the pensioners called back in, he said that he had been stoker on the same boat in 1925.

Some navigating officers came on board. The R.N. navigator was the teacher of the navigating officers. The R.N.R. navigator was the ship's navigator. 'Hands to stations for leaving harbour,' was shouted by the bosun's mate. I was one of the fo'c'sle (forecastle) hands. The dockyard party maties let go of the wires from the bollards. The fo'c'sle party pulled the wires in and coiled them around the bollards on deck. We lined the ship for leaving harbour, saluted the C in C, steamed out of the harbour and turned right, steaming into Spithead and the Solent.

I had received a Christmas card from Mum and the family. On the card it said that Dad was still working, as were Jock, Reg and Ron (who had obviously found a job). One of the chickens had to be picked out for Christmas dinner (Mum was not very happy about this!), otherwise everything was alright. They hoped I was keeping well, and were looking forward to seeing me. I was looking forward to seeing all of them.

Charlie Fox was cook of the mess. I was still chipping rust away. It certainly was a very strongly built ship. I chipped rust and then used the wire brush until clean steel could be seen, then we painted on the red lead. It was arm-aching work, but I was not the only one having to do it. At 1000 hours 'stand easy', time for a cup of tea and a fag. At 10.10 back to chipping until noon. Charlie had made a nice meal. Then at 1300 hours we were back to chipping again. All you could hear was the thud of chipping hammers. I wondered when the chipping had last been done!

The ship had started its return to Portsmouth Harbour, so we had to clean ourselves up, and change into our number three uniforms ready to line the ship for return into the harbour. The ship turned into Portsmouth Harbour, saluting the C in C as we passed the signal tower, we then turned into the basin and tied up to the *Plover*. The officers left the ship. It was tea time. All-night leave was given, so the locals were off. Tomorrow night was New Year's Eve and the ship would be off to the Nab Channel.

The shore leavers returned. We turned to at 0800 hours. P.O. May detailed some to carry on chipping and red leading, others were detailed to clean the heads and the washrooms and paint them. I was with the chipping party, we finished chipping, swept the fo'c'sle deck clean, ready to be painted black. P.O. May had gone paint happy!

At 1600 hours the ship slipped wires and left the basin, saluted the C in C and headed out. It started to rain and turned out to be a foul night. I managed to have some bread and cheese with Daddies Sauce. When the ship reached the Nab Channel the anchor was dropped, the gun crews closed up – that was the 12-pounder and the pom-pom. The gun crews had worked all day and now had to stay awake all night. At about 2100 hours the cook made a kettle of cocoa (kye) and some corned beef sandwiches and brought them around to the gun crews.

It was still raining although the wind had dropped a little – I had been working all day, had only had a piece of bread and cheese and Daddies Sauce. I was hungry, tired, cold and getting wet. I was moaning and groaning, when a voice shouted, 'Stop the moaning Beedie!' It was the gunner's yeoman, he was also a pensioner who had been called back. He was as hard as nails. He came over to me, thrust his face close to mine, 'Shut your trap, what's the matter with you!' I told him I was cold and hungry, he said, 'We all are.' He grabbed me by the lapels of my oilskin and pulled me even closer to his face and shouted, 'It's our job to watch and listen, you volunteered didn't you?' I said, 'Yes.' He snarled, 'If you can't take a joke, you shouldn't have joined.' He was very angry. I never moaned again, at least not when he was around!

Kye and sandwiches at 2100 hours, midnight and 0300 hours had always been the normal routine, but on this miserable occasion we could have done with some of Steve Connor's pot mess, why couldn't the cook make some cups of soup?

The gunner's yeoman had a workshop come cabin somewhere down of aft. I had never, ever entered it. After ticking me off he was gone, leaving leading seaman X in charge, and so the night went on. It was an ideal night for E-boats to motor silently in. The air raids had become few and far between, except for the snooper, high up going round and round, keeping everybody awake. This was becoming a bit of a risk for the German aircraft – our night fighters were becoming rather successful.

Dawn finally came. We upped anchor and made our way through the swept channel. The two mine sweepers were on their way out. The gun crews lined the ship, the 12-pounder crew forward, the pom-pom crew aft. Saluting the C in C we turned into the tidal basin and tied up to the south-west wall. The *Plover* had gone. I was too tired to eat, had a cup of tea, went for a wash then turned in to my hammock, which I had slung before going out to the Nab Channel. What a New Year's Eve!

Chapter Twelve

H.M.S. Alresford – January 1944–June 1944

The next day was New Year's Day 1944. The gun crews slept until noon, waking in time to have a wash and dinner. Leave had been given from noon 1st January to 08.00 in the morning on the 2nd January. All hands were back on board. The ship left the south-west wall tidal basin (S.W.W.T.B.) and made its way up to the coaling lighter. As soon as alongside, the cover was put over the skylight and trucks were handed down. P. O. May signalled me, Piggy Grant, Jock Towney and Charlie Fox down into the lighter. I held one sack and Piggy filled it with huge lumps of coal. Jock Towney held the sack that Charlie was filling. The bags were then hoisted over onto the quarterdeck where the truckers were waiting.

Stand easy came and went, there was no change around until dinner time. P. O. May said we were an hour later starting, so we would have to work harder if we were to finish by 1800 hours. Dinner came, corned beef and coal dust was washed down with tea. Change-around time came and the truckers took over in the lighter, those in the lighter took over the trucks. P. O. May said we were doing alright but would still have to work harder to finish by six. How many tonnes we had to shift I do not know. What ever it was we never made it! 1800 hours came and there was still quite a lot of coal in the lighter, but the bunker lids were put back in place, the trucks returned into the lighter.

Lines were let go, the ship turned and slowly steamed back down through Portsmouth Harbour. Out came the hoses and deck scrubbers. We looked like a load of miners scrubbing the decks! The ship turned in to the harbour and we tied up to the south-west wall. Steve Conner and Yorky had been detailed off to prepare a meal. There was still a lot of cleaning to be done before P. O. May was satisfied. Bulkheads had to be hosed down, the decks had to be squeegeed. At last he was satisfied and gave the order for all cleaning gear to be stowed away. When that was done, we were dismissed. I went to the wash room, undressed and washed most of the mess from my face with cold water. I had to wait a while before I could borrow Charlie's bucket. I filled it with water and had a good scrub and wash down. Dried off, dressed, then back to the mess deck for a nice meal produced by Steve.

The ship had two new additions. One was a leading seaman AA2, a second-class gunner named Selwood, he was a survivor off the *Royal Oak*, a battleship which was sunk in Scapa Flow, Scotland, in October 1939 with a great loss of life. After his survivor's leave, he was drafted to H.M.S. *Excellent*, where he remained until drafted to the *Alresford*. His nickname was Lofty, he was also to become the ship's comedian.

The other addition was Ordinary Seaman Orde H.O. There was a girl singer at the time, called Beryl Orde, so Ordinary Seaman Orde soon became 'Beryl'. They both became members of the 2nd part of port.

After helping to wash up and peel tomorrow's potatoes I played crib until it was time to turn in.

The next morning was 3rd January 1944. At 0800 hours, after falling in on the quarterdeck, the order was given to take in the lines, and we steamed out and moved up to the buoy. The monitor H.M.S. *Roberts* had entered and had anchored halfway up Spithead.

I had now been promoted to Bowman of the motor boat, the coxswain was Mike Johnson, the stoker was the same sailor that had been detailed to the motor launch back in 1925! About 1000 hours, the bosun's mate called, 'Away the motor boat crew.' I, Mick and the stoker reached the stern, climbed over into the boat and made our way around to the ladder, which had been lowered as soon as we arrived at the mooring. The Captain was piped ashore, he skipped down into the boat and told Mike to take him to H.M.S. *Roberts*.

There had been a hole especially made in the forward part of the canvas hood that covered the whole of the boat. I would stand as forward as possible, holding the boat hook upright. The *Roberts* was rather ugly to look at. She looked very squat, which enabled her to bombard in more shallow water. That's what she was made for. Her main armament was two 15-inch guns. As soon as Mike brought the boat alongside the ladder of the Roberts, the Captain climbed up the ladder and was piped aboard. I held on with the boat hood to a bracket on the side of the *Roberts*. Mike shouted let go, which I did.

Mike took the boat around and I tied up to the boom, alongside a magnificent launch. I was sitting in the stern with Mike and the stoker having a yarn, when there came a very angry bellow. We looked up and saw the very red face of a naval lieutenant. His eyes were popping out of his head. 'Get away,' he shouted, 'get away, lay off. Wait until you are called!' He obviously did not like our tatty-looking boat tied up to the boom. I let go and we drifted around for about an hour, until the quartermaster called us to come alongside. I wonder what the R.N. Lieutenant thought when an R.N. Commander D.S.O. was piped ashore and skipped down into our tatty little boat!

We returned to the ship, the Captain was piped aboard. I wondered what he had been talking about aboard the *Roberts*. It was becoming obvious that D-Day was getting closer. I and Mike had to help pump fresh water. Hands to dinner was piped, pot mess and dough boys – good old Steve!

In the afternoon, I went down and cleaned the boat; she was then hoisted on board, so I knew we were off to the Nab Channel. In the evening, we up anchored and the ship steamed round and made its way to the Nab. It was going to be a long night. There was a lot of activity the other side of Lyme Bay, there was none on the Portsmouth side of the Isle of Wight. The snooper turned up about midnight, keeping everybody alert. The gunner's yeoman came and went, thank goodness!

Large pieces of concrete were being towed into Spithead and sunk in every nook and cranny. They were for the concrete artificial Mulberry harbour that would play such a vital role during D-Day. The larger blocks had two Bofor guns, the smaller blocks had one. When the seacocks were open they were deliberately sunk. The Navy hoped that any snooping German aircraft would think they were gun positions (only part of the concrete block would be above water).

Back in September 1940, the *Alresford* had been anchored in the Nab Channel. The guns crews were closed up. The Commander, hearing an aircraft approaching, a Dornier, gave the orders – 'Angle of sight and range – Fire!' – Bullseye, one 1912 shell, one enemy aircraft shot down, one of the biggest flukes ever! The *Alresford* also served at Dunkirk and the massacre at Dieppe.

The night was still very cold, but the good ladies of Alresford town in Hampshire had knitted us balaclavas and mittens. They had also baked us a cake, it arrived in a biscuit tin. It wasn't exactly fresh by the time it reached us, but I was lucky enough to get a piece and it went down honey sweet – thank you ladies! I was also lucky enough to get a balaclava and mittens.

The sea was flat calm, no wind, a bright moon. Strange – all the activity was towards Lyme Bay again. At last dawn came, and the order to up anchor was given. We proceeded into Portsmouth Harbour, passing our two mine sweepers, doing their sweeping, and saluting the C in C signal tower as we passed. Turning into the south-west basin, we tied up to the *Plover* which was loaded with mines.

I had a good wash, had breakfast consisting of cheese and Daddies Sauce, then fetched my hammock, hung it and turned in for, with a bit of luck, four hours' sleep. Managed to get four hours, then went for a wash. Dinner was cottage pie prepared by Charlie Fox, with Manchester tart afterwards.

Mike told P.O. May that he thought the motor boat should be tidied up. P.O. May agreed. I fetched a bucket of soapy water to wash the boat, prior to painting it pussers' Navy grey. Mike trimmed all the rough edges and rubbed down the corners with fine sandpaper, where the boat had rubbed against the stern of the ship, saying, 'It will be just as bad in a few days, back down to the bare metal, but it will look nice for a few days at least!' He then gave me a hand to wash the boat. I went to fetch the paint from the paint store, looked after by another three-badge Able Seaman, called back in. He also looked after a caboose, which looked like a miniature ships' chandlers. He had a really cushy job, he deserved it – nobody bothered him. So, armed with a tin of paint and two brushes, off I went to the boat and Mike. We wanted to hang this job out!

The Captain, armed with his briefcase, had left the ship. I don't think that the first lieutenant was capable of taking the ship out. He'd taken her out once, a few weeks earlier – although Portsmouth Harbour is pretty wide, he managed to hit something, slightly damaging the starboard quarter.

Mike and I started to paint the boat with the dull Navy grey paint. I wondered how many coats of paint the boat had had since 1912! 1600 hours came, and hands were dismissed.

There was shore leave for those who wanted to go. Four of us, Steve Conner, Piggy Grant, Bob Jay and myself, decided to go ashore. I had not been ashore since joining the *Alresford*. Once ashore we had the dilemma of deciding where to go. The Golden Fleece was always choc-a-bloc, so we started to amble around. Portsmouth was slowly being cleaned up but was still in a awful mess. There were not many streets that had not been bombed. We passed the wreckage of the Princess Theatre – it was showing a film called *Mr. Wong At Headquarters* when it received a direct hit, which smashed the roof in. The theatre was full at the time and there were many children in there (not all children had been evacuated, some parents wanted to keep them at home, some children didn't want to go). Thankfully, there were not too many casualties. It was in Lake Road, which I knew well, it was one of the main roads in Portsmouth.

We ambled on, then finally found a pub, I don't remember the name. There were not many people in there. A few men at the bar; but sitting down were a few young women. Piggy, a bachelor, went over and started talking to them. Bob Jay and I went over as well. I sat and talked to a very lovely-looking girl. She was blonde, very slim and was wearing a lovely dress. We were getting on quite well together. I asked her what she did for a living. I expected something like a receptionist or typist as she was so immaculately turned out. She said she was a wire splicer in Pompey dockyard!

I nearly fell off my chair! I looked at her small hands and said, 'You surprised me!' She said, 'I enjoy it and it's not a hardship to me.' We had another drink. I can't remember if I bought her drink or not. I like to think that I did.

We then had to go, we were a long way from the dockyard. I said goodbye and thanked her for her company. I never saw her again. We had to get a move on, had to be back on board by 2300 hours. We all agreed that it had been a nice evening.

We started off back to the ship, passing bombed streets. Where had all the people that used to live in these streets gone? We passed ruined Aggie Weston's. Pompey was in a bit of a mess.

We finally reached Pompey dockyard, carefully made our way back on board ship and slung our hammocks and turned in. I lay watching an old stoker called Dell, who had been called back in, he'd been ashore and come back slightly under the weather. How he never fell down into the dock (it was pitch black), I'll never know, although it was the same for all of us coming back in the dark. Fortunately, it was still double summertime, so it was beginning to get lighter in the evening. Old Dell found his way down to the mess deck and undressed. He carefully stowed away a half pint of pale ale, which he would drink for his breakfast. He then climbed down into the hammock flat, struggling up with his hammock. Getting the hammock slung and ready to climb into was a challenge, but finally he did it. Sadly though, the effort was too much and he didn't have enough strength to get up into the hammock, so he ended up sleeping on a mess deck stool!

All hands fell in on the quarter deck at 0800 hours, Mike and I carried on painting the boat. We were told that there would be a boiler clean in March, meaning that each watch would get four days' leave. It was now late January. It seemed very hard for those living in the North and Scotland, they would have to find somewhere to stay for four days. I think there was a place called the Duchess of Albany where sailors could stay, though it may well have been bombed.

We had finished painting the boat, and Mike and I had to go to P.O. May for a job. The ship had a teak taffrail. P.O. May said it had to be sanded and canvassed, using a bucket of salt water, a bucket of sand and a piece of canvas about a foot square. The teak taffrail ran around the ship and stopped each side of the breakwater. I fetched a length of rope, a bucket of sand and some squares of canvas back from the old shipwright. Mike had the same materials. I was responsible for the port side and Mike the starboard. I tied the rope to a bucket and lowered it over the side, then pulled it up over the taffrail, accidentally tipping the water over the deck. As I was bending down to pick up the bucket, I got booted so hard I sprawled a few feet up the deck. Not a word was said. It was the hardest I had ever been booted, it was painful to sit down for a couple of days! I'd known the perpetrator would get me one day!

I lowered the bucket again and when full, pulled it up on board. I sprinkled sand on the taffrail, soaked the canvas in the water and started to scrub. Mike had started over on the other side. So we worked on, dip the canvas in the water, spread the sand, keep scrubbing. I had no feeling in my hands. At the stand easy, Mike complained that this was a summer job. P.O. May said nothing but put another hand, Beryl, to work a few yards in front of me. He wasn't much good at it, but it had to be finished. I just got on with it. P.O. May told us to put more effort into it (but that was to be expected!). When Mike and his mate Yorky had finished the starboard side, they came around and helped us finish the port side. The taffrail looked pretty good, worth the frozen hands, though Mike was still pretty angry.

When the buckets and sand had been returned, Mike said to me, 'Come on we will find something to do in the boat'. Ignoring P.O. May we climbed down into the boat and stayed there until it was time for us to be dismissed. I had pins and needles in my hands.

Mike and I went down to the mess deck, bread and jam for tea. Shore leave was given from 1800 hours until 0800 hours the next morning. The locals were off like a shot. Most of us stayed on board, there was not a lot to do ashore except find a pub. It would have been nice to see a film, but the only cinema that hadn't been bombed was the Tivoli over in Copnor, near where me and my family used to live – too far for us to get to. So we had few choices: crib, write a letter, do your dobeing, read a book or get your head down. I wrote a letter until it was time to fetch my hammock, hang it and turn in.

Next morning at 0800 hours, all the leave-takers had returned. Then it was the same routine. Out with the hoses and deck scrubbers and we gave both decks a good scrubbing.

The Captain returned and the order was given 'hands to stations' for leaving harbour. The ship left the south-west wall, hands lined the ship and saluted the C in C. We moored to the buoy just inside the harbour, the boat was lowered and tied up astern. The ship had taken some danbuoys on board, they had to be laid along the left-hand side of Spithead. A danbuoy is a sealed can, about three-feet tall with a flag pole coming off the top at the centre, with a small pennant on the top. At the bottom, coming out of the centre is a length of cable with a heavy weight on the end. It is used as a temporary mooring until such times as a permanent mooring can take its place.

The Captain told the first lieutenant, so the rumour went,

that there would be quite an armada gathering in the next few weeks. It was our job to lay the danbuoys, the navigational officers would be busy plotting the exact positions. The ship didn't have an echo sounder, the depth of water to the seabed would be measured in the same way as in Nelson's navy – lead and line. On the starboard side just behind the breakwater lashed to the side of the ship was a small platform; when lowered, it was secured by chains.

The lead was tapered and fourteen pounds in weight. The bottom was concave, thick grease could be placed in the bottom. When the lead hit the seabed it was possible to tell what sort of seabed it was. The line was quite long, the leadsman would whirl the lead line faster and faster, until it was about thirty feet above his head, then let fly. The lead would fly past the bow, giving the leadsman time to read the depth of water.

Small pieces of coloured cloth were pushed between strands of the line. This was done at certain points along the line. Five fathoms was white, seven fathoms red, ten fathoms a piece of leather with a hole in it, then fifteen fathoms back to white and seventeen fathoms back to red. In between five and ten fathoms, depths are called 'deeps'. I cannot remember how they were marked, but the leadsman would know the depth of water, above or below, a piece of cloth or leather, and would call out, 'Deep six sir.'

The water level would be about one foot above the five-fathom mark and four foot from the ten-fathom mark – at this point the ship should be still. The lead line would be up and down and the leadsman would shout, 'Ship stopped, sir.' Quickly the length of cable was altered on the danbuoy to suit the depth of water. If the ship is in the right position, the danbuoy would be lowered on to the sea and the weight would sink down to the seabed, leaving the can bobbing.

Piggy Grant, Charlie Fox, Steve Conner and Jock Brown

were the best leadsmen. They could heave the lead far in front of the bow. The secret of heaving the lead is not to look up while whirling, or you are likely to get a fourteen-pound lump of lead on your head! It's not a bad job on a fine day, not so nice on a cold, wet winter's day!

I had to take my turn as leadsman. I could not heave the lead as far as the others, so I was a little slower, to the annoyance of those on the bridge, who asked me to repeat the action a few times. It was frustrating for me too, but then I remembered I wasn't a proper sailor but an H.O.!

The ship would then go astern and the navigating officers would plot the next position, this was done three days a week. There were then four nights on the Nab Channel, and so it went on, day after day, night after night, including coaling the ship, pumping water and scrubbing the decks, until March came and the ship was due her boiler clean and we were all given leave. The starboard watch went first, from Monday 0800 hours until Thursday 23.55. Then the port watch from Friday 0800 hours until Monday 23.55. Some of the hands from the North were going to stay with their chums from the South.

I packed my little brown case plus an empty kitbag so I could bring back some old clothes for coaling, and a bucket. I was given my pay, plus ration tokens and railway warrants.

The Captain had gone away again leaving the first lieutenant in charge. Putting my gas mask over my shoulder I left the ship with one or two others. We walked out of the dockyard to Portsmouth Station. I warned my ship mates about the uniformed gorilla – I said he would be lurking somewhere! I went to the ticket office and used my warrant to get a ticket for Bournemouth. The others were going to London. The train arrived and we boarded. I changed at Southampton, saying, 'Cheerio' to my ship mates.

I crossed over to the platform and waited for my train and was soon in Bournemouth. Two buses and a long walk and I was walking indoors.

Mum was surprised to see me and gave me a big hug and kiss. The rest of the family were at work. Mum made me scrambled eggs on toast. Once I'd eaten, I went and had a long hot bath, then sorted out some old clothes. Jock later said that he had an old blue fitters coat which he would bring me from work. I sorted out a couple of old shirts, an old towel and most importantly a bucket! It was a galvanised one and I painted my initials, F.A.B., on it.

Mum made a cup of tea. I sat down in Dad's chair and fell asleep. Reg and Ron came in from work. Mum had made liver and onions and vegetables. We all sat down and had a nice meal. Jock was going straight out from work with his mates.

At 18.30 Dad came in, sat straight in his armchair. He changed into his working clothes when he started work, and changed back into his home clothes when he finished, so he was clean when he came home from work. Mum made him a cup of tea, he looked tired. Mum made him egg on toast. The hens were laying well. I said, 'We won't go out tonight Dad, you are too tired. I don't expect Paddy Daly or Mr. Habgood will be in the club tonight anyway.' Dad said, 'No they only go out on Saturday nights.' I said, 'We will have a quiet night Dad and go out tomorrow night.'

Dad said, 'I have been in the rattle!' When you have been put in the rattle in the Navy, it means you're in trouble! I knew that there were two maintenance fitters where Dad worked, who had been giving him a hard time for some time. They had been calling him 'pop', which he didn't like. To call Dad pop was like waving a red flag at a bull! They would pass him in the morning and say, 'Morning pop, oh sorry pop!'

After putting up with it for a while, Dad asked them to stop calling him pop, but apparently one afternoon they walked into the boiler room to do some maintenance, the door was open and when inside, they said to Dad, 'Shut the door pop, oh sorry pop!' Dad ignored them. When they had finished their maintenance work, they came down and said to Dad, 'Hey pop, why didn't you shut the door when we asked, it was cold up there working?' Dad said he had a son-in-law and a eighteen-year-old son in the Navy, and they should think themselves lucky to be in a reserved occupation. Then one of them said something derogatory about me, something like 'more fool him for joining up.' That did it, Dad knocked them both out, only two punches, a left and a right, and they were out cold!

Dad went and got the foreman and took him to the boiler room. The fitters were trying to stand up. The foreman asked them if they wanted to call the police. They said no, I think if they called the police, it might jeopardise their cushy jobs. The foreman said that all three of them would have to appear in front of the Commander.

The next morning, Dad and the two fitters were called into the Commander's office. The fitters both had black eyes. The Commander asked what had happened.

Dad explained how they had been calling him pop, which he disliked, and he had asked them to stop doing it, but in the boiler room the previous day they had deliberately called him pop when asking him to close the door. He had told them that they should appreciate that they had good well-paid jobs and that he had an eighteen-year-old son in the Navy. He told the Commander that the fitters had then been rude about me being in the Navy and that he had then lost his temper and before he realised it, he had knocked them out.

The Commander said to the fitters, 'Is that correct, that you have been calling him pop when he asked you not to and also that you said something derogatory about his eighteen-year-old son being in the Navy?'

They admitted it and he asked them if they wanted to call the police and make a formal complaint against Dad (Mr. Beedie). They said no and apologised, saying they did not realise they were upsetting Mr. Beedie.

The Commander said, 'I can tell you now, that you should know better, and I can easily get two more fitters, but I can't get another boiler man!' He then reprimanded all three as to their future behaviour, but they all kept their jobs. Dad said he was very lucky there!

I can only guess what was being said in the factory about an old sixty-six-year-old pensioner knocking out two younger men. There had been quite a few in the past who had got the same treatment. Before the war Dad had worked for many years on big liners sailing out of Liverpool with crews of Liverpool Irish. You had to be able to look after yourself and Dad was quite capable of that!

Dad started to nod off, he said he would like to go to the club on Saturday night. I said, 'That's alright, I have to be back on Monday night by 23.55, I'll go for a walk through the village tomorrow morning.' I sat there quietly reading. After a while Dad woke up and said he was going to go for a wash and go to bed, so off Dad went.

I sat talking to Mum. I said, 'That was lucky Dad keeping his job, those two must have really upset him!' 'Yes,' she said, 'he really thought he would have to go to Court and lose his job. I don't know what his work mates are saying. The boiler room is away from the workshop, so he doesn't see many of the workers. It's only when there is maintenance work required that he sees anybody. I don't expect he will see those two again!' I said, 'It's about time Dad retired, he is sixty-six now and still working ten hours a day – it's too much.' Mum replied, 'I think that the Commander realises that boiler men with the experience that Dad has are hard to find, and he appreciates having Dad. They seem to get on well, two old sailors together! Dad has said that he will do his best until the end of the war. He is certain that we are going to win!'

I said goodnight to Mum, had a good wash then went off to bed. The house was empty when I woke up the next morning. I asked Mum if I could have a bath, she said I could. It would be bucket baths for me in the weeks to come! Mum cooked me a nice breakfast. There seemed to be more food about. I put on my best number ones, gave Mum a kiss and said I was going for a walk through the village, which I had not done since my Home Guard days.

I walked past the dairy shop which was the Home Guards' HQ. Then past Crowson's the greengrocer's. Pauline Crowson was one of the Land Girls at Purchase and Vines Farm. I walked to the lodge gates; on the right-hand side of the road, was the large common where I had done mortar training with the Home Guard. I wondered if they still did the training there and decided that they probably did – perhaps they have real mortars now! I thought about Captain Pusey and wondered if Major Butt had had him dismissed. They did not seem to see eye to eye.

I walked back, went into the Kings Arms, it had a new landlord now, Albert Franklin, he turned out to be a fine landlord. His wife was the same. I did not know anybody in the pub. Two or three Canadian soldiers were at the bar. Albert was very friendly and we talked about cricket, which was my favourite sport. He was a scout for Middlesex cricket club and also for Arsenal football club. He was very knowledgeable. Dinner was calling, so I said cheerio to Albert, thanking him for chatting to me and telling him I would look forward to seeing him again.

When I got home, I ate my dinner, then sat down to read the daily newspaper. I wondered if there would be a cricket season. Would I see the likes of Hobbs and Sutcliffe, Ames and Hammond again? Mum said dinner was ready and we sat down to a lovely plate of stew and dumplings. After washing up I made a cup of tea for Mum and me, then I settled down in Dad's armchair and fell asleep.

I woke up at tea time. Reg and Ron would soon be in from work, so would Jock. There was plenty of stew left for them. Dad and I would have something light. Dad came in at 18.30, sat down in his old armchair and dozed off. Reg and Ron both disappeared. I sat down with Mum, she said she was missing her neighbours in Portsmouth, and that the shops were further away than in Portsmouth. Unfortunately, the road we lived on had no pavements and hadn't been made up, it was just gravel, so was very hard on her feet to walk on.

I said, 'Mum, you, Dad, Ron, Reg and Jock are safer here than in Portsmouth. We had some really scary nights and days there – we were lucky to survive! I don't have to worry so much about you now.' Mum said, 'I guess you are right, my son.'

Dad woke up, said, 'I'll get a wash now and get ready to go out.' I was ready when Dad came down. A 'cheerio' to Mum and we made our way up to the club. Mum was right about the walking, it was hard on the feet!

When we walked into the club we saw Mr. Habgood and Paddy Daly. They stood up and we all shook hands. Mr Habgood was a very nice man to talk to. Paddy brought us up to date about his son Harry, who had been wounded serving with the eighth army at the battle of Mareth. He was slowly getting better, which was good news to hear.

It was nice to sit down with a pint of beer and listen to these three men talk. About 22.00, Dad was ready to go home, so shaking hands again with Paddy Daly and Mr. Habgood, we said goodnight and I said that I hoped to see them in a few months' time. Dad and I made our way home. Mum made a pot of tea, but Dad did not want one. He was off to bed as he was working a ten-hour shift the next day.

I said to Mum, 'It's never right that at sixty-six, Dad is working ten hours on a Sunday!' Mum said again, 'Dad is determined to work until the end of the war.' She told me that Poole and Bournemouth had suffered from raiders now and again. There was a small shipyard in Poole, making landing craft to carry tanks. I don't think the Germans thought it worth a full bombing raid or they would have done it by now.

I kissed Mum goodnight and was off to a nice comfortable bed. In the morning, Dad and Jock had gone to work. I had a bath. Reg and Ron had a lie-in. Mum made me a nice breakfast. I got fully dressed and went for a walk in the garden and heard the sound of the Boys' Brigade band. Captain Pusey and his troops were marching up and down the main road. He was still in command.

I went for a walk through the village, down to the lodge gates and back up to the Kings Arms. It was quite full, mostly strangers to me. One or two locals were in and plenty of Canadians. I had a couple of pints then walked home. Reg and Ron came in, we all sat down to a nice dinner. After washing up, I sat down in Dad's armchair, Mum made a cup of tea, then I fell asleep, which was my favourite pastime!

Tea time came, I did not want a large tea, after such a big dinner. At 18.30 Dad came in. He looked tired. He sat in his old armchair. I said, 'Dad you are too old to work so many hours!' He just shrugged his shoulders and said, 'It won't last for ever.' Mum made him a cup of tea and scrambled egg on toast.

I said, 'You are too tired to go up to the club Dad.' He said, 'Yes son, I am.' Jock never came in, he had gone straight out from work with his mates. About 20.30 I got dressed, told Mum that Dad was still asleep and that I was going to walk to the Kings Arms. The pub was full of men and women I had never seen before and, once again, plenty of Canadians.

I had a nice yarn with Albert the Landlord. After a couple of pints I said cheerio to Albert and made my way home. Dad had gone to bed. I sat talking to Mum, then off to bed. I rose early to say goodbye to Dad and my brothers, said I hoped to see them in a few months.

Mum made breakfast, and after washing up, I helped her by doing the vegetables for dinner – carrots, swede, onions. The butcher had been very generous when Mum told him that I was home on leave and produced my meat tokens. Stews were the order of the day!

The weather was still cold. I told Mum that I was going to go for a last walk through the village. I was surprised when a couple of village girls ran up to me and touched my collar, for luck, then ran away. I had this happen to me in Portsmouth a couple of times and in Bournemouth too, when waiting for a train. I wonder if it works!

I walked into the Kings Arms, it was practically empty. The surly barman was in the public bar, so I went into the saloon bar. Albert was serving in there. I ordered a pint, went to pay, but Albert said it was 'on the house', which I thought was very nice of him. We had a good yarn about cricket, not so much football. He had such knowledge of sport, I could listen to him all day. I ordered another pint, and asked Albert to have a drink, but he said, 'No thanks.' After I finished my drink, I shook hands with Albert, wished him all the best, said thanks for the yarn, and that I hoped to seen him in a few months' time.

I made my way home, dinner was ready. I sat down and ate with Mum, then after helping to wash up, I had a nap in Dad's armchair. Mum woke me up a bit later and I went for a good wash, then packed my kitbag with the old clothes and the precious bucket.

Mum made what was now the easiest meal – scrambled egg on toast! The hens had become her pets, she looked after them as though they were children, that is why they kept laying so well, so Mum says! I ate my meal and Mum made a cup of tea, after which I packed my little case, collected my kitbag and gas mask, gave Mum a big hug and kiss, told her I would see her in a few months, then out the door and up to the bus stop I went.

A bus and two trains later, I was walking through the dockyard gates. I reported to the dockyard police, then walked through the dock to the SWWTB and aboard the ship. The bosun's mate gave me my station card and asked if I had had a good leave. I said, 'Yes thanks.' I don't know where he went for his leave as he was from South Africa.

I went down into the mess deck, produced my precious bucket, said anyone could borrow it but it would cost them sippers (rum), which produced a few boos! The first part of port were slowly drifting back. 'Drip Tin Watkins', as he was affectionately known, came back from London, and as soon as he came down the ladder he started to drip drip and moan moan, so we sang to him – 'If your Drip Tin overflows borrow mine!' – which would make him smile for a little while. He was a very nice bloke but hated to leave his wife and children and four days soon went by.

We sat nattering about our leave, then started to get our hammocks sorted out. I slung mine and turned in. Hands were called at 05.30 in the morning. At 07.30 hands fell in for leaving harbour. Up to the coaling lighter to coal ship, there was no way we were going to shift a hundred tons before 1800 hours. I was down in the lighter as usual. As I thought, there was still quite a lot of coal left in the lighter at 18.00. The ship left the lighter and the cleaning began. It was a bit of a comedown – one day home and nice and clean and the next day tired out and as black as a rook!

The ship made its way into the basin and tied up to the *Plover.* P.O. May did not dismiss us until he was satisfied that the ship was clean enough. Once we had finished, off I went to baptise my bucket! Not having to wait for a bucket meant I was quicker to get cleaned up. It was a job to get the coal dust out of our eyes. I used butter to remove it, otherwise I would have a black rim around them.

The locals were leaving to go to shore. I decided not to go, I was too tired. Piggy Grant had made a pot mess. More stew! I had my usual two or three platefuls. The meat from Argentina melted in your mouth. We had plenty of it.

I was keen for the ship to go out to the mooring, as Mick Johnson was letting me take the helm of the motor boat whenever we were going back to the ship empty.

The Captain was gone again, but was back next morning, so the ship left the basin and made her way out to the mooring. The motor boat was lowered and tied up astern. There was more activity in Spithead and the Solent. Buoy ships were putting down more permanent moorings. The large lumps of concrete were still being tucked away here and there.

The ship was back in the routine of going out to the Nab Channel four days a week. Three days' training navigating officers. The Navy seemed to want a lot of officers. There seemed to be more air activity. I think the Germans were wanting to know what was going on at Spithead and in the Solent.

The RN navigating officer was a real gentleman. At night he would stand on the quarterdeck and would talk about the stars and the universe to quite a few interested sailors. He had written two books about the universe. What that all Naval officers were like him!

About a half a mile on the right-hand side of Spithead was a jetty. The captain decided to anchor about five hundred yards from it, why I wasn't sure, as it was much further to the Kings Stairs to land the Captain or anyone else.

Nobody was very happy about it, as it meant that if going on shore leave, we had to get the Gosport Ferry across to Portsmouth Harbour. The locals could only go on shore leave if it was all-night leave and they would have to catch the early ferry back in the morning. If it was 11.00 leave, then they could not go. They were not happy! It was a strange decision to anchor there.

About three or four yards from the jetty, inland, was a mixed Ack-Ack battery (guns operated by men and women). There was a lane from the jetty to the main road. About half a mile along the road and around a corner was a pub. We soon got to know it! Some of us used the pub rather than go into Portsmouth. We soon got to know some of the girl gunners who also used the pub.

The liberty boat would land and about twenty liberty men would be taken to the jetty by the ship's whaler or lifeboat, towed by the motor boat. Some of the locals would make their way to the Gosport Ferry, moaning and groaning. Others would go ashore later and go to the pub. Some of the girl gunners would shout 'See you later!' from the open windows of the battery. What the Pongos (the Navy's friendly name for soldiers) thought about it I don't know!

There was never any trouble in the pub. Although the pub itself had the problem of not having enough glasses. We had to supply our own! I had an old marmalade jar with my initials on it, F.A.B. When not in use, it was kept on a shelf behind the bar with lots of others. We certainly outnumbered the locals, we must have been a god's send to the landlord!

I realised that anchoring where we were, made it easier for the Captain to visit other ship's captains, when required. The Armada was getting bigger. Mick was letting me steer the boat to the ship more often when we had the chance.

We did two nights up the Nab Channel and then had to coal ship again, not enough was shipped aboard the last time we coaled. Going to the coal lighter from the Nab Channel, the gun crews were excused until midday. I got about four hours' sleep. As the bags were too heavy for me to push on the truck, I went down into the lighter and relieved Piggy Grant from the sack filling and he went up to push the truck. By 1800 hours the lighter still had coal in it, but the ship made its way into S.W.W.T.B. When the ship was hosed and scrubbed to P.O. May's satisfaction we were dismissed and I went and got myself cleaned up. I was tired out. Charlie Fox made a roast with roast potatoes, pussers peas and Yorkshire pudding, followed by Manchester tart.

The locals were in a hurry to get ashore, it was much easier from where we were than having to catch the Gosport Ferry. I put my dirty gear in my bucket to soak, had a cup of tea and a fag, went and got my hammock, slung it and turned in – out for the count!

The ship stayed in the basin, as there were visitors coming

aboard. One was a Wren officer. Next morning, Mike and I made ourselves busy cleaning the boat. P.O. May never came near us.

After tea, four of us decided to go ashore: Steve Conner, Charlie Fox, Jock Towney and myself. We went out on the 1900 hours liberty boat. Handing in our station cards to the quartermaster on the way. We went out of the Marlborough Gate rather than the Main Gate. We had been tipped off that it was a 'safe' gate at 1900 hours. Some of the dockyard police used L/S Burns's father-in-law's pub. When they were on-duty, we could safely take cigarettes out or anything else. I would get two hundred cigarettes a week and a pound of either cigarette, pipe or leaf tobacco (for those who liked to make their own plug tobacco) a month.

L/S Burns told us the name of a pub that was still standing and where to find it. He said we could flog the cigarettes at two shillings a packet, so we put a packet of cigarettes in each sock, then I put another packet, with one cigarette out (that was the one I would be using), in the side of my blouse and another two packets on the other side of my blouse. The Rolls-Royce of cigarettes was the ship's Woodbines, followed by Senior Service, Gold Flake and Capstan, but everyone's preference was for Woodbines. I'm afraid I didn't have Woodbines, only Senior Service.

As I went through the door to the police office, I put a packet of Senior Service on the table, then walked out through another door into the street. The others did the same. We were not the only ones, it seemed easy to get things out. We could have taken the ship if we had been able to carry it on our backs!

Steve seemed to know his way about, and after an amble around we found the pub. Inside there were one or two locals; going up to the bar, Steve had a word with the landlord. He turned to us and gave us the signal. Myself and the other two, Charlie and

Jock, sat down at a table and quietly took the cigarettes out of our socks and blouse. Steve collected them and was paid £1/12 shillings. He then bought four pints of beer, which I think was about nine pence a pint. Steve brought the beer over to the table. It was decided that Steve could keep the change and pay for the night's rounds, then we would share anything left over.

After we had another drink, we decided to go for a ramble around. Saying goodnight to the landlord and telling him that we would be seeing him again, we left the pub. I wondered how much he charged for the fags!

Steve knew of other pubs, but they were now just piles of rubble. Heading off nowhere in particular, we eventually found a pub still in one piece. Inside was a woman on her own and beyond her there were two petty officers. Steve bought our beer and a pie each. Jock started talking to the woman, it was obvious that the two P.O.s had been talking to her also. It did not seem to make any difference to Jock that he was married!

It was getting near to drinking-up time, Jock was still talking to the woman. When time came, the three of us went out the door, slowly followed by Jock and the two P.O.s We were walking ahead, when we heard a bit of a commotion behind us. We turned just in time to see the two P.O.s collapsing to the ground. Apparently they had started an altercation with Jock, who had introduced them to what I think is called a 'Glasgow Kiss' with his forehead! Unfortunately for the P.O.s, two on to one did not work this time! Jock came ambling up to us, as if nothing had happened. The two P.O.s were struggling to get to their feet, no doubt wondering what had hit them!

We carried on with our ramble, now wondering where we were going to sleep. We came across a splinter-proof shelter and decided that it would have to do. Inside there were police lights, once our eyes became accustomed to the light, we could see quite clearly. There were long wooden benches down each side of the shelter and two across the middle. We settled down, one to each bench, stretched ourselves out and using our caps as pillows, soon fell asleep.

I'm not sure how long we were asleep, but something woke me up. I turned my head and looked straight into two large brown eyes belonging to a little tot of a girl about three years old. I sat up, the shelter was full of women, small children and a few men, all jammed together. I thought it typical of Pomponions to sit in discomfort, rather than wake four sleeping sailors. The little girl was still stood there looking at me, I felt somewhat embarrassed! I shook Charlie, who sat up, not believing his eyes. He quickly shook Steve and Jock who sat up. We all felt very embarrassed. We quickly offered our apologies and slunk out of the shelter. The siren must have sounded, not heard by us. Suddenly there was a putt, putt, putt sound, and looking up we saw our first V1 or doodlebug – horrified, we watched the flames coming from the rear of the bomb. Slowly, the flames went out and the V1 was falling, over a ton of explosives was about to land on innocent people. It was inevitable that there would be many casualties. A V1 landing in the middle of a row of houses would clear both sides.

We heard the explosion; slowly, not saying much we found our way back to the ship. I did not bother to sling my hammock, neither did the others. We just slept on the lockers.

I never went ashore with Jock again, he was trouble if he was drinking (not necessarily drunk) and would look for a fight. When he came back on board, most of us would stay out of his way. There were a few who would take him on, but not me! When not drinking, he was as good as gold.

On waking up, I part undressed and went for a wash. I still didn't shave. I changed into my working rig and fell in at 0800 hours. We had visitors coming to the ship, and P.O. May wanted both the upper deck bulkheads scrubbed extra clean. He even put on a not-so-scruffy pair of trousers, coat and cap and a polo-necked jumper! After the visitors had left, the ship got ready to go out to the Nab Channel. Steve shared out the change from the night before, about three shillings each. Quite a profitable evening! I wondered how the two petty officers were feeling this morning!

Air attacks were becoming more frequent again, we could see from the Nab Channel that Portsmouth was getting more attention, although the air raids were not as heavy as in 1941. The Solent was filling up with all types of ships.

The next day, we up anchored and made our way to the mooring inside the harbour. Mick had been teaching me how to handle the boat. The Captain had to be taken to several ships, so I had a chance to take over the tiller.

After a week or so of going out to the Nab Channel, we had to coal ship, so the boat was hoisted aboard and the ship steamed up the harbour to the coal lighter. After coaling, the ship made its way into the basin and tied up to the south-west wall. Once P.O. May thought the ship was clean enough, he dismissed us. The locals rushed to the washroom. I could not be bothered. I did not feel like going ashore. When I had washed down and changed into clean clothes, I put the dirty clothes into a soapy bucket of water, ready for dobeing. Piggy had made a nice roast, which was soon eaten. After clearing up, a cup of tea and a fag, I sat down to my second favourite pastime, reading – the first being sleeping!

The following morning, I was told by P.O. May that I had to take over as coxswain of the motor boat. I knew that this would not have been his recommendation. I think it would have been the R.N. navigating officer. Often when I got the chance, I would go up to the quarterdeck and he would be there, taking in the fresh air. He would soon have an audience and be telling us about the stars and the universe. I think, perhaps, it was because I showed an interest and asked him questions that he recommended me for coxswain.

I thought I could handle the boat alright as long as I had a good bowman. That's where P.O. May put the boot in – he made Beryl Orde the bowman. Two eighteen-year-old Ordinary Seamen H.O., not proper sailors in charge of the motor boat! Disaster was not long coming.

On our way back from the Nab Channel one morning, we tied up to a mooring just inside Portsmouth Harbour. The motor boat was lowered and the crew called away to take the Captain ashore. I told Beryl that at Kings Stairs, he would have to hold on to the rail, as the steps were hidden by water. We successfully landed the Captain ashore and returned to the ship.

As the day went on, the weather began to change. Bad weather was coming down the channel, it would soon reach us. The Black Can was hoisted at the harbour mouth, denoting that no small craft should leave the harbour. I kept an anxious eye on the Kings Stairs, knowing the Captain would want to come back to the ship. I could see small waves breaking over the steps. The figure of the Captain appeared at the top of the stairs. The quartermaster immediately called away the motor boat. Beryl, Stripy the stoker (thank heavens he was in the boat, he was the sailor who had been stoker in the same boat in 1925), and I reached the quarterdeck. I said to the stoker that when the boat reached the steps, he should keep the engine going slowly astern, to stop the boat from being swept on to the stairs, and he agreed. I said that the Captain was very nimble and at the first chance, would jump aboard. To Beryl I said, 'Hang that boat hook on to the rail and hold on to it for grim death, don't let go at any price!'

We made our way into the boat and made our way over to the Kings Stairs, the Captain was ready to jump. I took the boat alongside, the stoker kept the engine going slowly astern. The Captain quickly jumped aboard. Then disaster – Beryl let go of the rail too soon, the boat immediately swung towards the steps. The stoker quickly thrust the engine into reverse, but it was too late, the boat was swept onto the stairs. I could hear and feel the propellers grinding on the steps.

The boat swiftly went astern and I turned into the basin and headed out towards the ship. About halfway I looked down – there was about two inches of water, the boat was filling up. Beryl was waving to the ship that we were in trouble. The Captain was sitting cross-legged on the thwart. I thought we would sink in the middle of Portsmouth Harbour, the water was up to my ankles!

When we reached the ladder, the Captain jumped on to it. He simply said, 'Take the boat around to the falls.' The falls had been hoisted out ready, by those who had seen we were in trouble. I took the boat around as instructed and it was hoisted up high enough for us to get out. It was then left to drain out. Not a word was said about the damage. The propeller would have to be taken off. The shaft would have to be taken to see if it was out of true. The ship would be without a boat for some time.

I thought I would be in the 'rattle', but I was simply told I was being relieved of the job of coxswain of the motor boat. I was to relieve South Africa as bosun's mate, he was to go back to being part of ship under P.O. May. I don't know if P.O. May realised I would take South Africa's place in the watch-keeper's mess, and he would take my place in 1st part of port mess. It would mean the

South African would take my place at coaling ship and pumping fresh water. That would break his heart as well as his back! I had no more of either! Stripy was excused all duties. It was with great pleasure that I humped my hammock into the watch-keeper's mess. Beryl, I just ignored.

The weather was getting worse, the wind near a full gale. In the evening the Captain received an order for the ship to proceed at once. A Phoenix caisson, as those lumps of concrete were called, had broken its tow and gone aground on Littlehampton beach. The seacocks had been opened and the caisson sunk to the seabed to stop further damage by the huge waves on shore.

The ship was got ready, everything that needed to be was lashed down harder, including the whaler and the damaged motor boat. Then the ship slipped the mooring, turned and headed out of the harbour into a near full gale, which was blowing up her stern. She made her way in the dark, to Littlehampton beach. I expect the R.N. navigating officer helped to plot the course. When the ship arrived, I think that both anchors must have been dropped. A double anchor watch was kept, the engine room and boiler room were on standby. Nobody got any sleep that night. Our job was to guard the caisson.

There was a crew aboard the caisson, but they could not get off it, as the beach was filled with barbed wire and also no one knew if it was mined. They had to put up with it, until the gale abated.

Aboard the *Alresford*, there were no cooked meals. We had corned beef sandwiches. The cook said it was too dangerous to cook. He was a little bit strange. The trunking fixed on the galley's deck head was covered in old asbestos, probably the original from when the ship was built. There were plenty of cracks in it, nice warm places for cockroaches. Every now and again, a few would fall into the open cook pots and pans. So any of us could find a well-cooked cockroach in our stew! The cook could not be bothered to hook them out, he would say they added protein!! The ship had taken quite a battering, I had to be careful going to the heads and washroom.

After a day or so, the weather started to get better. A passageway was forced through the barbed wire on the beach and the crew of the caisson were getting ready to be towed off. This particular caisson was monstrous. I had never ever seen a lump of concrete so big before.

Finally, the weather was fine enough, and the tide was high enough to tow. The tow was fixed, and the signal was given to pump out, to raise the caisson from the seabed, but nothing happened! The pumps were not powerful enough to lift the caisson off the seabed! A signal was sent out by Admiral Tennant, who was in charge of Salvage Operations, to check all of the caissons, tucked away here and there, to see if their pumps were up to the job. The result was the same, they all failed.

Admiral Tennant said that a salvage expert was required to take charge of operations. An expert was found, and the hunt was on to find more powerful pumps. The search was throughout the country. When found, the new pumps had to be taken out to every cassion and changed in situ.

On board ship, we wondered what was going on, what with all the activity on the beach. Instead of two or three days, it was more like twelve days before the caisson was successfully towed off the beach. Had it not been for that bad weather in the channel a few weeks previously, D-Day would have been a disaster!

I wonder how many in the upper reaches of the Services were aware of the situation. It was said that Winston Churchill, who liked to be fully aware of what the Navy was up to, was not very happy, to put it mildly!

The ship escorted the tug and tow well up into Spithead, then moored to the jetty, much to the locals' disgust! This wasn't a problem for 1st part of port, who would all be going to the pub. I wondered if my marmalade jar would still be there on the shelf – it was!

The Germans' raids were becoming more regular. They were having a go at Spithead and the Solent. I believe the Government had some dummy arrangements on the mudflats nearby, and a lot of bombs landed in them. The sirens would sound off, some of the lads would go up to watch. The searchlights would start searching. I thought the Germans must be mad to try – what with all the shore batteries firing at them and every ship that could fire a gun having a go at them. The Ack-Ack battery near the jetty was deafening.

I never used to take any notice, and if not on-duty, would turn in. I remember Dad saying that it was the one that you did not hear that would get you. Any bomb landing in the water would resonate against the hull, this would happen every now and then. On one occasion I heard a sound and looking over the edge of my hammock, I saw one of the signalmen kneeling on the deck, with his head in his hands. I was going to tell him it was no good doing that, when I remembered that he was a signalman on a landing craft at the Dieppe massacre. The lads would soon come down from the boat deck. Shrapnel was falling from the air, and that was more dangerous than the bombing.

The ship's motor boat shaft and propeller were taken ashore by one of the many working boats. The shaft was found to be still true, but the propeller blades were a little ragged and bent. A new one was required, that was no problem. A new propeller and shaft were returned to the ship and refitted by the shipwright and an engineer. Piggy Grant was made coxswain, with Drip Tin

Watkins bowman. I moved into the watch-keeper's mess. A not very happy South Africa moved out.

The ship was in two watches, the quartermaster in the port was Stripy and I was bosun's mate. The starboard watch was a lad called Alderton who came from Tottenham, and an older chap, called Enoch. He was only about 5 foot 6 inches tall, slightly knock-kneed and very fiery. I never knew his proper name. There was a trio of comedians on the radio at the time, called Ramsbottom, Enoch and Me, that's how he got his name. He had brought a violin with him. In the evenings, when off watch, he would attempt to play it. Unfortunately it sounded like a cat being strangled. If any one complained, he was at them like a tiger!

I came to love old Stripy, I would not let him do anything. He was my hero. He had finished his twenty-two years in the Royal Navy before the war. He was happily married, had a nice house. He loved gardening. He never said if he had children. He worked as a porter on Blackpool Station, he was very happy. Then he got called back into the Navy. His first draft was to one of the four funnelled American destroyers lent to us from America. Stripy told me that first the showers were locked, then the water fountains taken away and then the refrigerators removed. The ships were built for the Pacific area, not the Atlantic.

The ship that Stripy was on used to leave Liverpool and meet a convoy, halfway across the Atlantic (this was in 1940), and escort them back to Liverpool. Stripy told me that one of the seaman aboard lived in Liverpool, so was quite happy to get home every couple of weeks, then he got drafted to another destroyer and asked Stripy if he would swap the draft. Stripy agreed and took the seaman's draft to the other destroyer. The destroyer he left went out to meet another convoy and was sunk by a torpedo and lost with all hands. The ship that Stripy was on was eventually sunk in the Mediterranean, but he survived. He then joined another destroyer, which was sunk in the mouth of Grand Harbour in Malta, when Malta was taking a terrible bashing from German and Italian aircraft. He was then sent to an army camp, halfway down the Suez Canal. He was told he would get a draft home, but all he got was a draft to the cruiser H.M.S. *Euryalus*, which was bombarding in front of the 8th Army in the desert. He was finally drafted home to the R.N. barracks in Portsmouth. From there he was drafted to the *Alresford*.

When he stood at the top of the ladder to the mess deck, he looked just like a gnome! He was about 5 foot 7 inches tall, about nine stone soaking wet, bald as a billiard ball with false teeth. He told us also that he was wounded, serving as a boy seaman on H.M.S. *Warspite* at the Battle of Jutland in the First World War. He was made a quartermaster right away when he joined the *Alresford*. Whenever I got a chance on watch at night, I would tell Stripy to get his head down for an hour or two.

It was well into April now, the routine was the same: training officers, then the Nab Channel. The Germans were still sending sporadic raids. We could only watch. We never saw any mines land in the sea. There was always activity in the Lyme Bay area.

At dawn, the ship upped anchor, and made its way through Portsmouth Harbour. We saluted the C in C and made our way to the coaling lighter, passing the two mine sweepers who were making their way out to the swept channel. It was a treat to see the Pirates of Penzance getting ready to coal ship, especially South Africa. What if he is told to go into the lighter with Mike Johnson! I think that leading seaman X will have to keep them apart!

After coaling ship, we made our way in to the S.W.W.T.B., tied up to the *Plover*. The routine was the same. The watch-keepers prepared their own meals, we found out that Stripy was good at making pastry. I made a pastry, but forgot to grease the pan, so, when cooked, it was stuck to the bottom! It took me ages to clean the pan, I think those in the mess wanted to throw it at me!

Stripy and I were on watch from 2000 hours to midnight. At about 2300 hours, the siren sounded, there came the familiar sound of a V1 or doodlebug. Stripy and I stood and watched it go overhead, then waited, horrified, for the explosion. There were innocent people out there, who only had a few moments to live. Then came the explosion. Soon the full air raid started, some crazy Germans were trying to bomb the armada below them. The Ack Ack was tremendous. The *Alresford* was alongside the *Plover*, which was full of mines, not a comfortable place to be during an air raid!

Someone shouted that the cook was up on the boat deck throwing spuds up in the air at the German aircraft. Sure enough, there he was, he had filled a bucket with potatoes and was throwing them high in the sky. I said, 'He'll be hit by shrapnel if he stays up there!' But who was going to get him down? It appeared that he had lost it, but how long for? Finally his bucket was empty, and he was ordered down. I and Stripy stayed on the quarterdeck. It seemed that the Captain had had enough, and a week or so later, a new cook came and replaced him and he was taken away, hopefully to get some help. At least we could hope that there would be no more cockroaches in our stew!

On 29th April, I was promoted to Acting Able Seaman, H.O., so I still wasn't a proper sailor. I can't remember how much pay rise I was given, might have been sixpence or a shilling.

In May, there was one more air raid over Portsmouth and the armada and some serious damage was done. In the middle of May, all leave was cancelled, we knew then that D-Day wasn't far away. 27th May was my nineteenth birthday. I couldn't go ashore to celebrate it. Stripy gave me half his tot of rum, that was enough for me.

There was an incident that we did not think was fair. Steve Conner's wife was having their first baby, there were some severe complications and Steve applied for compassionate leave, which was refused. The R.N.V.R. navigating officer had a brother, who was a member of an air crew, and sadly was killed when his aircraft was taking part in an air raid over Germany. The R.N.V.R. navigator was given compassionate leave to attend the funeral. The argument was, was it fair that Steve wasn't given leave? Steve's wife had the baby, but it was touch and go. Steve was very angry.

Chapter Thirteen

H.M.S. Alresford –
June 1944-February 1945

The ship had been coaled and was tied up to the *Plover*. The weather wasn't very good, 6th June came, and the Armada left Spithead and the Solent and headed for France. That meant that the *Alresford*'s part in preparing for D-Day was over. No more Nab Channel, no more laying buoys, no more guard ship, no more gunnery shoots, no more escorting and no more use for the *Plover*.

The ship now resumed its duties as the official tender to H.M.S. *Dryad*, the navigational school for the Royal Navy. Those duties included teaching officers to become navigators and also teaching Dartmouth cadets and Naval cadets. The ship would go out to Spithead and the Solent and around the Isle of Wight area for five days. On the other days, the ship was more or less moored alongside the harbour wall in Portsmouth Harbour or the S.W.W.T.B. I do not know how long a navigational course lasts, but I would think it rather long.

One morning a coach drew up alongside, full of Wrens; they had been underground in Fort Southwick , under Portsdown Hill, for a number of weeks, prior to D-Day. They came aboard ship and we took them down to Spithead and the Solent and around the Isle of Wight, to blow the cobwebs away. I only recognised one of them – I saw her doing sword fencing once or twice, on the sea wall at Frazer Battery. I think they enjoyed themselves – the sailors enjoyed their company, too.

So, life went on and the weeks passed, doing the same jobs, coaling ship, pumping water – jobs which I didn't have to do any more. I can't say I missed P.O. May!

The ship was due a boiler clean in August. We had now gone into summer routine, which meant white front shirts and white caps. The leave was now seven days for each watch. I think that that meant that most of the ship's company could get home for a few days. Four ship mates took over our watch. Stripy and I, and our two opposite numbers took over again, when we returned from leave.

Leave was very quiet. Dad was still working ten hours a day, no more incidents with the workforce. Dad said they seemed to look at him in a different light! My brothers were all working alright. Mum was still Mum. I walked through the village, after first doing the vegetables for dinner, and called in at the Kings Arms, quiet now the Canadians had gone. Had a pint and a yarn with Albert. I could have gone to the Odeon in Bournemouth, but it meant two buses and a long walk – I did not think it was worth it, for a Boris Karloff film. I was quite happy to walk about the village, hoping to meet somebody else on leave, but I never ever met any of the lads who were home on leave at the same time as me, including my old Home Guard chums.

Saturday night, Dad said he would go up the club, to have a drink and a yarn. I said, 'Alright, I have to go back on Sunday.' So, we said cheerio to Mum and made our way up to the club. Mr. Habgood and Paddy were sitting at their regular table. Mr. Habgood rose as usual, putting out a hand to shake and saying,

'Hello son.' Paddy also shook hands, there was a nice atmosphere about the club. Very friendly. It was nice to be here with the three of them, discussing the war. A year ago Britain was losing hundreds of ships. Dad was a little happier now that the Navy was doing better in the battle of the Atlantic. Paddy's son, Harry, was almost well again. I thought that Paddy was great, considering what he went through when the gasworks was bombed.

When 10.00 came, Dad said, 'Come on my son, I have work tomorrow.' Rising, I shook hands with Mr. Habgood and Paddy, said, 'I will see you again in about five months.' That would be around January. We had been told that there would be no Christmas leave again. Nobody knew why.

Getting home, Mum made a cup of tea. Dad said he was going to have a wash and go off to bed. I sat talking to Mum, who said it was all quiet now. No more raids. I knew Mum would like to go back to Portsmouth. She missed the hustle and bustle. She could not get used to village life. Dad was gone all day, seven days a week. Mum missed walking around to Mrs. Fletcher – her door was always open and Mum would go in, and they'd make a cup of tea, sit down and listen to the latest serial on the radio. The serial I remember at the time, was called *Stella Dallas*, a real tear jerker!

It was a good thing that Mum had the chickens to look after and keep her busy. I said, 'Never mind Mum, things will change when the war is over. When we lived in Portsmouth we were lucky not to be bombed!' I gave her a hug and said I was going to have a wash and turn in.

I rose early to say goodbye to Dad, said I would see him some time around January. My brothers were still in bed. I had a nice hot bath, the last for a few months, the bucket would have to come into use again! I helped Mum to do the vegetables for dinner, which were now very plentiful, thanks to Reg. Saying cheerio to Mum, I went out the door and walked into the village. No sound of a bugle band, had Captain Pusey been dismissed? I walked up to the farm, no sign of the old horse, no sign of the Home Guard either. I walked back to the village, it was very quiet. I could understand why Mum wasn't very happy with village life. I walked up to the Lodge gates and then back again, never passed a soul. I expect my brothers found it boring as well.

The Kings Arms was now open. I went into the saloon bar, not the public bar. Now the Canadians had gone, the surly barman could not get 'confused'! There was nobody in the saloon bar, only Albert. Where had all the men and women gone? Something to do with the Canadians perhaps. Albert must be quite down in his takings. I ordered a pint, asked Albert would he join me in a drink. He said, 'Thanks' and had a half pint. I said, 'Things are very quiet Albert.' He replied, 'Yes, the Canadians certainly livened the place up, though I never had any trouble with them at all.'

One or two people began to come in, nobody I knew, though. Albert said that when the war was over, he would like to start a village football team[4], which he did, but I was elsewhere and anyway, I was no good at football. Cricket was my game.

I had another drink, then shook hands with Albert and said cheerio. Told him I hoped to see him in a few months. I made my way back home to a nice roast dinner. After all the clearing up was done, my brothers shook my hand instead of the usual clout, then with a 'cheerio' to their mum, they vanished.

It was a lovely summer's day. I sat in Dad's armchair and Mum made a cup of tea. I must have dosed off, and when I awoke, Mum was sitting quietly doing some knitting. About 1600 hours, Mum made scrambled egg on toast and after eating, I got ready to leave. No need for a greatcoat. Putting my gas mask over my shoulder, I gave Mum a big hug and kiss, then picked up my little case, telling her that I would see her in a few months. Out the door I went and up the road to the bus stop, leaving Mum on her own. I could see her point of view about village life. Her neighbour on the right-hand side of the bungalow was a little way away. The occupants were Londoners, who had come down to Dorset to get away from the Blitz, and were very noisy. There was only one bungalow on the left-hand side, a young woman lived there. She was a little strange, almost a recluse and not neighbourly at all. No wonder Mum was a bit down. She never said anything about being unhappy to Dad or my brothers, only to me.

I caught the buses and trains and was back on board ship by about 20.00. The rest of the watch were slowly drifting back, including Drip Tin. When all leave was over and boiler cleaning was finished, the ship could concentrate on training. She became very busy, coaling ship was needed about every ten days.

The coxswain should have given the job of steering the ship in and out of harbour, and out to the coal lighter and back, to the quartermaster, but Stripy was considered too old and I was too young. I think it was L/S Selwood who was given the job of helmsman. Stripy and I got on very well. I would do everything, he looked so old. There were two watch coats, shared by all the quartermasters and bonsun's mates. When Stripy put the coat on, it would almost touch the deck! The sleeves were about three times too long as well!

I had a very good hammock billet, tucked away where it wasn't bumped. Being the last to join the ship, there were not that many good billets, where you didn't get bumped about by shipmates passing by. Stripy had a billet that got accidently bumped about by liberty men, coming back at night, so I changed with him and got bumped about instead! When I transferred into the watch-keeper's mess, I changed billets with South Africa, he wasn't very happy. Stripy decided to stay where he was.

One night, during the middle of the watch, a bell rang and a light appeared above the cabin number of the R.N. Navigating Officer's cabin. I said to Stripy, 'I will go down', so off I went. I knocked on the door and a voice said, 'Come in.' I entered, saying, 'Yes sir?' The navigating officer was in his bunk, sitting up, he said, 'Beedie.' I said, 'Yes sir.' He said, 'How is the weather?' I replied, 'Quite calm sir'. He said, 'What are the air and water temperatures?' I told him.

He then asked, 'How are the moorings?' I said, 'They are alright sir.' He then said, 'Beedie.' I said, 'Yes sir.' He said, 'I have received a phone call from my wife, saying that our son, a Major in the Royal Marines is missing presumed dead, but he is not dead Beedie.' I said, 'I hope not, sir.' He continued, 'I know our other son is dead, he was Captain on a destroyer which was sunk with all hands.' I said, 'I am sorry to hear that, sir.' He said, 'Get me my writing pad, I am going to write a letter telling my wife that our son is still alive.' I went to his desk, took a pen, writing paper and an envelope and took them to him. He said, 'Thank you Beedie, that is all.' I said, 'Aye aye sir' and left his cabin and went back to the quarterdeck to tell Stripy the sad news. Stripy said, 'I hope he is right.' The navigating officer was a very good officer, the other officers loved him because he never wished to go ashore. When his bell rang, the duty quartermaster knew that he would ask about the moorings, weather and temperatures.

The ship would always moor up in the S.W.W.T.B., so regular night leave was given. There was no more tying up to the jetty and no more company from the A.T.S. in the pub. Wonder what happened to my marmalade jar?!

I would have thought that the Captain could have looked

for a better ship to command, it must have been very boring doing the same thing week after week, month after month. Unless he decided to carry on in command when the war finished, he would retire. He was the King's Harbour Master in Singapore. When the Japanese captured Singapore, he broke both his legs during the evacuation. He was very nimble now though.

The locals were very happy, one of the starboard watch had a cold fish shop. On long leave, he could be seen in his shop, in his white coat and apron. As it happened, when we lived in Portsmouth, our house was about three quarters of a mile from the shop.

Sometimes, when I got home from school, Mum would say, 'Your Uncle Wilfred wants a pair of bloaters.' I would say, 'But Mum, I've got my paper round!' but she would say, 'Even so, you'll have to get them!' So I would have to run like blazes to get them. Uncle Wilfred lost a leg in the First War and had thirteen body wounds. He was always grumpy. I never got any thanks, but a clout if he thought I was late! I never realised that the fishmonger and I would be future shipmates! If we had any leave at weekends (08.00 Saturday morning until 08.00 Sunday morning), he would soon be home and behind the counter. He was a very happy H.O.!

The wireless office staff consisted of a P.O. telegraphist, a leading telegraphist and one ordinary telegraphist. A speaker had been fitted into the mess deck, and in the evening, the telegraphist would tune in to a popular radio station. We would have first-class band music to listen to. Plenty of Vera Lynn, although I preferred Anne Shelton. The ordinary telegraphist was a fitness fanatic, he never went ashore. There was plenty of deck space in front of the wireless office. He rigged up a self-made punch bag, a good one too, and all he did was skip and punch the bag. He never wanted any company. He was also an H.O. perhaps he hoped to become a boxer when he was demobbed.

The ship left S.W.W.T.B., all hands were on board, except a stoker who had gone A.W.O.L. He had always been very quiet and hardly ever went ashore. It must have been three weeks or so before he was brought back on board, by two naval police officers. He should have been court-martialled and sentenced to ninety days in the naval prison. Milton was also a civilian prison, but I think the Navy must have taken it over for a while. However, the Captain found out that the stoker was aboard H.M.S. *Cambletown*, which, with its bows filled with explosives, had rammed the German submarine pen gates at Saint-Nazaire in France, pretty much a suicide mission. All prisoners taken were manacled and taken away. At noon the following day, the *Cambletown* blew up, killing many high-up German officers, who were standing on the bow and also causing a major problem in the Atlantic for the Germans. The stoker managed to escape in one of the few motor launches that were left.

Bearing in mind what the stoker had been through, the Captain arranged for him to be sentenced to fourteen days in cells in Portsmouth Naval Barracks. The stoker was a very grateful prisoner! All the ship mates were pleased to see him after he had finished his sentence. There were not many left, after that heroic action. The Captain was a very sympathetic officer, he was well liked by all the crew.

The ship carried on training navigating officers. The advanced courses must have been very hard and were very long. The weeks went by and one day when Stripy and I were on the 08.00 to midday watch, the R.N. navigating officer came up to me and said, 'Beedie.' I said, 'Yes sir?' He replied, 'Do you remember the conversation we had some weeks ago, I told you that my son a Major in the Royal Marines, had been reported missing, presumed dead?' I said, 'Yes sir', and he carried on, 'My wife has phoned me (there was a phone line connected to the ship when we were tied up to the S.W.W.T.B.) to say she has received a card from the Red Cross, saying that he is a prisoner of war and is uninjured. I told you Beedie, didn't I, that he was still alive!' I said, 'Yes sir, what a relief for you and your wife!' 'Indeed Beedie, it is,' he said and then turned and walked away. I think he was quite emotional. Stripy was pleased to hear the news.

Christmas was almost on us – no Christmas leave again, as the ship would have a boiler clean in January and leave would be granted then. Mick Johnson had come back with a lovely black eye after the last leave. There had been a march in Belfast, celebrating the Battle of the Boyne in 1690 (where the Protestant forces of King William and Mary of Orange defeated the Catholic forces of King James II). There was still rivalry between the two sides. Mick was a firm follower of King Billy, as he called him, and had been caught up in an altercation. South Africa was absolutely delighted! I think Mick would have liked to give him a black eye!

Christmas arrived, ship mates had been bringing back greenery purloined from various bushes around Portsmouth when on night leave. The locals were alright – port watch were on leave from noon on Christmas Eve to 08.00 on Christmas morning. Starboard watch from noon Christmas day until 08.00 the following morning.

The port and starboard messes were decorated out. The cooks of the mess, the experts, were busy getting Christmas dinner, a roast, ready. The cook on our mess was busy, too. He was quite the opposite of the previous cook, no cockroaches, thank goodness! We had a roast with pussers peas and sprouts brought in by one of the locals, and Yorkshire puddings. This was followed by apple tart and custard. A mess kettle full of hot soapy water was ready for washing up.

There was a Londoner called Smithy on board, who must have been saving his tot of rum (rum could be preserved by putting sultanas in it and watering it down) for Christmas. Smithy, for some reason no one could understand, shared a bottle, down in the hammock flat, where the kitbags and hammocks were stored, with the most obnoxious character on the ship, 'Yorky' (he was from Yorkshire). Yorky received an extra threepence a day for being 'temperate' (not drinking rum), but he would always be ready to drink someone else's!

Apparently, everyone was ready to start their meal, when up from the hammock flat came Yorky, drunk as a skunk! He promptly kicked the mess kettle over, flooding the mess, and collapsed. Jack Towney, Jock McDonald, Piggy Grant and Charlie Fox leaped around the mess table, grabbed and dragged him, bump, bump, bump up the ladder – then lifted him up and bodily threw him, he came down with a thud on the deck. It was quite a cold day, and he only had his boiler suit on, but he was left there to sober up. They went back down to the mess and sat down to eat the rather lukewarm Christmas dinner, with their shoes in soapy water. Afterwards, they washed up and mopped the deck.

I was in the watch-keeper's mess, so wasn't involved. Nobody in the port watch was worried about Yorky, and as for Smithy, he kept out of the way as well as he could. That was Christmas dinner 1944!

In January everyone was looking forward to seven days' boiler cleaning leave, especially the fishmonger – he was in the starboard watch who went first, including Yorky, who was so full of rum on Christmas Day that the cold never affected him – he was sent to Coventry by the first part of port for spoiling their Christmas lunch! Smithy apologised, but never gave the reason why Yorky got so drunk.

I was ready to go as soon as the starboard watch came back. Their leave finished at 23.55 Sunday night. The port watch started their leave at 08.00 Monday morning. The port watch were soon on their way to Portsmouth Station. I caught the London train, left it at Southampton, and caught the Bournemouth train, and after two buses I was home. Nothing had changed, Dad was still working ten hours a day, my brothers were still working and Mum was still tired. I gave her a big hug and kissed her, asked if I could have a bath – the first since August. Mum said, 'Of course you can.' Whilst I had a bath, Mum was preparing a cottage pie, which we shared at dinner time. Reg and Ron would have theirs when they came in from work.

It was Monday, and after dinner, I sat in Dad's old armchair and Mum made a cup of tea. She sat down and I asked her how she was feeling. She was some what down, she hadn't been anywhere for years. Dad had been working ten hours a day for almost three years. He was sixty-seven. Apart from the allowed holidays, he had never had a day off, not a day sick. He was as hard as nails.

Mum was now sixty-one years old, and had had a hard life, and could do with a jolly good holiday. Looking after four men was not easy. Her only daughter, my sister, Jean, lived in Portsmouth, if she had lived closer, it would have made all the difference. Jean's husband, Bill, was now a C.P.O. in the Indian Navy.

I told her that things would change when the war was over. The boys did their share to help Mum, but a daughter to talk to would have made all the difference. Mum had also not seen her grand-daughter. She sighed, sat down and started knitting. I sat and read the paper that I'd bought in Portsmouth train station. Soon, as usual, I dosed off and the next thing I knew, two of my brothers were in. Jock was working overtime. Mum gave Reg and Ron their meals and after eating, they went up to their rooms. I slept on a camp bed in Jock's room – my choice.

Dad came in, tired out, he took off his coat and sank into his armchair. It would not be long before Mum made him a light meal, then he would go for a good wash, and soon be off to bed. I sat on the settee, and talked to Dad about the war. The Army was now in Germany, the V1 and V2 bases had been destroyed, and I did not think that Germany would last many more months. The R.A.F. were giving Germany as much bombing as they had given us, if not more.

Dad asked me how long on leave I had, I told him, seven days and that I was lucky to be a bosun's mate as I didn't have to coal ship. He said that when he was on the liners, they would burn over a hundred tons of coal a day! His life had been hard even before working in a factory boiler room.

I said, 'You don't go out much now Dad?' he said, 'No, it depends on the weather, but I'll go out with you on Saturday night.' I said, 'Alright Dad.' We sat and yarned a bit, while he ate his supper and then he said, 'Well my son, I'm off to have a wash and go to bed now', and off he went. Mum soon followed.

I didn't go very far on leave, the weather wasn't all that good. One morning, when the weather was better, I decided to go to Winton. I caught the bus, got off at a crossroads, turned left and was soon in Winton. I window-shopped as I walked and after a while I came to a British Legion. I went in and was made very welcome and I decided to join. I had a couple of drinks with my new friends, then left the club and found a small café – they only made – you got it – cottage pie! I think cottage pie was helping to win the war! I sat at a table anyway and the cottage pie arrived, it was actually quite nice! The other customers seemed to enjoy it, too.

When I came out of the café, there were quite a lot of people about, and I decided to walk home and stretch my legs. I walked back to the crossroads and turned right. Two young girls ran up to me and touched my collar, then ran away laughing. I walked until I came to the long road that led into Wallisdown village, where I and another member of the Home Guard used to patrol in the dark. I walked passed the post office, deciding not to go in, in case Captain Pusey had been dismissed. The Kings Arms wasn't open. I carried on walking until I reached home. I had enjoyed the walk.

The week was soon passing. One morning, I walked up to the Kings Arms and had a drink and a yarn with Albert. He thought that the end of the war was in sight and that the Home Guard had been stood down. He said that he thought that Captain Pusey had been dismissed, although Captain Pusey wasn't one of Albert's customers. I had another drink, then said cheerio to Albert and walked home to a nice dinner.

Saturday came. In the morning, I caught the bus to Winton. I walked down to the British Legion, there were no servicemen in there. I ordered a drink and was challenged to a game of snooker by one of the members. I was well beaten, it was a long time since I had played snooker. I bought him a drink, then sat down with some members and played cribbage. It was a nice friendly club. Finally, I decided to go, I said cheerio to my friends, saying that I hoped to see them again sometime. I went into the little café, and ordered cottage pie and a cup of tea. I had told Mum that I would eat while I was out.

I decided to walk home again and at the crossroads, which was called 'the banks' because there were banks on three corners, I turned right and walked home through the village. There were not any villagers about, the weather was still miserable. Reg and Ron were indoors, it was too miserable for them to go out. They had had dinner. It was toast and jam for tea.

At 18.30, Dad came in, cold and wet. I said, 'Dad, we are

not going out tonight, I will see Mr. Habgood and Paddy next time I come home. I doubt they will come out tonight anyway.' I think Dad was quite thankful.

Jock was out with his friends. He could afford nice clothes now – he was becoming quite a skilled engineer. He was a good son and looked after Mum.

So that was my last night at home with Mum, Dad and my brothers. Sunday morning, I helped Mum to do the vegetables for Sunday dinner. Dad had gone to work, I had got up early to say goodbye to him. I watched him make his way up the hill in the poor weather. Dad had been a hard Dad, but I was rather proud of him.

After dinner, I sat in Dad's armchair until it was time to pack my case. Mum made egg on toast for tea, then I put on my greatcoat, grabbed my case and gas mask, gave Mum a big hug and kiss, told her it shouldn't be long now. I said, 'Keep your chin up Mum!' Then I was out the door, up the hill, two buses, two trains and I was walking through the dockyard gate.

I reported to the dockyard police, then made my way back on board. The rest of the watch were slowly drifting back. Stripy appeared, then a signaller and a telegraphist. One of them made a tea kettle of tea. Drip Tin appeared, moaning that 'the bloody war will be over before we get another leave!' which would be June.

Stripy and I were due to go on watch the next day. I felt he should have stayed at home. We all had a cup of tea, then I fetched Stripy's hammock out of the hammock flat, along with my own. Stripy slung a deep hammock, all you could see when you looked up at him was his little bald head.

One of the first things that hands had to undertake was coaling ship. Then there was an increment of officers to be trained. The ship then returned to the S.W.W.T.B. and normal duties resumed.

Chapter Fourteen

H.M.S. Rochester

February 1945 came and one morning, the ship returned from duty at Spithead and tied up to the wall in Portsmouth Harbour. Stripy and I had just come up on deck to start the 0800 hours to twelve noon watch. Hands were following up, to fall in on the quarterdeck. A sloop started to come alongside, hands quickly took the lines and the sloop, named H.M.S. *Rochester*, was secured alongside. A lighter appeared and tied up alongside the *Rochester*. The skeleton crew on board, soon transferred their gear onto the lighter.

The crew of the *Alresford*, including me, were ordered to take all their gear and themselves over on to the *Rochester*. A skeleton crew were named and stayed aboard the *Alresford*. She then sailed to Milford Haven, where she waited to be sold to Belgium for mercantile use.

Apart from the fact that we were losing leading seaman Selwood, and four seamen – Mick Johnson and Piggy Grant from the first part of port and Alderton and Yorky from the first part of starboard – as shipmates, the remainder of the crew were delighted to be leaving the *Alresford*, including myself! No more coaling ship or pumping fresh water – the heads and washrooms were inboard, we wouldn't know ourselves! The *Rochester* also had radar and echo sounder, much more effective that a lead and line! She was built in 1931.

I was glad that I was still a bosun's mate, as, after the Captain had inspected the ship from stern to stern, he decided that the deck had not been looked after properly, and ordered it to be holystoned (a lump of sand stone, used for scrubbing the deck), which brought some groans from the crew! Out came the holystones, which must have been in the back of the shipwright's store on the *Rochester*.

After a couple of weeks under the watchful eye of P.O. May, the deck had been holystoned and then scrubbed down with soapy water. Then the hoses came into play. What needed painting was painted. P. O. May was in his element!

One morning in March, I and Stripy came up on deck with the other hands at 0800 hours. We could not believe our eyes, the dockyard mateys were all dressed in clean white boiler suits! – then we saw the reason why. Being drawn by eight sailors on each rope was a gun carriage, on which was a very large coffin. Marching either side of the carriage were three very big chief G.I.s. The gun carriage stopped at the ship's quarterdeck and the six chief G.I.s lifted the coffin off the carriage and carried it aboard. It was a struggle as it was a very large coffin. The chief G.I.s then unscrewed the top of it – on the inside of the coffin were slots in which the chief G.I.s slid large pieces of lead. The coffin top was then screwed back on. A burial board appeared from somewhere, one end rested on the taffrail, two strong legs supported the other end. The board was greased with soft soap. The coffin was raised up onto the burial board. On top of the coffin was a raised wooden cross, under the cross was a glass window, about 3 feet by 4 inches in size, through which could be seen the uniform of a full

Admiral. His name was Admiral Tupper.

The gun carriage and the chief G.I.s departed. Stripy and I and two other shipmates were told to hold the four corners of the white ensign, which was draped over the coffin. The ship slowly left the harbour wall and headed out of the harbour. As the ship passed other naval ships, all saluted the dead Admiral. The battleship the *Duke of York* was tied up beneath the C.I.C. signal tower. A bugler on the battleship sounded the 'still'. The C.I.C.s also saluted from the signal tower. The *Rochester* slowly steamed out of the harbour. The bugler sounded 'stand easy'. It must be the first time the C.I.C., and a battleship saluted an old sloop. The salutes were answered by the coxswain, with a bosun's call – a whistle, made to a special shape enabling it to make various calls, before an order was shouted. I got quite efficient at recognising these calls, under the auspices of Stripy.

The ship steamed slowly through Spithead, being saluted and anwsered by naval ships that were at anchor. As the ship slowly made its way round the Solent and into the Channel, the Captain called all the other officers, except the 1st lieutenant, to attention. The Chaplain then read a lesson. At a given order, we carefully lifted the burial board and the coffin slowly slid down into the water with a large splash. Then a Royal Marine bugler sounded the last post. There was only one mourner, a lady dressed in black. After the last post, the lady was escorted to the wardroom. The ship returned to the S.W.W.T.B.

If it had been peacetime, Admiral Tupper would have had a much more senior ship to take him on his final journey. The burial board was cleaned and delivered back to the *Duke of York*, where it came from. Who the lady in black was, we never learned.

After the excitement of seeing the dockyard mateys in white boiler suits, normal duties were resumed. There was another bit of excitement when the ship pulled alongside an oiler. A stoker armed with a spanner ran up and connected a pipe to the oiler. A cheer went up from those watching, how much easier than having to coal ship! This probably meant losing our shilling a day 'hard lying' money, though.

I did not get to find out, as on the 14th April, P.O. May told me I was being drafted to the Royal Naval Barracks on 15th April, the next day! I went down into the watch-keepers mess and sat down, somewhat stunned. I could not understand, with the war nearly over, why I, an H.O. would be drafted to the R.N.B. Perhaps I was going to be kicked out. The *Alresford* was a hard ship, but I'd enjoyed the fifteen months on her, and the brief spell on the *Rochester*. With the exception of one or two people, you could not find a happier ship. The officers were great, the Captain was a very fine officer, as was the R.N. navigating officer.

I started to pack my kitbag, thinking where will I find ship mates like Steve Conner, Charlie Fox, Drip Tin Watkins, Jock McDonald, Jock Towney and many more, but most of all Stripy. I had grown to love that old sailor – I only hoped that he would be quickly demobbed.

The next morning, I washed, dressed, lashed my hammock and finished my packing. I gave my bucket to Stripy. At 0900 hours, the little white canvas-topped van arrived. My kitbag and hammock were carried up for me. I had my greatcoat on, gas mask over my shoulder and little brown case in my hand. Most of the seamen were on the quarterdeck. I shook hands with them all, even P.O. May. I put my arm around Stripy and said goodbye. My gear had been taken down and placed in the van. I walked down the gang plank and over to the van. Gave a last wave to my shipmates, got into the van and off we drove. Gone were all my shipmates, I would never see them again.

Chapter Fifteen

The Royal Naval Barracks

We soon arrived at the R.N.B. The van drove to the drafting office and I reported in. A drafting petty officer took my details, which were not many, and told the driver to take me to one of the large blocks of mess decks. I can't remember which block or which mess deck. The driver was good enough to give me a hand with my gear, up to the second floor.

The mess was about three quarters full. I hoped to find a bunk somewhere near the middle, away from the door. I found one, and dumped my kit next to it, the driver did the same, I thanked him for his help and off he went. It was a bottom bunk, nobody on the top. Over in the corner of the barracks there were a few elderly sailors who had somehow managed to evade the draft. They were called Barrack Stanchions, they never moved – encouraging young sailors to play a game called Crown and Anchor, which was illegal. Those who did play, soon lost their pay.

I sat on my bunk wondering what was going to happen next. I talked to a couple of sailors who were in the same position as me, they had been there for a few days and it was they who warned me to keep away from the Crown and Anchor crowd. They also told me that a messenger from the drafting office came over every lunchtime and placed draft chits on the mess deck table.

I asked, 'So what do I do?' They said, 'Nothing, that's the trouble, we all have to keep scarce. Fall in at 0800 hours on the parade ground. You answer your name, then a chosen few are given jobs. Then the parade is dismissed and those without jobs have to make ourselves scarce. We are not even allowed in the mess decks in the mornings!'

The next morning, at 0800 hours, I fell in with the same two sailors. Our names were called, and we answered. After 'stand easy' and the 1000 hours' break, a chance came up to get into the mess. The mess deck patrols couldn't look in every mess, and if they did come into the mess we were in, we would hide until they were gone – like a game of cat and mouse!

At 12.00 midday, it was dinner time. After dinner, we were allowed to stay on the mess deck. When 'hands to dinner' was piped, I followed the horde and was soon sitting down partaking in the Navy's finest pea soup. It was still the finest soup I ever tasted! I can't remember what the main meal was, probably cottage pie! After dinner, I went back to the mess. No draft chits on the table. I opened my hammock, and spread it over the bunk, there were hooks where I could sling my hammock if I wished. Then I sat and talked to my new friends. There did not seem to be any 'get up and go' feeling anywhere in the barracks. No sharpness.

On 18th April, I found a message on the mess deck table, telling me to report to the drafting office. On reporting, I was told I was being drafted to H.M.S. *Excellent* for fourteen days retraining on four-inch guns. I was to have my gear outside the drafting office by 1400 hours. Just before 1400 hours, I said goodbye to my new-found friends. One helped me with my gear to the drafting office. Sure enough, up rolled the little white van. The driver went into the drafting office and came out with some paperwork. I thanked my friend for helping me with my gear and he wished me good luck.

I jumped into the van and off we went to Whale Island. I wondered if the disgraceful P.O.G.I. was still there. I didn't think I would recognise him if he was. After reporting to the regulating office, I was back in the van, and off to a mess-deck block. When I walked into the first-floor mess deck, I thought of Buncie, did he survive those awful injuries – what had happened to him. How were his parents taking it? I would never know.

A P.O.G.I. came into the mess deck, asked my name, and told me to find a bunk. He said that I would be there for two weeks with a few others, for a short course on the twin four-inch gun, plus other subjects. He instructed me to fall in on parade at 0800 hours and that my name would be called by a P.O.G.I. who would be my instructor.

At 0800 hours the next morning, I fell in with three more gunnery ratings, the same as me. A P.O.G.I. took charge. 'You will double between classes, as you did when doing your third-class gunnery course. At the end of fourteen days, you will return to the R.N.B.,' he told us. So, that was it, after fourteen days of doubling here and there, renewing old subjects, especially gun drill (which was taken by the smallest P.O.G.I. I have ever seen, who had a voice like a foghorn), I returned to the R.N.B.

On 4th May I reported to the regulating office, gave my name and was told that I had been given ten days' leave. I was given ten days' ration vouchers, plus my up-to-date pay and a railway warrant. I was told to report back on 14th May. With my greatcoat on and carrying my various gear, I made my way to the railway station. No uniformed gorilla, he must be lurking somewhere else! I changed my warrant for a ticket and made my way to the Waterloo platform. I found a seat and sat pondering why I and others, also H.O.s, should have to do a short gunnery course when the war was almost over. Ten days was the longest leave I had ever had while in the Navy. What was going on?

The train arrived and I changed at Southampton for Bournemouth, caught two buses and I was home, to a surprised mother. I told her I had been given ten days' leave for some reason or other. I settled in and for the first few days did not do very much. Then on 8th May 1945, peace was declared. The church bells rang. The lights came on, there was dancing in the streets. Victory in Europe! Dad would be able to put his notice in. Jock would be called up at sometime for his National Service. Nobody would want to go to work, why should they? The war was over! Was I going to be demobbed? I hoped so.

The village came alive with coloured bunting and flags flying from windows. I helped Mum to peel the vegetables for dinner. I said to Mum, 'I don't think the boys will be in very early, people will be going out and partying in the streets. I expect Dad will come home early though.'

I did not go out. We could hear the church bells ringing, the bell ringers must have been getting tired! It was still double summertime. The street lights would be coming on later. I sat reading a magazine. Mum said, 'Dinner is ready.' Minced beef with vegetables, followed by rice pudding with a dollop of strawberry jam on top – very nice! After clearing up and washing up, Mum made a cup of tea and we sat down and quietly listened to the radio. The broadcaster said that at 1500 hours, the war in Europe officially ended. I said to Mum, 'I expect there will be a church service tonight.' The sound of cheering coming from London filled the room. I thought of Buncie and Bertie and then my mind wandered back to life in Portsmouth during the war and my best friend Ronnie Stout.

Ronnie and I grew up together. We were like eggs and bacon, always together. We used to talk about what we were going to do when we grew up. I said I wanted to join the Navy. Ronnie said he wanted to join the Naafi (which stands for the Navy, Army and Air Force institutes). The Naafi was like a seagoing general store and sold most things, like toiletries and cigarettes etc. There was a Naafi on all ships of a certain size. There were also Naafis on all shore bases.

Ronnie and I were never separated – we always went out together after work. One lovely summer evening during the early part of the war, Ronnie and I were mooching about, about three streets from where I used to live. One of the roads was called Drayton Road, and there was an Infants School there. The infants had been evacuated and the school had been turned into a first aid post. Ronnie suddenly shouted, 'Look up there!' I looked up and high in the sky, glinting in the sun, were what looked like a shoal of silver fish. Then he shouted, 'They are not ours, run for the shelter!'

We both started to run for the shelter on the corner of the road. By then the sirens had started to wail, the guns opened up. We reached the shelter and ran in, there was a mighty explosion and the blast hit the shelter. Ronnie and I stayed sitting in the shelter. The noise of the guns was deafening. Finally the guns grew quiet and the 'all-clear' was sounded. Ronnie and I then went back to where we had been mooching about. Sure enough, Drayton Road Infant School had been hit. Thirteen doctors, nurses, police and others had been killed and many more injured.

Mr. Richardson, our baker, and his brother had a small bakery. Bread was baked in a wood-fired oven. They also had a full-time delivery man. The bread was absolutely wonderful. Mr. Richardson did the books and ran the business. He and the delivery man had bicycles, with a very small front wheel. Coming up from the wheel was a V-shaped structure that took a large V-shaped wicker basket. The basket would be packed with freshly baked bread. The loaves would be stacked in the basket in order – the bread for the last house to be delivered to, would be packed in first, the second last next, and so on, until the basket was full. The bike had to be leant up against the customer's front wall to stop the back wheel from lifting up off the ground.

Mr. Richardson would wear a collar and tie, a tweed suit, highly polished shoes, a brown smock coat and a bowler hat. His brother baked the bread. He was also a volunteer heavy rescue worker. After the bombing of the school, he made his way to Drayton Road to see if he could help with the rescue. The heavy school door had been blown off. Rescuers had been tramping in and out. When Mr. Richardson and others lifted the door, there was a poor soul lying under it. Whether he was alive when the door landed on him but died after the door was tramped over, it was not known.

Mr. Richardson told his brother about what had happened at the school and his brother told my mother. That year, he and his brother cooked Christmas dinners for those who could afford turkeys but did not have the facilities to cook them.

This was not the first time that Ronnie and I had to run for it. There was a threepenny matinee at the Tivoli cinema, which had not been bombed. We decided to take a chance as there was a good Western on. We got to the cinema and paid our threepence, saying that we were under sixteen. We found our seats and settled down to watch the film. About halfway through the programme, the film stopped, the manager came out and shouted that we were all to leave the cinema. We started to file out. The sirens were wailing. The Tivoli was on a main road and there wasn't a shelter nearby.

Ronnie said, 'We'll have to run for it'. I agreed, so off we ran down the main road. The guns started firing. We ran faster and turned right onto a long road; after a while we turned left into an alley, on coming out of the alley, Ronnie turned left and then turned right into Percival Road (Marsdens were on the corner of Percival Road) and headed for home. I turned right and then left, into Byron Road and at the end of the road, was our house, number one.

Shrapnel was falling all around me, I could hear it clattering about. The air was full of the sound of aircraft engines. I ran into the house and straight through into the garden and down into the shelter. Mum gave me a good telling off. If she hadn't been there, Dad would have given me a clout for worrying them!

So what had happened to Ronnie, did he join the Naafi and survive the war? I never found out, as unfortunately it was at this time that we moved from Portsmouth, and although Ronnie would have been home from work at 5.30, our brave furniture movers insisted that we pack up and get out of Portsmouth by 5 o'clock, so I never had a chance to go and say goodbye. Mum never had a chance to say goodbye to Mrs. Fletcher either.

Mum got up to make another cup of tea, and I came back to earth. I wondered what Mum was thinking. She had lost her first husband, Jimmy, when the battleship H.M.S. *Bulwark*, which he was serving on, was sunk in the First World War. She sat quietly, doing her knitting. Dad came in at his normal time of 6.30 p.m., as the coach that picked up the workers had arrived at the same time as usual.

I said to Dad, 'You'll be able to give that job up now Dad.' He said, 'Aye.' Then I asked, 'Do you want to go out tonight

Dad?' He said, 'No, it's madness out there!' I said, 'Alright Dad, I won't go out either.'

Mum made Dad a cup of tea and I made some toast. Dad told us that his works canteen had made sandwiches and tea, and the Commander had come down and thanked all the workers for their war efforts and that they would have to wait and see what would happen in the future, but that they should all come in to work as normal the next day. He told the workers that lived nearby, to clock out and go home. Dad and the others, who relied on transport to get home, had to wait.

So, Mum, Dad and I had toast and marmalade and sat quietly listening to the radio. Reg and Ron came in late. Jock didn't come in until the early hours. Whether they went to work or not, I can't remember.

I sat talking to Dad, I said, 'Dad, did you ever hear of an Admiral Tupper, during the last war?' Dad looked at me, steam coming out of his ears, I thought he was going to explode! I can't write down what Dad called him! After he calmed down, he told me (this is from memory) that Admiral Tupper was in command of the 10th Cruiser Squadron in Scapa Flow. Apparently, he ordered all of the public houses to be out of bounds for sailors. They were to be for officers use only. The sailors only had one canteen to use. He must have been the least popular Admiral in the Navy!

I said, 'Well Dad, the Admiral has passed away and the ship I was on carried his body out to sea, and he was buried in the Channel near the Needles. He only had one mourner, a lady dressed all in black. So he couldn't have been very popular at home either!' I think that made Dad's day!

Dad told me that he was going to put his notice in, in the morning. I was very pleased to hear that. If ever there was someone who had done their bit for the war effort, it was Dad.

We sat quietly talking and listening to the fireworks which were going off, even though it wasn't dark yet.

I said to Dad that I wasn't very happy, I did not like the two weeks at Whale Island. What was the reason for me being there? The European war was over and I was only an H.O. Dad said that it did seem strange, but the Navy acted in strange ways sometimes, and I would just have to wait and see. With that, he said goodnight and went off for a wash and to bed, leaving Mum and I. Mum was quiet.

I said, 'There are a lot of happy people out there, but also a great many sad ones.' She said, 'Yes.' I knew how she was feeling, so went and made a cup of tea. Then sat quietly with her until it was time to turn in.

The next day, I had a lie-in, then got up and had a bath. My brothers and Dad had gone off to work. After breakfast, I went for a walk. The village had come alive. I walked up to the Lodge Gates, then turned back and called in at the Kings Arms. The public bar was almost full, a lot of laughter, I went into the saloon bar, there was a happy crowd in there too but nobody I knew. I was pleased to see Albert and his wife. They bought me a drink. I said to Albert, 'It should not be too long now before you start your village football team.' 'Yes,' he said. 'There are a few that are interested, and we might be lucky and get a field to use at the farm' (which they did).

I said, 'Have you been very busy?' He replied, 'Yes, but the problem is that there is a shortage of beer. Some pubs are only opening part time. I won't be open tonight. I'll be closing up shortly and hoping for a delivery soon!' I had another drink and then said cheerio to Albert and that I hoped to see him again soon.

I made my way home for dinner. After we'd eaten, Mum and I sat down with a cup of tea. She said, 'You don't seem very happy.' I said, 'Well Mum, at the moment, I am trying to fathom out why I have been sent on a course to Whale Island, what is the point of it? What is the Navy up to?' Mum said, 'You'll soon find out when you get back.' I told her, 'That is what I am concerned about!'

Reg and Ron came in, their work was not affected by the war ending. They had their meal, washed and changed and went out to join the festivities. Jock came in and did the same and was soon out with his mates. His hours of work were to be cut. Sunday work was finished and Saturday work would finish at noon. That would make quite a difference to his wage packet.

Dad came in at six thirty, tired as usual. I asked him if he had put his notice in. He said, 'Yes, but I have told the foreman that I'll carry on until he finds another boiler man.' I said, 'It could take weeks for them to find another boiler man!' Dad just shrugged his shoulders and said that the foreman had been very pleased. Mum said, 'And so he should be!' and that was that.

I told Dad about the beer shortage and that the Kings Arms was not open that night and that maybe the club was in the same boat. The issue being that if the club was closed, the members could use the pub, but if the pub was closed, the pub users could not use the club unless they were members.

Dad said, 'The club will be sure to be open on Saturday night.' I said, 'Albert told me that he was waiting for a delivery, so the Kings Arms should be alright this weekend, though if the club is open, I would like to go there Saturday night.' Dad said, 'Alright, we will go.'

Mum made Dad a light meal and then we all had a cup of tea. Dad told us that he would now be working from nine until five during the week with an hour off for lunch. That meant that he would be home a good hour earlier, which Mum was very pleased about. He said, 'I expect it will take a little time before things are properly sorted out.' The same would apply to Jock, who could now look forward to his National Service. Dad then went for a wash and went to bed. Mum and I soon followed.

The next couple of days passed quickly. I would go for a walk in the village and call in at the pub. Albert had had his delivery, but he was going to have to restrict his hours, to make it last. I decided not to go to Winton. I did not fancy all the walking, only to find that the Legion was closed.

On Saturday, I did the same, calling in at the Kings Arms to say cheerio to Albert. I said, 'I don't know when I will see you again, I hope it won't be too long.' I shook his hand and made my way home. Dad was home, the first Saturday he had not had to go to work for three years.

Of course, the vicious war in Burma was still going on. One lad in the village, named Claxton, nicknamed Dingle, was out there in the 14th Army.

Dad enjoyed his dinner, knowing that he could enjoy his first afternoon nap for some time! That night Dad and I made our way up to the Conservative Club. It was fairly full. The Kings Arms was open as well. Paddy Daly was there as was Mr. Habgood. They had saved a seat for Dad and I managed to find a chair and squeeze in between Dad and Paddy, who was very pleased that his son Harry was almost over his wounds and hoped to be home soon. His oldest son, Jim, was serving in the Navy and was also alright.

Mr. Habgood, as usual, stood up to shake hands and say, 'Hello my son.' There was a very happy atmosphere in the club. An old Irish policeman named Mulligan, who had a battered face and had enjoyed his fair share of the golden amber that night, attempted to stand on a table, which was on top of another table, to give us a rendering of an old Irish ballad. He finally made it, his head almost touching the ceiling. He was great, got a good hand of applause from the packed bar. His problem now was how to get down! He decided to fall, and was caught by half a dozen members! I bet he'd knocked a few heads together when he was a policeman!

It was so noisy in there, I had a job to hear what was going on. It was nice to see Paddy and Mr. Habgood so happy after all the worries of the war and to see Dad relaxing after all of his concerns about the war effort in recent times. And so the festivities and the singing carried on. Just after ten, Dad said that it was time to go, and after shaking hands with Paddy and Mr. Habgood and saying that I hoped to see them in the not too distant future, we left a very happy crowd to their jollities.

We walked home and were soon sitting down indoors. Mum asked us if we wanted a drink, but we said no. I said, 'I am going back to Portsmouth after dinner tomorrow, I want to do the joining routine in the afternoon, so that I get a decent billet.'

The next morning I had a lie-in. My brothers had not come in until late, and were still out for the count. I got up and had a bath – when would my next bath be? I wondered. I got dressed and helped Mum with the vegetables for dinner and then went for a walk in the garden. It was lovely and peaceful, the bees were buzzing around Reggy's garden. The chickens were clucking, Mum's pets! I sat there on a old garden chair, at peace with the world. One of my brothers appeared, I can't remember who it was, and gave me a glass of cider, the first cider I had ever drunk. It was lovely. I sat there until Mum called me in for dinner. A nice Sunday roast, then apple pie and custard. After all the clearing up had been done, we all sat down and enjoyed a cup of tea together.

My brothers were all going out to Bournemouth in the

afternoon, to enjoy the party atmosphere which was still going on. I shook hands with them all, and they wished me the best of luck. Dad settled down in his old armchair for his nap. I then got ready to go. My dobeing had been done and ironed, so I collected up my things and gave Dad a gentle shake. He woke up and I said, 'I'm off now Dad, I guess I will soon solve the mystery of what is going on!' He said, 'I hope it is not bad news.' We shook hands and I turned to Mum and gave her a big hug and kiss, saying, 'I don't know how long it will be before I see you again Mum', little knowing that it would be sixteen months!

Then with a last 'goodbye and take care' I was out the door. Two buses and two trains later, I was back in Portsmouth and on my way back to the R.N.B., it wasn't far to walk. I walked into the barracks and reported to the regulating office, where I was given my station card, and told my mess block and mess deck numbers. Someone showed me the way to the mess block and told me to report to the baggage office to collect my kitbag and hammock.

Once I had my gear, I humped it to the mess block. I made my way up to the second floor, having made a couple of rest stops on the way. There were quite a few sailors in the mess, and I was shown a spare bunk, on which I dumped my luggage. I was shown where I could sling my hammock, which I preferred to a bunk.

I had missed tea, so I slung my hammock and asked where the galley was. I followed the instructions I had been given and found my way to the galley, where there was a P.O. cook. I explained that I had missed tea. I was given a mug of tea and a corned beef sandwich, which I enjoyed.

When I got back to the mess, I asked a fellow mess mate what the routine was. It turned out to be the same as before. Fall in at 0800 hours, answer your name when it was called. A chosen few would be given jobs. The rest of the parade would be dismissed, and then we should make ourselves scarce.

I said to my new mess mate friend, 'How long have you been here?' 'Only a couple of days,' he replied. 'All the sailors here are waiting for something to happen.' There were about twenty of us, and they were all just as mystified as I was.

I decided to go for a wash and turn into my hammock. I had a nice clean blanket. There was an old stoker on the *Alresford*, nicknamed Sidi Bish, who would scrub your hammock for a shilling, wash blankets for one and six, mattress cover for a shilling. Being a stoker, he could dry these in the engine room. A seaman had to almost grovel to put any dobeing in the engine room!

I washed, came back and laid my uniform out on the bunk, ready for the morning. I turned in – at 2200 hours, pipe down and out lights. The mess decks were patrolled at night, and a P.O. walked through the mess deck shouting to everyone to turn in. He switched out the lights even though it was still dusky outside.

We turned out at 0600 hours. I half dressed and went for a wash, came back and finished dressing. I lashed my hammock and left it slung, then sat down and waited for 'hands to breakfast'. Ate porridge and bread and jam, then at 0800 hours, it was 'hands on parade'. We all clattered down the stairs and fell in as a squad, the tannoy sounded and called us all to attention. Our names were called, and we were told that there would be others joining us in the next few days. He still kept what was going on under his cap. One of the squad asked what we were waiting for, but the P.O. said he didn't know. The days went by and other ratings were slowly joining us, stokers etc.

One lunchtime, I came back to the mess and there was a draft chit, telling me to report to a Bay-class frigate, H.M.S. *Bigbury Bay*. This surprised me and the others, I grabbed my cap and made my way to the drafting officer, only to be told that the draft had been cancelled, and to report back to my P.O. Which I did. He said he was not surprised. A few days later, there were about forty of us.

One day, after falling in on parade, the axe fell, and we were told that we were to be the advance party to join a Bay-class frigate called H.M.S. *Whitesand Bay*. She was being completed in the Harland and Wolff shipyard, Musgrave Channel, Belfast. She was being prepared to join the British Pacific Fleet in Hong Kong. There were gasps of dismay, a lot of them from H.O.s like me! We all knew that the war in the Pacific was still going on, but for how long?

The P.O. said, 'There is no more leave for you, it has been cancelled. You will place your station cards on the mess table tomorrow morning. They will then be collected. You will all now fall in down below, where I will march you to the sick bay, where you will receive injections for serving in foreign climes.' More groans could be heard. We trooped downstairs and fell in, in three ranks. The P.O. then marched us off to the sick bay. There was a room adjoining it, with chairs set out. We were told to take off our jumpers and take a seat.

The P.O. said, 'You will go in, in alphabetical order', so that will be me first, I thought! We took our jumpers off and sat down. A voice called 'Beedie'. I thought so! I marched into the surgery and was told to sit down. I was given three injections. I thought that was bad enough, but some poor souls had a jab in their stomachs as well. They were going somewhere different.

I was told to put my jumper back on and go and sit down. My arm was beginning to ache painfully, so putting my jumper back on wasn't as easy as taking it off! I sat down to wait for the rest. One or two fainted, they were picked up and taken off to a ward like room, where they were put on beds, and left to get over it. They had to have the three jabs, whether they liked it or not! My arm was still sore and had swollen up, but it wasn't as bad as the jab I had when I joined up.

I didn't have to wait long, as those who felt ill were left where they were until they felt well enough to complete the injections. The rest of us went back to the mess. Some of us struggled to get our jumpers off. Some stalwarts struggled to get their jumpers on to go to dinner. I decided to forego my dinner, I would only miss the soup! Others decided to do the same. The P.O. came into the mess and said, 'You can have a "make and mend" afternoon, if any of you feel ill, report to the sick bay, you will probably be given a couple of aspirins. You have got to be fit by tomorrow, as you are all off to Belfast. I won't be going with you, so good luck!' With that he departed.

I spread my greatcoat down on the bunk and got my head down, as did the others. By teatime, my arm was not so painful, so I managed to get my jumper back on and went to tea. In the evening, the P.O. came into the mess he said, 'At 0800 hours tomorrow morning, you have got to be ready to go, kitbags packed, hammocks lashed. A lorry will arrive, you will go down with your gear, and load it on to the lorry. It will then be taken to Portsmouth Railway Station. You will be collected by coach and also taken to the railway station, where you will proceed to unpack your gear from the lorry and take it to the platform for the train going to Waterloo Station. You will be watched. I suggest you get a good night's sleep, you will need it! Good night.'

My hammock was still slung, I went for a wash, then turned in. At 0600 hours the next morning, we all turned out, arms still aching, half dressed and went for a wash, finished dressing, lashed hammocks then waited for breakfast. Toast for a change with jam! Lovely! The cooks excelled themselves getting toast for forty men.

They had heard where we were off to – their efforts were much appreciated.

I returned to the mess deck and finished packing my hammock and brown case. I carried my gear down the stairs and out of the mess deck. Others were doing the same. There was a P.O. outside, who appeared to be in charge. A lorry arrived which was then loaded with our kitbags and hammocks. We retained our brown cases and gas masks. Once the loading was complete, we fell in as a squad. Our names were called, and we answered, 'Aye aye, P.O.' After our names had been called, the P.O. found out who was the most senior rating, and put him in charge, telling us all that we must respect this rating.

A coach arrived and we all boarded. The P.O. wished us the best of luck and then we were off to Portsmouth train station. On arrival, we were met by a chief regulating officer, who told us to unpack the lorry and place our kitbags and hammocks on to the porter's trollies, and wheel them right to the end of the platform, which he showed us by pointing. He also told us that we were being watched in case any of us should think of doing a runner! I wondered if the uniformed gorilla was around!

We loaded up all of our gear and wheeled it to the end of the platform. We were then told to wait, so I sat on my hammock, the others doing the same. The regulating officer said nothing more. A P.O. came over to us, carrying a large bag. The train came in, the last carriage was empty, next to that was the baggage van, then the guards van. As soon as the train stopped, the kitbags and hammocks were loaded into the baggage van, whilst this was going on, a P.O.G.I. appeared, with his gear on a trolley, pulled by a porter. He was to be the ships P.O.G.I. He had come from Whale Island. He turned out to be one of the best P.O.G.I.s I ever met.

The loading finished, the chief regulating officer had a rota list and proceeded to call out our names. As each rating stepped forward, answering his name, the P.O. with the big bag put his hand in the bag and produced a 'bag meal', which had a fruit pie, packet of Smith's crisps, a packet of biscuits and an apple. We all received a bag, it would have to last us until we reached the ship in Belfast, sometime the next day. On receiving our bag meal, we were asked to sign our name, and then told to board the train. This routine was performed until every rating was on board the train, including the P.O.G.I. All the carriage doors were locked. The regulating officer then walked the length of the train, checking the doors. At the end, he turned, took one more look and then waved at the train guard – job done, he departed.

The train then started its journey to Waterloo. I took my apple out of my bag, managing to pack the rest of my bag meal into my little brown case. I sat munching my apple and staring gloomily out of the window at the countryside passing by, remembering the many times I had made this journey with Frederick Hotels, but there was no tea and toast today. Some packs of cards and crib boards were found, and using the little brown cases as tables, games of crib ensued.

The train reached Waterloo, and the doors were unlocked. We all disembarked and the P.O.G.I. detailed some of us to fetch porters' trollies, which were then loaded up with our kitbags and hammocks, then pulled to the front of the station, where a lorry waited to be loaded. Once loaded it took off to King's Cross station. An old coach was also waiting to take us to King's Cross.

On arrival at King's Cross, we loaded our kitbags and hammocks on to porter's trollies and pulled them right to the end of the platform, where we unloaded them. I knew that we were being watched – no doubt they were still worried that someone

178

might do a runner! There were no refreshments. I sat on my hammock and waited – same as all the others. The P.O.G.I. spoke to the regulating officer but was told that no refreshments had been laid on for us.

The train pulled into the station and, as before, the baggage van was loaded, our names were called, and we boarded the train and the doors were locked. We had not had anything to drink since breakfast and now had a eight- or nine-hour journey to Carlisle, before going on to Stranraer. We were all going to be hungry and thirsty by the time we got there!

The train left the station and the crib schools started. I settled down and tried to get some sleep, as did some of the others. There wasn't a lot of moaning, everyone knew it wasn't the P.O.G.I.s fault, he was as thirsty as we were. The train wended its way along, the hours slowly passed and finally we arrived in Carlisle. To our surprise and gratefulness, the wonderful, wonderful, ladies of Carlisle had tables set out with plates of sandwiches and homemade cakes, and best of all, tea! Tea and sandwiches and cake were passed through the windows. How they knew a train would be arriving, full of hungry, thirsty sailors, I never knew. We thanked the ladies of Carlisle and the train pulled out and made its way to Stranraer.

We arrived at the Stranraer Ferry and found the offices still open, but the last ferry had gone. We would have to sleep on our hammocks and kitbags until the morning. Thankfully the ferry offices stayed open, and allowed us to use the toilets and to wash our faces. We didn't have any towels, so dried our faces with toilet paper. We were beginning to look a sorry lot. After a restless night, trying to sleep, the morning eventually came, and the ferry arrived. There were passengers waiting to board. They must have thought what a pretty scruffy lot we were. We hadn't had a proper wash or shower, our uniforms were a disgrace and it wasn't over yet!

Once again, we had to borrow trollies to load our kit on board. Once on board, we stayed as a group. I wondered what the passengers thought of us. Pretty disgraceful, I expect!

On reaching Larne, there was a lorry waiting to take our kitbags and hammocks. We then fell in to three ranks, as instructed by our G.I. A regulating P.O. told our G.I. to march us to Larne Station. Off we marched, soon reaching the station. When the train came in, as before, the last carriage was empty. The same routine as before commenced – load the baggage van, answer our name when called by the regulating P.O., board the train. The doors were locked and off we went to Belfast.

The Navy had changed from winter routine to summer routine, which meant we were wearing a white front and white cap. On reaching Belfast, we all disembarked from the train, and fell in to three ranks, as instructed by our G.I. We stood looking around for a coach, but there wasn't one. We were told we had to march to the Harland and Wolff shipyard. None of us had washed or shaved. Our uniforms were creased and untidy. Apart from the very welcome tea and sandwiches at Carlisle station, we had not eaten since breakfast at R.N.B. We looked a mess, what would Warrant Gunner Pantlin think of us if he could see us? He would explode!

The P.O.G.I. had a rough idea of where the docks were; if we got lost, we could ask a policeman! So off we marched, holding our little brown cases in our right hands. There was a saying in the Navy that the Royal Marines would march past in a column of route, the Royal Navy would march past in a bloody great heap! How true!

People came out of shops and looked out of windows. Girls

looked at us with fascination, or was it horror? Cars coming out of a side road cut the column in two. By the time the cars had finished turning, the front column was about fifty yards in front, they never bothered to wait, just kept ambling on. Those of us in the rear followed suit.

Chapter Sixteen

H.M.S. Whitesand Bay – Belfast

Eventually, we reached the dockyard. I can't remember if the G.I. had to ask for instructions, but finally, we arrived, and there she was, H.M.S. *Whitesand Bay*, looking in a pretty sad state.

The front column came to a halt, waiting for the second half to catch up, and we were ordered to turn right and stand easy. Names were called alphabetically. My name was called, I answered 'here' and was given a card, telling me which position I would be on, on the ship. I was on A gun. It also told me which watch I was in, and which mess.

Our kitbags and hammocks were in a pile on the dockside, by the ship. We were told we could collect them at any time. I decided to have a wash, but then thought I'd go and get my hammock and find a place in the mess to sling it first. I went ashore and rummaged around until I found my hammock. Going back on board, I was shown where my mess was by an Irish docker. I found a place in the corner of the mess and slung my hammock, took off my jumper, collar and white front and put them on top of a locker, then I wandered off to find the washroom. I was amazed and delighted to see three shower cubicles – I went for a closer look, then groaned – they were locked and stayed locked the whole time I was on the ship!

On the shoreside of the ship, things were in a bit of a pickle, with electric cables and welding cables snaking around everywhere. The hull of the ship still needed to be painted, bulkheads also. The upper structure had to be cleaned then painted. The inside of the ship was finished.

I returned to the mess deck, where others were doing the same as I had, slinging their hammocks and going for a wash and shave. There was no hot meal that day. So it was corned beef sandwiches and tea, made by a caterer. In the same mess as me, another six had arrived. We were the port watch. There were others arriving, who would be the starboard watch. I soon got to know them all (of course there were a lot more to come). After eating my sandwiches and drinking my tea, I set to, cleaning my uniform, giving it a jolly good brushing.

The P.O.G.I came into the mess deck and told us to sort ourselves out, lights would be out at 2200 hours. Hands to rise and shine at 0600 hours in the morning for breakfast, and then fall in on the dockside in boiler suits at 0800 hours. He told us that there was no quartermaster or bosun's mate, but there was a night watchman. He then departed. I went out and fetched my kitbag. The ship seemed well catered for, so the crew would be able to start preparing proper cooked meals soon. The first thing though, was a good night's sleep.

So far the port watch consisted of the following Able Seamen, some were like me, Acting Able Seamen: Hill, Brighton, Fripp, Lacey, White and Yarker. Fripp and White had all the hallmarks of being proper sailors. All our hammocks had been slung. I went for another quick wash, came back, said, 'Good night', and turned in.

At 0600 hours, the P.O.G.I. came into the mess deck

shouting, 'Come on my hearties, rise and shine!' I turned out, grabbed my toilet gear and made my way to the washroom. My shipmates were doing the same. After washing and dressing in a boiler suit, I lashed my hammock and waited for breakfast. There were seven hands in the starboard watch, on the other side of the mess, who were doing the same thing.

Breakfast consisted of bread and jam, a cup of tea and a cigarette. At 0800 hours, we fell in on the jetty. There were fourteen of us. We answered our names when called and then waited. There then appeared, a lieutenant R.N.V.R., a sub-lieutenant R.N.V.R., a coxswain, a chief stoker, and a chief engine-room artificer. I assumed that they had been staying in accommodation somewhere nearby, to watch the ship being built.

The lieutenant R.N.V.R. turned out to be the ship's First Lieutenant. He told us we were the advance seaman working party. It was our job to get the ship spick and span before the rest of the crew arrived. The P.O.G.I. took charge, any gunnery ratings, like me, were set to cleaning the guns. The rest started to clean the ship inside and out. As stated on my card, I was to be Number 1 of A gun twin, these were four-inch forward guns. The P.O.G.I. provided me with the cleaning gear, plus Brasso. I was quite happy cleaning the guns, it was better than scrubbing bulkheads etc.!

Shore leave was given from 18.00 to 10.55. I decided to go ashore with Fripp, who became Frippy, and Hill, who became Brummie (he came from Birmingham). I stayed as Fred! We had tea of bread and cheese and Daddies Sauce and then the three of us went ashore. At 1800 hours, we caught the liberty boat. Some of the others in the watch had decided to go ashore later.

We walked out of the shipyard and down what seemed to be a main street. We found a small tea shop open, so went in and had a nice cup of tea and doughnuts. The people in the shop were very friendly. Brummie must have been an H.O., as he had just got married and was living with his newly wed wife at her mother's. Brummie was a little bit worried about that arrangement. Frippy was not married, he became the ship's comedian.

Leaving the tea shop, we walked down the road, there seemed to be a friendly air, one or two people passing by wished us a good evening. I wondered where Mick Johnson was, this was his home town. Then Frippy said, 'Let's try the famous Guinness.' It seemed to take the barman quite a time to serve the pints – quite a lot of froth passing from one glass to another, before we were served. The Guinness was as black as coal and was so thick, it almost had to be chewed.

There were shipyard workers in the bar, who were very friendly. Now that the war was over, ship building would be cancelled. They must have been concerned about their jobs. We had another pint, then saying 'Goodnight' to our friendly shipbuilders, we made our way back to the ship.

Falling in at 0800 hours the next morning, the R.N.V.R. lieutenant informed us that the King and Queen would be paying a visit to Belfast. The cruiser H.M.S. *Dido* came into the basin to see if it could fit alongside the dock wall, opposite to where the *Whitesand Bay* was situated. It was successful and so back out she steamed. The officer then told us that the ship side of the *Whitesand Bay*, looking across the basin, had to be painted in Pacific colours. A light green and cream, with a slight bow wave effect.

So all hands were put to work – all the upper works had to be cleaned and painted. The ship's whaler, or sea boat, was given a coat of Pussers' grey. All guns were cleaned and barrels set at the right angle. Then at 1600 hours, or the first 'dog watch', all the hands had to line the ship with their caps, to practice cheering their majesties when they arrived.

The sub-lieutenant instructed us he would lead the ship's company in cheering ship. He told us, 'It will be hip, hip, hurrah – at the hurrah, caps will be raised. This will happen three times, we will then have a slight break, then we will start again and carry on until I say stop.' And so, we all hip-hip-hurrahed across the empty basin. There were one or two shipyard workers on the dock, they must have looked up and across the basin and been amazed by what they saw. Then one or two, at the 'hurrah', doffed their caps and bowed. This caused some merriment with the crew. The sub-lieutenant wasn't at all happy. Shouting at us to 'Keep quiet!' This happened again on the following evening, with one or two more shipyard workers looking on as the ship's company lined ship. At the first 'Hurrah' some of the workers doffed their caps, some pulled the side of their trousers and curtsied. More choked merriment from the crew – the sub-lieutenant was livid! Before lining ship on the third evening, the sub-lieutenant gave us a warning that we would be put on report if there was any more laughing.

He was saved any problems, because, on the fourth evening, the ship's company were told that the King and Queen would be flown over. However, this left the ship as a perfect example of 'before and after' and I'm afraid that all the seamen taking part in the cheering were now in the sub-lieutenant's bad books.

It wasn't long before the ship was spick and span, and the first lieutenant was satisfied. The great day came, a coach drew up alongside the ship, and the rest of the crew disembarked. The ship's crew then numbered a hundred and ten. The Captain finally came aboard. We had heard rumours about him. Apparently he did not like H.O.s. He wanted a crew of proper sailors. I expect that all the H.O.s on board were like me, only 'acting able seamen'.

With the Captain, there was an R.N. lieutenant, a gunnery officer, a navigating officer, a RNVR surgeon lieutenant, a RNVR midshipman, then there was the first lieutenant and the RNVR sub-lieutenant. Joining the crew were some leading seaman. One of them did not want to go abroad, so he picked a fight with the P.O.G.I. who did not retaliate. The leading seaman was apprehended, and the coxswain informed the Naval Barracks in Belfast. Two naval police came aboard and the leading seaman was taken into custody. He was eventually court marshalled and sentenced to ninety days in Milton Prison, what a fool! The port watch had a leading seaman called Jessy. The forecastle P.O. was in his forties and chubby faced, he looked like the actor Charles Laughton. I cannot remember his name.

The Captain ordered 'clear low deck' and we all assembled on the forecastle. He then told us that he had come from the crack R-class destroyer HMS *Racehorse*. He had been the first lieutenant and had built up a first-class, well-trained crew. He intended to do the same with us. He went on to tell us that there would be engine trials, after which there would be exercises, before going to Tobermory on the Isle of Mull for further exercises. He then told the first lieutenant to carry on.

The Captain did not seem very happy with what he saw. I don't know about stokers, but the majority of the seamen were under twenty and were all H.O.s. The Captain wanted proper sailors – and look what he got!

The first lieutenant said, 'You've all got your cards, they tell you where your mess is.' There were seamen's messes either side amid ships, as well as in the forecastle. First part of port was in the forecastle, the second part of port was amidships. Likewise, the starboard side. I was in the first part of port. The majority of the advance party were in the first part of port. The rest of the crew sorted themselves out. The coxswain picked Fripp as the port watch quartermaster. White was the starboard watch quartermaster. They were both 'active service', whilst Mosely was bosun's mate, port, Yarker bosun's mate, starboard. Both were H.O.s.

At noon, 'hands to dinner' was piped. I can't remember what was for dinner. Cottage pie I expect! After that, 'make and mend' was piped, which gave everybody a real chance to get to know each other. The communication branch, signalman, telegraphists, had their own mess. The first part of port seemed to be a nice lot of young seamen, but they would never come up to the *Alresford* crew.

As we talked about the ships we had been on, I asked if they had ever had to coal ship. They looked at me as if I had come from a different planet! 'Yes,' I said, 'we were down in the coal lighter having to shift a hundred ton of coal in nine and half hours. Then had to scrub and hose down the ship from stem to stern! A nice job in the middle of winter – although we were given a shilling a day hard lying money! We had to do that every nine to ten days and after finishing, wash down in a bucket of soapy water! What's worse, I come aboard a brand new frigate and find the showers locked, so it seems like I'm back to a bucket, or at best a sink!' Some did not seem to think much of that!

The Captain decided to inspect the ship, he came in to the forecastle mess with the first lieutenant. All stood to attention. He had a piercing eye and studied every one and the mess deck in detail, then nodded to the first lieutenant, who said, 'Carry on.' They then vanished up the ladder, the Captain said not a word. We carried on, wondering what was ahead of us.

The coxswain, who came from Poole, same as me, did not hide his disapproval that he had a number of H.O.s in his crew. He had huge black bushy eyebrows, which made him look quite sinister. After tea, he came to the mess deck, he looked us over, said,

'Anybody stepping out of line will answer to me!' then he vanished up the ladder – which gave us all something to ponder about.

That evening, after sorting out hammock places, we all decided that we had seen and heard enough for one day, and turned in. Before I knew it, the tannoy was telling me to 'rise and shine'. Then there was the usual rush to the washhouse, after which, dressed in boiler suits, we had a breakfast of bread, jam, and a cup of tea.

We had not yet prepared the food for that day's dinner, so after falling in at 0800 hours, one hand was detailed off, from each mess, to prepare the day's dinner. They had to go to the Leading Supply Assistant store, where they were given vegetables and meat. The easiest meal was pot mess. Everybody knew how to prepare that. The only difference from the *Alresford*, was that we never had a 'cook of the mess', but we had a proper supply assistant. The ship had been fully fuelled by a small tanker which came alongside (no coaling, thank goodness!).

The order was given for hands to prepare to leave harbour, the forecastle P.O. taking charge of the forecastle party. The same would be happening at the aft end. I am afraid I can't remember much about the quarterdeck crew. Lines were let go, and the ship slowly left the harbour wall and made its way up Belfast Lough.

When the ship was fully underway, the forecastle P.O. detailed some jobs. Lamen A.B., H.O. was a nice chap, though a bit slow, he was made the mess deck dodger. His job was to keep the mess deck clean and tidy. Humphreys A.B. was put in charge of the paint store, plus all cleaning gear; he was active service, came off H.M.S. *Nelson*. A.B. Tristram became the Captain's servant. Leading seaman Jessy made coxswain of the motor boat. I became bowman. There were many more in the mess deck whose names I cannot remember.

The P.O.G.I. whose name was Flint (Flint by name, Flint by nature), but a very good P.O.G.I. detailed all the gunnery ratings to the position on their cards. I was Number 1, of right A gun. There was a gunnery rating, same as me, on the left gun. I gave the orders and worked the contact breaker that put the red light in the transmitting station. The G.I. had to sort out ratings for gun loading; six were wanted, three for each gun. The same had to happen on Y gun, which was on the aft part of the ship. There were also twin Bofers, port and starboard, behind the funnel. Also two twin Oerlikons aft of the Bofers, and two twin Oerlikons on the port and starboard wings of the bridge; these were manned by Ack-Ack ratings.

The ship steamed up and down Belfast Lough, carrying out speed trials at 20 knots. How long would it be before the Captain was satisfied? As soon as he was satisfied, and the ship became his, it would start exercising in Bangor Bay. The ship would then have two weeks before going to Tobermory, in the Isle of Mull, for more training.

The P.O.G.I. knew that A and Y gun crews were well trained, having recently come back from Whale Island. The same went for the Ack-Ack crew, who had also recently come back from training. All crew had to learn 'fire drill' and other seaman seamanship such as, 'away sea boat' and 'man overboard'.

The worst was learning how to use the kedge anchor. This was used if the ship had no power, and had to move away from danger. There was a kedge anchor, lashed to some part of the ship. This had to be hauled to the quarterdeck, then lashed to a wooden structure. This was then lowered over the side, and under the sea boat, where it was secured. A wire hawser was attached to the kedge anchor, and ran to a winch on the forecastle of the ship.

The sea boat was manned by some strong seamen, who then

rowed the sea boat away from the ship, pulling the hawser. I don't know how many yards they had to row. Then the kedge anchor was released from the wooden structure, and dropped to the seabed. The winch on the forecastle would then winch the ship away from danger. I'm not sure if I have got this right, as it is some seventy-three years ago since I watched it being done. I cannot remember how the kedge anchor was lowered to the sea boat – but I think what I've described is a rough idea of how to 'kedge'.

For two weeks, we were kept at it. The H.O.s were not all that enthusiastic, the war had finished, not just started! After two weeks, we sailed for Portsmouth – we were there only long enough to fully store ship, top up oil, and load up ammunition. Once this was done, we set sail for Tobermory.

Chapter Seventeen

H.M.S. Whitesand Bay –
Tobermory and The Sound of
Mull

As soon as a ship enters Tobermory, it is being watched, points being awarded for how well tasks are completed. The Commodore had been given a nickname. Sadly I cannot remember it! His ship was called the *Western Isles*, crewed entirely by Wrens. About a third of the way up the mast of the *Western Isles*, a platform had been fixed. On this platform were the Wren signallers.

The *Whitesand Bay* lost points before ever gaining any – this was because the Wren signaller used semaphore! That caused a flap – how long was it since our signallers had used semaphore! This was one thing not practised. One of the signallers came from a merchant ship and was a little slow. That put the Captain in a temper, and we had only just arrived! It was only a case of our signallers being a little rusty, and they soon became top rate, but unfortunately the damage had been done. The ship found its anchorage. There were also a Royal Naval sloop and a Polish destroyer at anchor.

The Captain was never asked to visit the Western Isles, all messages from her were by semaphore, or ten-inch signal lamp. The gun crews were kept busy exercising. The A gun had six strong ratings as the gun loaders. The exercises were the same as I had done with the Kiwis, only no drenching! The crews had to fire ten rounds each gun, with dummy projectiles. The time it took to fire was fairly slow by the Kiwi's standard. Would only get better with practice.

The ship carried out most of the seamanship and gunnery in the Sound of Mull. Submarine hunting by Asdic – very slow. Hurling life belts in to the sea. Calling away the sea boat. A sea boat's crew had been picked beforehand. This was being timed by a R.N. lieutenant. Fire and flood drill down below – the stoker's exercises. The dreaded kedge anchoring exercise was pretty ragged.

P.O.G.I. Flint was very pleased with A and Y gun crews. Every man on each gun knew each other's job. He had no fears about us. He also had a crew doing depth charge drill. A month ago, the ship's crew did not know each other, or what was expected of us – so we were doing pretty well. Then there was Bofers' gun drill and also the Oerlikons.

One morning, nearing the final drill day, there was live gunnery drill. The AA guns firing at drogues, pulled by an aircraft. The four-inch gun target was on a wooden framework, similar to the one used when I was on the *Alresford*. One of the drills that the guns crew practised most was the 'misfire drill'. In the event of a misfire, I would shout, 'STILL, MISFIRE, GUN CREW BEFORE THE GUN', which meant that the crew had to run very quickly in front of the gun's shield, in case the breech blew up.

A gun started to fire at the target, timed by an elderly R.N. lieutenant gunner. Hardly into the shoot, the left gun had a misfire. Before I could shout 'STILL' the lieutenant gunner ran across, opened the breech, caught the projectile from the sloping barrel and hurled it right over the side. He turned to the crew, saying, 'Don't any of you ever do that!'

After the shoot, the gun's crew got together for a chat. Was the lieutenant gunnery officer a complete maniac, risking our lives, plus his own? The crew all agreed, that whatever it was, he had scared the life out of us!

I think that A-gun crew did pretty well. I would say in the top half of ten. Which, bearing in mind that we did not have any anti-flash gear on, or ear muffs, only tin helmets, wasn't bad.

The drills were finally over. Next was the final exercise in the harbour. The ship entered harbour and dropped anchor. After tea, there was shore leave given. Not many went ashore. Those that went said that the inhabitants showed a greater affection for the Polish sailors than the British sailors, there was quite a bit of resentment about it. I never heard of any trouble with the Polish sailors, at least not with any of our crew. There did not seem to be a very happy atmosphere anywhere. I decided that I would be glad when we left.

I went for a wash, slung my hammock and turned in, not looking forward to the next day. I soon fell asleep. 0600 hours came, 'All hands heave ho, heave ho, lash up and stow,' shouted the tannoy. The day had come. I washed, dressed had breakfast and then waited. The tannoy then shouted, 'All hands fall in on the quarterdeck', which we did.

The quartermaster was keeping a sharp look out for the launch which would come across to us from the Western Isles. When it was spotted, all the officers appeared on the quarterdeck. The launch came alongside the ladder. The bowman's boat drill was as smart as a guardsman on parade. The quartermaster piped the Commodore aboard. The Captain and officers saluted. The Commodore stepped on to the quarterdeck (it was said that on one ship he boarded, he threw his cap on the deck, calling to the quartermaster, 'That's an incendiary bomb!' The quartermaster promptly kicked it over the side! Whether that story is true or not, I do not know), he saluted back and then addressed the crew – 'This is your final day here. I expect you to be trained and ready for today's exercises.'

He turned and spoke to the Captain for a short time and then the officers, before addressing the crew again – he said, 'Now this is the situation. You are in Piraeus Harbour in Greece, being heavily bombed. You have no power in your engines. You have an injured man in the crow's nest, this is the "communications branch problem". You have to send a landing party. There are German paratroopers heading your way. There is a ship drifting towards you which is on fire. You have to kedge your way to a mooring buoy a hundred yards away, out of danger.' The Commodore turned to the Captain, saying, 'That is the situation, now carry on.' He then turned towards the ladder. His launch came alongside, and he left the ship. The quartermaster piped him over the side, all the officers saluted and off he went back the Western Isles. Some how, the forecastle P.O. had made me the bridge messenger for the exercise. I did my best to make myself invisible, hiding away somewhere.

Whilst the seamen were at their problems, the engineers had been given their problems, which we on the quarterdeck didn't hear, I hoped their problem would not be that we were sinking! The P.O.G.I. got the landing party ready. None of the party had boots, they each had a rifle and also a really awful weapon similar to the Sten gun, I think it was called a Stirling. None of the landing party had handled a rifle since their training days.

I wondered how many of the landing crew would fit in the sea boat, bearing in mind the sea boat crew, it couldn't be many. It would have been better to have the motor boat tow the sea boat, without the sea boat crew. I and A-gun crew should have been firing at the enemy aircraft. Finally the sea boats had been lowered, filled with the P.O.G.I. and as many of the landing crew as could fit in the boat, without getting in the rower's way. Then they were off to fight the German paratroopers, with the midshipman at the tiller.

Meanwhile, seamen were getting the kedge anchor plus the wooden structure ready for when the sea boat returned. The Captain was pacing the bridge, like an angry tiger. I looked over to the lochside. There was a bank that had to be climbed, not very steep. The front rower was trying to lower his oar, so he could take the sea boat's rope, get ashore and keep the sea boat alongside the bank. The landing party were trying to scramble ashore. The sea boat's crew were trying to hold their oars upright. The landing party finally got to the top of the bank, where I expect they were promptly shot!

The sea boat started to make its way back. The ship's boat falls were hanging so that the sea boat could hook on, ready to be hoisted, so that the kedge anchor and structure could be slid underneath. The midshipman made a hash of it, missed the falls somehow. The midshipman then had to race around and come back under the falls. The arc he was making was too big. The Captain raced past me, he looked at me, but I'm sure he did not see me. I have never seen eyes like it, they were blazing! He leapt to the wing of the bridge, and called the midshipman a most awful name. The Commodore and the crew of the Western Isles must have heard – and it must have cost us points!

By the time the midshipman had got the sea boat under the falls, it was too late. The drifting ship, which was on fire, hit us. That was it, all hands had to fend the ship off – and what about the poor devil in the crow's nest? He had to be got into a Robinson stretcher, without any of his rescuers falling down from the crow's nest! Finally they got him down. I think they did a pretty good job, didn't think the Captain could criticise them too much.

The landing party had to be brought back. No one on the bridge seemed to need my services. I quietly made my way down to the mess deck, thinking that on today's showing, the ship had failed. Personally I thought that the A and Y guns and the Ack-Ack guns' crews had put up a pretty good show. The P.O.G.I., thought so, though what he thought of the crazy gunnery officer, he kept to himself.

Did the Captain apologise to the midshipman, who came from a very wealthy banking family, for his language? I doubt it. Unfortunately, he also used to reprimand his officers in front of the men, which was not appreciated.

The decks needed to be cleared, the kedge anchor and wooden structure had to be stowed, the sea boat hoisted inboard. Tomorrow, the ship was off to Gibraltar. At tea, all decided that the Captain had ruined the day.

Chapter Eighteen

H.M.S. Whitesand Bay – Gibraltar to Port Said

In the morning, the Captain passed his last messages to the Western Isles, and the ship sailed out of Tobermory and headed for Gibraltar. The journey turned out to be uneventful. The Bay of Biscay was quite calm. We moored alongside the harbour wall. I don't think the Captain could have received the results of our stay in Tobermory, as leave was given.

I heard that the Hunt-class destroyer H.M.S. *Ledbury* was in dock. My ex shipmate Bob Jay, a signaller on the *Alresford*, had been drafted to her. I went ashore and wandered around until I found her, propped up in a dry dock. I went aboard and found Bob getting dressed in to civvy clothes. He and others were off into Spain. I said to Bob, 'How lucky can you get!' We had a brief chat. Bob was very surprised that I had been given a draft to a ship going out to join the B.P.F. I said that he was no more surprised than I was! I then left Bob to enjoy the Spanish delights.

The *Whitesand Bay* did not stay very long in Gibraltar and was soon on its way to Malta, and more exercises – who was it said that the war had finished, not just started! On arriving in Malta, the ship headed into Salima Creek, then anchored. There was no shore leave. Had the Captain received the results of the three weeks' exercises in Tobermory, or was he being vindictive?

After a day or two, the ship sailed out into the Mediterranean Sea, to start exercises with the cruiser H.M.S. *Norfolk* and motor launches. I have no idea what the exercises were for, but perhaps they were more for the *Norfolk* than us. When the exercises were over for the day, the *Norfolk* sailed into Grand Harbour. The launches went into Salima Creek. The *Whitesand Bay* sailed into Marsamxett Bay and anchored for the night. This was to happen every day, until the exercises finished.

One evening after the day's exercising, the ship entered Salima Creek for fuel. As the ship entered the creek, it signalled immediately, volunteering as 'Duty Destroyer'. This could be any type of frigate or sloop, that stands by in either two, three or four hours' notice, in the event of an accident or if an aircraft should crash into the sea. 'Duty Destroyer' was granted. The ship that had been 'duty destroyer' was very pleased! Again no shore leave for us!

The ship moored to forward and, after buoys, so she remained still. The tannoy shouted that if anyone wanted a swim, they would be allowed to. I decided I would go. There were rocks between the ship and the shore, I and others dived in and swam to the rocks and climbed up onto them. The shore road was no more than fifty yards away, so the shops, cafés and honky-tonks could be seen and heard. The midshipman was not very popular – he'd lost the points that lost our shore leave! He wouldn't care, he wasn't that keen on H.O.s.

The following day, the ship left harbour for more exercises. When the weekend came, the ship entered Salima Creek – tied up to the harbour wall. The Captain relented and allowed shore leave, to the port and starboard watch on Saturday and Sunday. What had happened to him?

I went ashore with Brummie Hill, the place had sure taken a pasting. Reminded me of the pastings Portsmouth had taken and the terrible night when the city was set on fire. Some 25,000 incendiary bombs were dropped. I remembered Dad and Mr. Stribley with the old lady in the wheelbarrow. Helping Dad and Mr. Stribley put out incendiary bombs, watching my old school burn. Jock coming in late, Mum and Dad being really worried about him – he was filthy dirty, because he and his mates had spent the night helping the rescuers – he had simply had a good wash and a cup of tea and slice of toast and made his way off to work. It had been a night of horror. I certainly knew what the Maltese had gone through!

There were small cafés on shore. Brummie and I went into one. Some of our shipmates were in there, they were certainly whooping it up – glad to get away from the ship for a little while. Brummie and I sat down at a table and had a nice cool beer. I said to Brummie, 'They had better watch it, or they will be trotting up and down between the bow and the breakwater, holding a rifle above their heads!' Brummie replied, 'I don't think they care!' On the way back to the ship, we bumped into Leicester and Yarker, and we had our photograph taken by a street photographer.

The exercises were now finished. There were a few defects in the engine room to be sorted out. After two or three days, the ship left Malta for Port Said. It was a few days after that that disaster struck, the sick berth attendant went down with appendicitis. The doctor said it was too rough to operate. The Captain had no choice but to sail to Tobruk. The harbour was full of wrecks. The Captain did a good job navigating his way through. I don't know if the sick bay attendant survived or not, he certainly had some rough handling until he finally reached an Army hospital. He was a great loss, a vital part of the ship's company.

Fig 1. Malta, with Brummie, Yarker and Leicester

The ship finally sailed into Port Said. One of the telegraphists was rather large, he was covered in prickly heat spots, and was in agony. The doctor could not do much for him, so the Captain arranged for him to go ashore to hospital, where it was decided he should be sent home, to serve in home waters only. We now had lost the L/S, who was in prison, the S.B.A. to appendicitis and now a telegraphist to prickly heat. Able Seaman Tristram, the Captain's servant, had been a member of the St. John's Ambulance, he was promoted to S.B.A. – he could issue aspirins four times a day!

Fig 2. Port Said

Chapter Nineteen

H.M.S. Whitesand Bay –
Suez to Colombo

Leaving Port Said behind, the ship slowly made its way to the Suez Canal. We waited in a convoy. When the convoy moved forward, we followed. The coxswain was steering the ship, with the wheelhouse door open. I stood looking out to the shore. I could see Arabs on camels and a few British soldiers. In the centre of the Suez Canal, it seemed to broaden out, like a lake. Here was a place called Ismailia (it was here that Stripy was sent, hoping to be going home, but the Navy sent him to a cruiser instead!).

We waited at Ismailia for homeward-bound ships, coming the other way, to pass through. A troop ship passed, full of soldiers who were shouting and laughing, some jerking their thumbs towards the way they had just come. Eventually it was the convoy's turn to enter the second half of the canal and we passed uneventfully into the Red Sea.

The ship slowly made its way through the Red Sea to Aden; the ship was now on eight knots, economical steaming to save fuel. Slightly different to the Captain's ex H.M.S. *Racehorse*! At Aden, the ship took on water, it was absolutely awful to drink and we had a tank full of it!

There were more defects in the engine room, so we were stuck in Aden. What a pit! There was no shore leave. I don't think anyone would have wanted to visit this awful place anyway! The ship finally left and started to wend its way to Colombo. The P.O.G.I. kept the gun crews training. The Captain never allowed live shooting. When not exercising, I was cleaning the motor boat, which was much better than the *Alresford*'s ancient old boat.

Fig 3. Me and the P.O.G.I. aboard the Whitesand Bay

Nearing Colombo, the Captain told the first lieutenant he wanted the wings of the bridge washed, before entering harbour. There was quite a heavy swell, the ship was rolling a lot, doing eight knots. The first lieutenant told the Captain that he did not think it wise, as the ship was rolling so much. The Captain told him to tell the duty P.O. to tell the duty watch to rig stages. The duty watch said, 'No way!' The Captain was face-red with anger that the duty watch had refused to rig stages. He turned to the first lieutenant and said, 'I will have the wings washed, even if you have to do it!' He then told the first lieutenant to clear the lower decks.

Meanwhile the ship had turned and headed out to sea. The seamen all collected on the forecastle and the Captain told us that he intended to have the wings of the bridge washed, before he entered harbour, would any seaman be prepared to do so? Nobody moved. He then told the first lieutenant to clear the lower decks of everyone. The ship was rolling its way back to Aden. Once everyone was on deck, he asked the same question, would anyone be prepared to wash the wings of the bridge. Again no one moved. A few raspberries were blown, I think from the stokers' section. The Captain decided not to be defeated, and ordered the midshipman and the sub-lieutenant to do the job.

The first lieutenant dismissed the ship's company, except the duty watch. I went back down into the mess deck. I was later told that the duty watch rigged the stages, which started to swing backwards and forwards, they then lashed the stages to the ship's sides and prepared for the midshipman and the sub-lieutenant to go over the side, down on the stage, and to prepare to lash themselves to the staging. By then, the ship had turned a large circle, and was heading back towards Colombo again. The staging was still banging about against the ship's side, and at last the Captain saw reason and decided it was too dangerous to attempt the cleaning job. He told the duty P.O. to haul the stage inboard, much to the relief of the midshipman and sub-lieutenant!

The tannoy piped 'hands to get ready to enter harbour'. We all had to change into our number three uniforms. Then the tannoy piped 'hands to line ship, ready for entering harbour'. As the ship entered harbour the quartermaster sounded the still, and all hands came to attention. After a while, the tannoy sounded 'all hands dismissed, duty watch to standby to tie up to harbour wall', which they did. Who the ship saluted, nobody knew!

There were mutterings that the ship's company were getting fed up with the way they were being treated, that a statement should be written saying that the crew was tired of this and had no confidence in the Captain, then the crew could sign it. The P.O.s said that that would be mutiny, better to apply individually for a draft. This was done, all the lower deck, cooks, stewards, the communications branch – all made out a chit for a draft. That only left the officers, C.P.O.s and P.O.s and anyone else on that level. The coxswain's eyebrows must have bristled when all the draft chits were handed to him, to give to the first lieutenant – these he had to show to the Captain. Not a word was said to the crew, no 'clear lower deck', nothing. I could imagine him telling the first lieutenant to destroy them and to carry on as normal.

Then, to everyone's surprise, the tannoy stated 'shore leave will be granted to the port watch from 1800 hours to 22.55', which amazed all of us. After tea, some of the port watch got ready to go ashore. At the weekend, on the Saturday, shore leave was given from 12 noon to 22.55. After dinner, Brummie and I went ashore. Colombo was a very clean place. Little traffic. We walked around and found a small green-grassed park. We sat on a bench, nice and quiet and peaceful. Brummie was worried about his newly wed bride, hadn't had any mail since Malta and there was none here in Colombo. I wondered how Mum and Dad and my brothers and sister were getting on. They were all alright at the last mail call. Thankfully, the war was over.

Brummie said, 'Let's go find something to eat.' Leaving the peace and quiet of the park, we wandered in to where there was more noise and bustle and found a café and enjoyed the local fair. Brummie said, 'Do you think we will get sent home, now both wars are over?' Atom bombs had been dropped in August 1945 on Japan, which had ended the war in the Pacific very quickly. This was wonderful news to us, and would save thousands of lives and the cost of war. I said, 'We'll have to wait and see if the skipper we've got will volunteer for anything. I don't think he's the type to help us go home!' Brummie agreed. We left the café and found a quiet bar and sat and had a couple of beers before wandering back to the ship. It had been a very pleasant afternoon and a nice change from being on board ship.

The atmosphere on board was strange, everyone was walking about on egg shells, waiting for an explosion that never seemed to come. If the news of the draft chits got out, there might be some trouble. The sub-lieutenant and the midshipman were throwing their weight around a bit more. As for the coxswain, he seemed to leave everything to the P.O.s.

The vile water from Aden had finally been used and the Colombo water tasted better. I don't know what we were doing in Colombo, there were no exercises. We just stayed tied up alongside the harbour wall. The ship was washed, painted, polished from stem to stern. Humphreys, who was a proper sailor in charge of the paint store, had done quite a bit of bartering in Malta, with the Maltese boatmen. A bicycle appeared in the paint store among other things.

The ship topped up with oil and fresh stores and there was talk that we would soon be off to Singapore. Nothing happened about the draft chits, the P.O.s, chiefs and officers acted as if nothing had happened. One morning the tannoy piped 'hands to stations for leaving harbour'. The ship left harbour and at eight knots limped its way to Singapore, leaving the draft chit saga behind us, or so it seemed, although I and the rest of port watch did not think that we had got away with it, and things would get better. The Captain was not that sort of officer.

Chapter Twenty

H.M.S. Whitesand Bay –
Singapore to Hong Kong

The journey to Singapore passed without anything untoward happening. Guns' crews were kept training – the P.O.G.I. did not think we would get much better.

On reaching Singapore, I don't remember much about it, because I had caught a flu-like bug and was confined to my hammock, on two aspirins four times a day – I felt really grotty. I don't even remember how long the ship was in Singapore. The ship's company was now being issued with a mepacrine anti-malaria tablet. It was a rather large tablet and its one fault was that after a while, our skin started to turn yellow. The whites of the eyes also turned yellow.

The forecastle P.O.s decided that Fripp and I should take turns at being quartermaster and boat's crew. Fripp would take the ship to Hong Kong, then I would take over. Strange that the same had happened on the *Alresford*. The other watch was to stay as it was.

The ship slowly wended its way up the South China Sea towards a place called Subic Bay on the western tip of the Philippine Islands. It was a huge bay. There were a large number of American war ships already anchored there. Our ship was the only Royal Navy ship.

It was late afternoon, and before we anchored, the Captain decided to have a depth charge dropped. I cannot imagine what the Americans thought about a Royal Navy ship coming to the bay and dropping a depth charge! However, one was dropped, boats were then lowered and went fish gathering, being careful of sea snakes. Between them, the two boats had quite a pile of fish, which were thrown onto the quarterdeck. Hoses pumped sea water over the fish to keep them as cold as possible. The yeoman of signals then sent a general signal around the other ships in the harbour saying, 'Anyone wanting fresh fish to come and help yourself'; boats soon started to come, and kept coming until all the fish were gone. Then some came back with fresh vegetables, large tropical tomatoes, all different shapes and sizes. Tins about one foot high by about ten inches wide arrived – when opened, they were full of potatoes about the size of a small satsuma orange – every potato was the same size, kept in some sort of oil.

I have never seen a cook so happy, he had fresh fish, lovely vegetables and proper potatoes! All we'd had up until that point was dehydrated potato, carrots and cabbage, which had to be soaked overnight, then strained before being boiled in fresh water. This concoction ended up in a mash of potatoes and veg with no goodness in it at all. It could almost be drunk! The Americans certainly knew how to look after their sailors. It seemed that it was a good idea of the Captain's to drop the depth charge and share the subsequent fish!

Another small landing craft came alongside, with cases of cans of beer. These were quickly stowed into the 'hedgehog' magazine. The cover of the magazine was in the wheelhouse, it was the size of a large dustbin. Unlock the cover, lift it and then down into the magazine went the beer – then the cover went back on and was locked. The troops never saw any of those cans! Dinner the next day was wonderful, fish, vegetables and potatoes – we needed to make the most of it while it lasted!

The weather was now very hot, up in the ninety degrees – no air conditioning. British warships were not made to work in such conditions. Nearly all the crew wanted to sleep up on deck but had to wait for the decks to cool down first.

What we were doing in Subic Bay I do not know. We just anchored there and sweated – we could not swim, because of the sea snakes – the second-most venomous snake in the world. One bite and that's it, you are gone, having suffered hours of terrible pain. Coming up the South China sea, we could look over the side and see shoals of them, their striped bodies seemed to keep up with the ship – there was no antidote if bitten.

There was no shore leave, Look left, then right, all there was to see was a sandy beach with trees almost down to the sea edge. Hula-hula girls? You've got to be joking! Then one morning, the tannoy signalled 'hands to stations for leaving harbour and to line ship'. The rig of the day was now white fronts, white shorts, black socks that came up to the knee cap, black shoes and white cap. We lined the ship, the anchor was winched up and the ship slowly left the bay. I don't know what our American friends thought, as we slowly steamed away – I only hope they enjoyed the fish!

We made our way across the South China Sea to Hong Kong, it took about four days, at eight knots. We entered the harbour and anchored not far inside, on the left. The area was called Aberdeen, and was where the 'sampans' (flat bottomed Chinese wooden boats) in this corner, all lived. It was like a sampan village, the occupants were born, lived and died in their sampan.

Behind them on the land was Tai Kow dockyard. There

was a ship in dry dock when we arrived, it was still there when we finally left! There was a wooden jetty which cut the sampan village into two. We were allowed to use it, as the main landing jetty was further up on the left-hand side. Our liberty men were allowed to use this jetty, although it was a little further to walk into Hong Kong.

I think it was from time immemorial that naval ships inside Hong Kong had a 'side party'. This is a sampan that is chosen from the village. I don't know who did our choosing, but our sampan consisted of a husband, wife and two children. Humphreys made a flag with the ship's name on it. This was fixed to a wooden staff, which was then fitted to the sampan's stern. The sampan would be tied up astern all the time the ship was in harbour. It was their job to keep the ship's sides clean. In return, the ship would look after them. I do not know if they were paid or not. It was amazing, the ship could be away for weeks, but as soon as it returned, and had anchored, within fifteen minutes, the side party's sampan would tie up astern. They were a nice little family in our sampan.

The harbour which seemed to be tidal, was heavily polluted with dead animals and all kinds of rubbish. If any liberty man had the misfortune of tumbling down into the water, he would be pulled out and escorted to sick bay and introduced to a stomach pump. This would be the sick bay attendant's job, and as we didn't have one at that time, it was the doctor's job, if he was on board. If he was ashore, poor old Tristram would have to do it – I hope he had been shown how!

I had now taken over as quartermaster, with acting A.B. Kevin Lacey H.O. as bosun's mate. I and Kevin were on the first watch, 2000 hours to 12.00 hours midnight.

There were three crew members who were all from Newcastle, and were trouble. Unfortunately they were all on the same watch, so got to go ashore together. One calm, clear moonlit evening, with the sea like a mill pond, Kevin and I were on watch. We heard the liberty men coming back, and then heard laughter and a loud splash. We wondered what was going on. The motor boat went to pick the liberty men up and bring them back to the ship. The Geordies were laughing their heads off, it turned out that they had come back to the harbour by rickshaw – instead of paying, they had heaved the rickshaw into the harbour with a splash! The following night, two liberty men were coming back, when they were waylaid by China men with lengths of bamboo. Both had to be taken to one of the two hospital ships. They had been badly beaten.

There was one depot ship, the real hospital was at the top of a mount; it had been destroyed by the Japanese – the same hospital where, in December 1941, the Japanese had rounded up, raped and bayoneted all the nurses and female staff. Bayoneted all the patients in their beds, did the same to doctors and patients in the operating room, they spared no one.

When the atom bomb was dropped on Japan, it was said that the Supreme Commander, Lord Mountbatten, ordered a Marine Commando unit, either the 41st or 42nd, on a fast mine-laying cruiser, either H.M.S. *Apollo* or *Manxman*, capable of over forty knots, to get to Hong Kong and occupy before the Americans; this they did. Pieces of the hospital had tumbled down the mount and the Marines were now ordering Japanese prisoners of war to carry them back up.

For some unknown reason, all cooks and stewards were taken off the ship and Chinese cooks and stewards took their place. Our cook was a little bit strange. His head was as wide as his shoulders. He was absolutely petrified of the Japanese. He had found his wife lying in a gutter, completely disembowelled, she had probably been raped beforehand – no wonder the poor man was the way he was. He turned out to be a very good cook, considering the rubbish he had to cook with.

The only depot ship was H.M.S. *Berry Head*, where we could get fresh bread which had been made on board, but that was all. Apparently, the Americans told the Royal Navy that if they wanted to be here, then they had to be self-sufficient. Sydney and Brisbane, Australia, were a long way away. Fuel oil and water were in short supply.

The Americans built a shore base on an island called Manus in the Admiralty Islands, it was a festering, malaria-ridden place – in no time at all, the American Seabees had the place bombed with mosquito killer, until there wasn't one left. Concrete piers were then made and storage areas built.

The Royal Navy were allowed anchorage off shore. Potatoes were brought up to Manus from Australia, the ship was allowed so many pounds. I don't know if any other stores were brought up from Aussie. There was no other fresh food. After a week of bread and potatoes, it was back to Coronation or Nestlé condensed milk, dehydrated potatoes, carrots and cabbage, bully beef, ship's biscuits and an awful American product called soya link, which was like compressed sawdust – it was made from soya beans. I don't know if it had to be fried, boiled or roasted, I only know that it was awful!

The two badly beaten ratings came back aboard, their faces badly bruised, as were their ribs and backs. They were excused duty, what they and their mess mates thought of the three Geordies I don't know. I was glad they were in the amidship messes. I think there was only one H.O. amongst them.

After tinkering around in the engine for a couple of days (there were no spares, any required would have to come up from

Brisbane or Sydney), the ship was ordered to meet a passenger cargo steamer coming to Hong Kong from Shanghai, so leaving our side party's sampan bobbing up and down astern of us, we made our way out of the harbour and into the East China Sea. The *Whitesand Bay* was much easier to steer than the old *Alresford*.

We had been lucky with the weather, did not experience any rough seas. We were still steaming at eight knots. After about four days, we met the steamer. She had to cut her speed down to suit ours. She was glad to see us, even though she was well prepared for pirates, having barbed wire wrapped around all the ladders, especially the bridge ladders. The front of the wheelhouse was reinforced to stop machine-gun fire. All doors opened from the inside, so could only be opened by crew members.

One afternoon, the Captain decided to carry out an exercise, he threw a lifebelt over board – we had steamed a few miles ahead of the passenger steamer. A shout went out, 'Man overboard, call away the sea boat.' The sea boat's crew rushed over and climbed into the sea boat, which was hurriedly lowered and dropped into the sea. The crew then rowed across to the unfortunate lifebelt. The boat's falls – the ropes to pull the lifeboat up – were run along the deck, like 'tug of war' ropes – there were two sets, one for each end of the sea boat. The ship stopped to pick up the lifebelt. The fore and aft boats' falls were hooked to the sea boat, then the whole ship's crew of seamen picked up the falls, gripping them tight. The order was given 'hoist away', the crew started to run, pulling the falls, until the pulley blocks fore and aft on the sea boat reached the pulley blocks on the top of the davits, which were then secured. Out climbed the sea boat's crew and the rescued lifebelt. There can't be many who can say that they rowed a sea boat in the East China Sea!

The ship then hastened along to catch up with the passenger

steamer. After another day or so, the passenger steamer was safely delivered into Hong Kong harbour. We then made our way to Aberdeen and anchored. Within ten minutes, our side party were tied up astern.

I went ashore with Brummie for a walk around. There wasn't much in the way of cafés. From a small shop, I bought two beer mugs. They were made in Macau, a little way down the coast from Hong Kong. I don't know what they were made of, some sort of soft metal, I don't think it was pewter – I wouldn't like to think that they were lead! They had dragons carved on them, and glass bottoms. I never had a chance to drink out of them. I had my name 'Fred' engraved on one of them, the other was engraved 'Dad'.

It was now December. Christmas 1945. Sadly, there was absolutely no Christmas spirit, it was my third Christmas away from home. There was very little activity on board, which gave the engineers plenty of time for maintenance work. I don't think the Chinese celebrate Christmas, so it came and went.

If the Captain was waiting for orders, then they arrived on New Year's Eve. The Captain ordered, 'Clear lower deck', and when we were all assembled on the quarterdeck, he said (and he may have been gloating a little), 'If any of you H.O.s thought you might be going home, I'm afraid you have another think coming, it is now our job to protect ships from piracy. Tomorrow the ship will proceed to the Balabac Strait, south of Palawan. There we will meet an Australian collier and we will escort it to a place called Cam Pha in French Indo-China.'

There was a stunned silence, he turned to the first lieutenant and said, 'Carry on.' The first lieutenant dismissed us. Both wars had been over for eight months, but instead of going home, we were going to look for pirates! I had heard of them – apparently they were rather ruthless and very cunning.

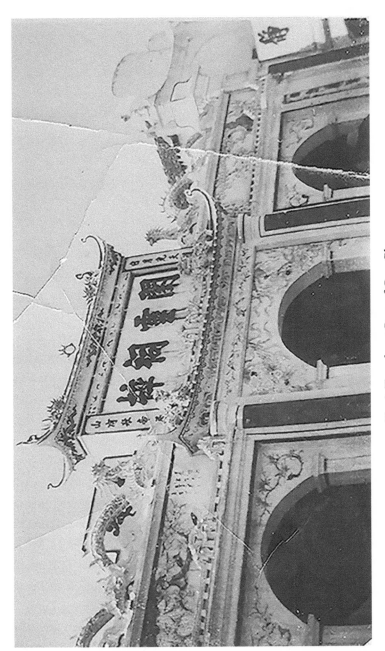

Fig 4. Temples at Port of Cam Pha

Chapter Twenty-One

H.M.S. Whitesand Bay – The South China Sea

The next morning, the ship topped up with oil and water and made its way down the South China Sea. As we steamed along, it seemed that the sea was empty, we never passed anything. The pirates' sampans could be picked up by our radar close to the shore. The pirates would only come out if any shipping went too close to the shore. They were well armed with machine guns fitted on the forecastle of their boats and were powered with diesel engines. The danger to an unescorted ship was that pirates would mingle with passengers, their weapons hidden in passengers' baggage. At a certain point in the voyage, the pirates would attempt to take over the ship. Then their mates would come out in their sampans – the passenger ship stood no chance. It would be steered into one of the many coves or inlets and run aground. The ship would then be ransacked. Within forty-eight hours it would be bare bones. What happened to the crew, the old and the young male passengers, could only be guessed. The woman and girls were taken up to Nanking or places like that and sold.

On her way up from Australia, an attempt had been made by pirates to board the collier, but the Chinese pirates found that the

Australian crew were a different kettle of fish! Although she had now asked to be escorted. There was quite a lot of disappointment and anger on board the *Whitesand Bay*. Some H.O.s had good jobs waiting for them back home. It would not have been so bad if conditions on board were alright, but they were not. The temperature was up in the high eighties. The mess decks were like ovens. The wheelhouse, with a door open each side, wasn't too bad. The officers on the upper bridge, must have been roasted.

I and my opposite number steered the same course for days at eight knots, it became quite boring. What it must have been like in the engine and boiler room, I can't imagine, almost unbearable I would think. I was glad I wasn't a stoker! I didn't know if there were any stoker H.O.s.

The ship finally reached the Balabac Strait, after a few hours, the collier came into view. When she reached us, she had to cut her speed to ours. She was quite modern. Pirates must have been pretty fearless to tackle her. She went ahead and we followed, across the South China Sea into the Gulf of Tonkin. We reached Haiphong, where we moored up to fore and aft buoys. In front of us was moored an American D.E., 'destroyer escort', on loan to the French Navy from the U.S.A. The Captain invited the French officers to come aboard for drinks. I don't know if the French Navy was allowed alcohol on board, like we were in the Royal Navy, or not. All of the French officers accepted the invite. Our Captain and the Duty Officer greeted the French Captain and his officers. I piped the French Captain aboard with my bosun's call, it was about eight-thirty in the evening. It was a very quiet night, no movement at all. Just before twelve midnight, all the French officers appeared. They seemed to be on good terms with our officers, there was a lot of shaking hands and goodbyes/au revoirs. Their motor boat came alongside and the officers climbed down into it. Their Captain went last, and I piped him over the side. Away went the boat and our officers departed, I assume to the wardroom. It was then time for me and the bosun's mate to go off watch.

The ship stayed another day, perhaps she had to get permission to go further. However, at 0800 hours the next morning, the collier weighed anchor and started to turn left into the Cam, or Forbidden River. The *Whitesand Bay* slipped her moorings and followed her. The collier had been here before. The Cam River is one of the shorter tributaries of the Thai Binh River. This river starts in the north-east of French Indo-China, then flows into the South China Sea.

The collier steamed for about two hours, then turned to the right and entered another tributary of the river; we followed. Looking through the open starboard wheelhouse door, I could see temples. After a while, the collier entered a large open area of water and steamed across it to a manmade canal, about the same width as the Suez Canal. The *Whitesand Bay* had hardly entered the canal, when there was some very fast activity. The bridge rang down with instructions to slow down, almost to a stop. Apparently there was signalling from up in the hills. A white ensign was hoisted to the mast head. The union flag was draped over the side of the ship. After a while, the collier slowly moved away and the *Whitesand Bay* followed. Eventually the collier tied up to a coaling wharf. As soon as the collier was secure, the *Whitesand Bay* tied up alongside her.

We had been alongside the collier for a short while when the sub-lieutenant came up to me and said, 'Beedie, I want you to cross the collier and wait on the wharf for two Chinese officers, when they arrive, escort them over the collier and bring them down to the ward room.' I said, 'Yes sir', then made my way across the collier, I stepped off the gangplank on to the wharf, straight into two bayonet tips, on the bayonets of two rifles, held by two of the most villainous individuals I have ever seen! They were dressed in grimy pantaloons, their bare feet in dirty sandals, black toe nails sticking out, grimy blouses, with crossed bandoliers of bullets, turbans on their heads, what teeth they had were black. I looked at them and they kept prodding me in the stomach, then prodding the holster of the unloaded Colt 45 I had in there.

I nodded and said, 'I get it, the message is, you don't want me to land, armed?' They kept prodding, I turned, went back across the collier. The sub-lieutenant saw me and came over, said, 'Beedie, why aren't you on the wharf?' I pointed over towards the wharf and replied, 'There are two villainous characters with rifles and bayonets, they don't want me to land on the wharf armed.' 'But you will be out of the rig of the day Beedie!' the sub-lieutenant protested. I said, 'I'm sorry sir, but I am not allowed ashore, armed.' Stalemate. The Chinese officers found their own way over, by then I was off watch.

I went down to the mess for dinner, which consisted of a mish-mash of dehydrated vegetables and bully beef or soya links. For breakfast we had ship's biscuits and cheese or jam. Tea was the same. We were all beginning to lose weight and starting to get a brownish yellow tan.

After a number of days, the collier was finally emptied, and ready to leave. The *Whitesand Bay* let go her stern lines and the collier slipped out astern, crossing the harbour, before turning right and heading for the canal. The *Whitesand Bay* let go the forward lines and followed the collier, leaving my unsavoury friends behind!

The two ships soon left the canal and crossed the stretch of open water to the River Cam, turned left and headed towards Hai

Phong. No stopping. The collier headed for the Balabac Strait, I expect she wanted to get a move on, time is money for a merchant ship, but she had to put up with eight knots, all the way down the Gulf of Tonkin, across the South China Sea, to the Balabac Strait, where we signalled 'goodbye' to her. She sounded her horn in reply and headed off down the straits.

The *Whitesand Bay* turned left and plodded her way up the full length of the South China Sea. It was sometime later, that I found out that those crummy looking articles back at the canal were Communist Vietnamese guerrillas, under the command of General Giap. They gave the French a hard time, until finally beating them at the Battle of Dien Bien Phu, at which point French Indo-China became Vietnam – well, they were a fearsome-looking lot!

Steaming up the South China Sea on the same course for days – the sea was empty. Not a sign of anything. Genuine sampan traders were too frightened to go down the sea, pirates would have them in no time. One day, while I was off watch, and up on the upper deck, I looked over the side to see striped sea snakes, they seemed to be keeping up with the ship.

The poor old cook was at his wits end, trying to make something with the rubbish he had to cook with. Frippy made dough boys and a Manchester Tart, as well as the inevitable Chinese wedding cake!

At last, we reached Hong Kong and anchored in the middle of the harbour (don't know why). Our side party were soon tied up astern. Unfortunately, we received bad news, we were losing our Number One. He had been so patient, accepting the Captain's comments as only a gentleman can, so helpful to the crew, never raised his voice to us. He knew what we were going through, he treated H.O.s as though they were proper sailors.

No H.O.s left the ship at this point – 'Where are we going next?' we all wondered. Now more bad news, a catastrophe really, the Number One's replacement is a Royal Navy lieutenant, who had been court marshalled and dismissed from his ship, a sloop, for verbally abusing a stoker H.O.. He had been saved by the *Whitesand Bay* losing her first lieutenant. So now we had a Captain, first lieutenant, sub-lieutenant, midshipman and coxswain, all who disliked H.O.s! I was glad that I was a quartermaster, with Kevin Lacey as bosun's mate.

The motor boat had been lowered, ready to take the captain ashore. Liberty had been given from 1800 hours until 22.55 in the evening. I thought that the first thing the liberty men would do would be to find something decent to eat! I managed to have a good bucket bath (borrowed the bucket) and did a bit of dobeing. I began to feel human again, but what I wouldn't do for a cold beer and a plate of salad! But no, it was potatoes, fresh at least from the depot ship, and bully beef or the dreadful soya link!

The engineers were busy maintaining the engines, getting spare parts was still difficult, they had to come up from Brisbane or Sydney and be stored in Manus, then brought up to Hong Kong. Admiral King, the Commander in Chief, did not like the British, he did not want the Royal Navy out here, this area and the Pacific were his patch.

There was just one thing that helped the Royal Navy with small bartering, and that was a bottle of Scotch whisky. American ships were dry, an American Captain would give anything possible for a bottle of Scotch. Any large items would require an order, which would have to come from Washington and Admiral King – no doubt such orders would go to the bottom of the pile! I wonder why Admiral King never liked the British? I believe his parents were Scottish. Certainly, not liking us made our life harder!

I went ashore with Brummie, didn't fancy Chinese food and no steak, egg and chips available! We walked around, and I bought a silk scarf for Mum, Dad had his mug. Brummie and I had our photograph taken. We ended up in a bar, which was full of sailors. Some were laughing their heads off – blimey, what a change it was to hear laughter! The canned beer was American, nowhere near as nice as a pint of bitter, but we were glad to have it. Where the bar got it from, I don't know.

After another couple of beers, Brummie and I headed back to the main jetty and waited for the liberty boat. It soon arrived and in no time was full of sailors that were a lot happier than when they went ashore! When we got back on board, some nice new bread from the depot ship had arrived, so I made myself a sandwich with cheese and Daddies Sauce. Brummie did the same.

There was a lot of anger on board, that no H.O.s had been relieved; it seemed that our draft chit requests had simply been ignored. To make matters worse, the Captain now had a first lieutenant who disliked H.O.s more than he did. I couldn't understand why they disliked us so much. When at sea, or ashore, there was no way anyone could tell the difference between an H.O. and a proper sailor. The new first lieutenant had called the stoker on his previous ship an H.O. b*****d. Some H.O.s were as educated as him, if not more. Perhaps that's why H.O.s were not liked?

The ship was, as usual, washed, scrubbed and painted from stern to stern. Some of the officers had the sea boat lowered and went sailing. After an afternoon's sailing, the sea boat would be tied up astern, keeping the sampan and the motor boat company. One morning, the Captain ordered the motor boat to take him ashore, I piped 'away motor boat crew'. The crew hurried and scrambled over the stern, into the motor boat, then with the engine started, leading seaman Jessy brought the boat around to the ladder, I then piped the Captain ashore.

Some of the crew were happy, because our mail had caught up with us at last. I had a letter, everyone at home was fine, Dad had retired at last, and still went up the club on a Saturday night with Mr. Habgood and Paddy Daley. At the time of writing Jock had not been called up. Reg was still enjoying his bike riding, Ron was around with his friends, Jean was fine and had sent Mum a photo of her little girl, who looked lovely, her husband Bill was still in India. Mum's arthritis was playing up. She hoped to see me soon.

Most of us were still down in the dumps, especially the married H.O.s. Brummie was quiet, and I left him alone. We would soon know where the ship was going, when the motor boat returned and tied up astern. After about two hours the officer of the watch came up to me and told me to call away the motor boat crew, to fetch the Captain, which I did. I then piped 'all hands to dinner'.

After dinner, the Captain ordered me to pipe 'clear lower decks'. We all mustered on the forecastle. The Captain said, 'The ship will escort three BYMS to Manila in the Philippines.' He also said, 'There are over six thousand American sailors there, if anyone gets into a brawl, they will be severely punished, no matter whose fault.' The first lieutenant then dismissed us – I never knew what the letters BYMS stood for, but they were a class of small wooden minesweepers, used to sweep harbours.

I piped the forecastle hands to weigh anchor, and the P.O. ordered a hose pipe to be run up the deck. Two seamen then leant over the side, and as the stoker winched the anchor cable up, the two seamen hosed it clean. The anchor was also given a good hosing, while it was being secured.

The ship then made its way to an oil tanker and topped up with oil, then we crossed over to the water tanker and did the same. Once this was done, the ship slowly left the harbour, as did the three BYMS. For some reason, the doctor was drafted (was the drafting officer aware that the ship did not have a sick bay attendant?!).

Fig 5. Escorting the B.Y.M.S

Chapter Twenty-Two

H.M.S. Whitesand Bay – Hong Kong to Manila

The ship, still travelling at eight knots, made her way down to Manila. The heat was up in the nineties and over. The sea quite calm. They must have been feeling the heat in those small BYMS. After two days, there was no more fresh bread or potatoes, so we were back to the mish-mash, although we now had some tinned tomatoes and beans. We never seemed to be short of bully beef!

The trip down to Manila was quiet. No sampan to be seen, the sea was empty. On arrival in Manila, the BYMS made their way to where they were required. The ship anchored near a jetty. There was not a proper building in sight, the place had been flattened. The only structures in view were a few hovels made up of bits of board and tin and anything else they could find. The battle for Manila was one of the most vicious. Over one hundred thousand Filipinos were killed. The only other building to be seen turned out to be the U.S. Navy canteen.

I piped 'hands to dinner', such as it was. The Chinese cook had made a bully beef cottage pie, tried roasting the dehydrated potatoes on top of the bully – all you could say is that it was a change! Leave was given from 1300 hours to 2100 hours. The port watch liberty men lined up on the quarterdeck, an awning had been made and rigged up to cover the quarterdeck, which was a blessing. Stokers one side, seamen the other. The officer of the day was the sub-lieutenant. He said, 'Off caps' – the stokers and seamen were then like children getting their Friday-night pocket money – he slowly and religiously placed one American dollar on each cap. The stokers all threw their dollars on the deck. A pack of cards was found, the stokers then cut the cards, and the two highest cards shared the money between them. At least the two winners would have enough money to have a decent time ashore, although there did not seem to be much life around. A few of the sailors said that it was alright. No wolf whistles.

The following afternoon, I, Brummie and two others decided to go ashore, we were religiously awarded our one American dollar. The motor boat took us to the jetty, where a few America sailors were loafing about. They took little notice of us. We walked to the canteen, which was full, and went up to the bar. I had my beer mug with me. We found that one American dollar bought ten cans of Schaefer canned beer, all the way from Milwaukee!

Brummie bought ten cans and we found a table. Only one comment came our way, from the back of the canteen, but no one took any notice. I had a feeling they were as fed up as we were. A burly sailor sitting opposite me saw the beer mug. 'Hey buddy,' he said, 'that's one helluva beer mug, can I see it?' I said, 'Yes' and handed it over to him. He looked at it every which way, handed it back to me and said, 'I sure would like to buy it, will you sell it?' I replied, 'Well, I bought two, they come from Macau, near Hong Kong, one for me, one for my dad.' He said again, 'I sure would like to buy it, I'll give you thirty dollars American.' I said, 'Alright.' He handed over the thirty dollars and I handed him the mug. He and his shipmates were just the same as us, a long way from home!

We drank a second can of beer. The Americans were not very happy, apparently there was no Coke this month. Leaving two cans of beer on the table, we shook hands with our burly shipmate, said, 'Cheerio' and made our way back to the ship.

We were sitting in the mess deck, when someone shouted down, 'The ship's writer has cracked, he's gone crazy, he's stalking the decks, swinging a three-foot fire axe! Nobody can get near him!' I said, 'I'm getting out of here, in case he comes down here!' The others in the mess deck agreed, and we got up the ladder pretty quick. The P.O.G.I. was trying to pacify him, but he wasn't taking any notice, he was still swinging the axe. He was normally such a nice chap, very quiet, well educated, looked after all the ship's documents.

The P.O.G.I. was walking backwards, away from the writer and towards the forecastle. He was talking over his shoulder, saying, 'I will try to get him to the open forecastle, two of you get up on A-gun deck. As soon as he comes clear, drop on him, but try not to hurt him.' The G.I. continued walking backwards, talking quietly to the writer, until eventually he came clear. Two of his mess mates were waiting up on A-gun deck, they had to be careful that they didn't drop down into a swinging axe! As the axe swung downwards, they dropped down onto the writer, each taking a shoulder. It took four hands to get the axe off him and get him into a Robinson stretcher (I think that is what it was called). They soon had him trussed up. If there had been a doctor on board, he could have sedated him.

The Captain had to decide what to do with the writer. Would the U.S. Navy take care of a crazy British sailor? Yes they would. An ambulance was sent for, and he was taken ashore, like a trussed-up chicken, to wait on the jetty in the burning sun, with curious American sailors looking on. The ambulance finally came, and off he went, we would not see him again. Like the S.B.A. at Tobruk, the telegraphist in Port Said, then the doctor, and now the writer. I hoped that an officer from the ship went with the writer. If the Captain ever heard what had become of him, he never told the ship's company.

It was now time to leave Manila. The forecastle party soon had the anchor secured, and the ship slowly left what was a shattered, miserable place. Then at the usual eight knots, we plodded our way back to Hong Kong. On arrival, we anchored in the middle of the harbour. The ship's desalinating plants were playing up. I hoped they didn't need spare parts! The ship's engineers were working on the engines. They were turning the 'screws' (propellers) whilst at anchor. They would suddenly give the engines a burst, which caused the ship to swing about.

Myself and Kevin Lacey had the afternoon watch, a cutter came alongside, manned by a Chinese crew. Standing in the stern sheets was a chaplain and a surgeon lieutenant, who shouted up to me, 'Do you know where the sloop H.M.S. *Woodcock* is lying?' I replied, 'I do not know, but if you come aboard, the ship is turning screws at anchor. I will find out.' They both came aboard. I told the Chinese coxswain to lay the cutter off. I then phoned the bridge and asked the duty signaller where the *Woodcock* was lying. He answered back, saying he would ask the P.O. yeoman.

Whilst I was waiting, a ship mate came up to me and said, 'Do you think the doctor would come and have a look at Wiggy?'[5] I said, 'I will ask him.' I approached the surgeon lieutenant, saying, 'We do not have a doctor on board, and one of our ship mates seems very ill. He is having eight aspirin a day but nothing else.' The doctor replied, 'Certainly', and off he went with my ship mate. He wasn't gone five minutes, before he came back to me, saying, 'Your ship mate is very ill, send for a hospital boat as quickly as possible.'

I immediately phoned the bridge and told the signaller to tell the yeoman that Wiggy was very ill and to send for a hospital boat immediately. Which the yeoman did. Whilst waiting for the hospital boat, the yeoman found out where the *Woodcock* was lying. Actually, she could be seen from the ship. I pointed her out to the doctor, thanking him for seeing Wiggy. He thanked me for my help, and then left the ship with the chaplain.

Meanwhile, Wiggy's mates were wrapping him up in a blanket and taking him down to the quarterdeck. The hospital boat arrived and Wiggy was carefully lowered down into it. The engineers had been told to stop turning the screws whilst this happened. The hospital boat then took off, and that was the last we saw of Wiggy.

Chapter Twenty-Three

H.M.S. Whitesand Bay – Hong Kong to Labuan, Borneo

For a week or more, the ship swung idly around the anchor. Again, no H.O.s were relieved. Frippy and I had changed places; he was now quartermaster, with Yarker as his bosun's mate. The day after Wiggy was taken away by the hospital boat, the ship left for a little island called Labuan, off the north-west coast of Sabah, North Borneo, in the company of H.M.S. *King Salvor*, a naval salvage vessel. We were to protect the *King Salvor*, whose job was to tow a Japanese salvage vessel with a large crane on it back to Hong Kong.

Frippy was now on the helm, I was back on the boat with leading seaman Jessy. We were given the bad news that the ship's desalinators were not producing enough water, due to defects in them. So water would have to be rationed. There would be two hours of water, twice a day, 0600 hours to 0800 hours and 1800 hours to 2000 hours. Water priority would be given to hygiene and cooking. The engineers, we were told, were working hard to keep the desalinators working. I thought that we should turn back – no chance!

Suddenly, there was a change of course, something had been

spotted on the radar. As the ship drew closer, we could see that it was a drifting sampan. The ship drew alongside. There were three bodies lying on the bottom of the sampan. They had no heads. The sampan had been ransacked, where were the heads? The usual procedure in these circumstances was for someone to go down into the sampan and with an axe, smash a few holes in the bottom, and let it sink. No one was volunteering to go down into this sampan. The bodies were badly decomposed – so it was left to drift. I wondered where it would end up.

The ship then resumed its course, and it was then that we received the signal that Wiggy had died, on the 13th April 1946, of a malignant malaria, which it seemed, was immune to the mepacrine tablets. We later found out that Wiggy had been buried in a naval cemetery, some of his mess mates had visited his grave. I believe that one of them had a camera, and took some photographs of the grave, but I am not sure.

There was much sorrow and anger aboard. The two wars had been over for nine months, all H.O.s should have been relieved from the Navy. If we had have been, Wiggy would still be alive. Instead of being relieved, we were going to some godforsaken place that no one had ever heard of.

The water was turned off, the leading seamen of all messes made sure that every man played by the book, and used water fairly. Mess kettles were filled, to be used as drinking water from 1600 hours to 1800 hours. As we drew nearer to Borneo, the weather got hotter, now in the late eighties to early nineties. Some ratings were getting prickly heat, sweat rashes and some nasty boils.

Reaching Labuan the *King Salvor* steamed around to the other side of the island, where the crane ship lay. I couldn't understand why the Japanese never scuttled it. We steamed on, then turned right. The beach was long, shaped like a walking stick. The ship had turned right, towards the bend, then steamed towards the centre of the bend. There was a high sand dune on our right and the beach on our left. The Captain ordered us to line ship, as if we were going into Portsmouth Harbour!

All along the long beach was the debris of war, Australian soldiers and Japanese prisoners. Needless to say, the Chinese cook had vanished. The Captain gave the order for the anchor to be slipped. The stoker P.O., with a large hammer, hit what I think was called the Blakes slip stopper, which was holding the cable tight. He gave the slip a mighty swipe, the anchor flew off the end of the cable and the ship slowly steamed forward until it buried its bow into the sandy beach, which startled some Australian soldiers, although they soon got over it and acted like typical Aussies, falling about laughing! I am not going to write about the Captain's reaction!

The ship slowly went astern to its proper anchorage, and dropped the other anchor. The Captain had the ship drag for the lost anchor, back and forth, for a couple of days, then realised the fuel situation and gave up. So if any scrap iron dealer needs an anchor, there is one lying somewhere on the seabed in Labuan Lagoon! I hope the Captain got a right rollicking for losing it!

Midway, on the left side of the long beach, was a small tributary, in which the Australians had built a small wooden jetty, similar to those on beaches back in Britain, 'Any more for the Skylark?'

The motor boat had been lowered and brought around to the ship's ladder, which had been lowered. The Captain told the first lieutenant to carry on. Frippy piped him over the side. He stepped down the ladder, into the boat and told leading seaman Jessy to take him ashore. This he did, taking the boat to the small wooden jetty. The Captain told him to wait for him, though he did not know how long he would be. I secured the boat to the jetty.

On shore, there was a group of Australian soldiers, and a sergeant, who saluted the Captain as he approached, which surprised me, as the Aussies don't normally use such formalities. The Captain saluted him back, then started a conversation with him. They walked together along the beach, until the sergeant pointed out a gap in the bushes, which led to a path that crossed to the other side of the island. The Captain took the path and vanished.

The soldiers were on the island to help make the Japanese prisoners clear the debris. Nobody was very enthusiastic, it was far too hot – although you would think that the Aussies would be used to it. The sergeant walked towards me, coming close, he said something like 'Hello mate.' I said, 'Hello, would you like a cigarette?' He replied, 'I sure would!' I offered a Senior Service. He said, 'A Tailor Made, I haven't had one of these for ages.' He took one, I took one and gave him the packet. We got talking, his company at Labuan was part of the 9th Australian Division, famous for it's defence of Tobruk in April 1941. They held out against Rommel's Panzer Division for seven months. After which the Division were sent back to Australia for Home Defence.

Leading Seaman Jessy preferred to stay in the shade of the half cabin, at the rear of the boat. The stoker stayed in the engine room. I found some shade in the bushes, where I could see the entrance to the path which the Captain had taken. The sergeant, who seemed to be a pretty tough customer, had been in the army some years. I half squatted, half sat in the bushes, the sergeant did the same.

I looked around, said to the sergeant, 'Where are all the

natives? I can only see your mates and the Jap prisoners.' He replied, 'They have taken to the hills, the Japanese have infected all the women and girls with syphilis, which cannot be cured, we haven't got the drugs. So they have gone up into the hills to die.' I was horrified and said, 'But that will leave only men and boys!' 'I'm afraid so,' he said. 'How can anybody be so terrible to do that to innocent girls and women?' I asked. He said, 'These Japanese are capable of the worst tortures invented!'

He then told me things which I cannot describe here as they are too evil. Although, I will tell you about two forms of torture which were supposed to be not so bad – they would lay a prisoner on the ground, put some painful apparatus in his mouth to keep it open, then rig up a hose pipe just above his mouth, so a trickle of water was going down his throat. He would then be left in the sun. It would take about two hours for his stomach to distend, until he looked like a heavily pregnant woman, then a Japanese soldier would get a stool and put it next to the prisoner. He would then stand on the stool and jump on the prisoner's distended stomach, until the water spurted out of the prisoner's nose, eventually choking him.

The other torture is where a prisoner is made to stand to attention, and then outstretch his arms, like an aeroplane's wings, looking up at the sun. I tried to do this, but never lasted more than five minutes – you try it! As soon as the prisoner's arms start to drop, he is beaten. This continues until he is beaten to death.

After the sergeant told me about these things, I asked him, 'Doesn't this make you want to retaliate?' He said, 'The Commander in Chief, Lord Mountbatten, has said that no Japanese prisoners are to be ill treated – otherwise it will prove that we are as bad as them.' We sat talking until the Captain reappeared. I said, 'Cheerio' to the sergeant and made my way back to the boat.

The stoker started the engine, leading seaman Jessy was

ready. The Captain approached, and I saluted him (it is not the man you are saluting, it is the King's uniform); he saluted back to me and stepped into the boat. He and leading seaman Jessy saluted one another, then leading seaman Jessy shouted to me to let go the lines. That I did, then stepped on to the bow of the boat, which headed back to the ship.

The boat was steered alongside the ladder and the Captain left the boat. Knocker White, the quartermaster of the starboard watch, piped him aboard. Leading seaman Jessy took the boat around to the stern and I tied her up. We all then clambered aboard the ship.

The cook had been found, it was a hard job to get him to cook the rubbish we had to eat – it was a waste of time, as no one felt like eating. I had corned beef with ship's biscuit and a cup of tea. As soon as the cook had finished his jobs, he vanished. I don't know how I, or anybody else, would feel if they found their wife disembowelled by Japanese soldiers. I told the mess deck about the infecting of the woman and girls. They could not believe it. I said, 'That is why there is no sign of the local people.'

I noticed that there were no soldiers swimming. On board, there was a fear there might be sea snakes in the sea. Nobody was prepared to take the chance, even though a swim in the sea to cool off was very tempting. It was time to get our heads down. A lot of the mess decided to sleep on deck. I slept on the mess deck table. Sleeping in a hammock was out of the question – it was miles too hot!

I still wasn't shaving, so in the morning, just had to have a face wash. I and L/S Jessy had to wear a white front, a white shirt, black socks up to the knee, black shoes and a white cap. I had a job to keep them washed and ironed. Breakfast consisted of a cup of tea, biscuits, cheese and Daddies Sauce. The mess deck leading seamen made sure there was plenty of water for tea making. The mess decks were beginning to smell. There was no air. The ports were open but there was not even a breeze.

Myself and L/S Jessy waited to be called to take the Captain ashore. He always looked immaculate. We were sweating and itchy. I was lucky to have the chance to get away from the ship. The Captain seemed to prefer to stay on the *King Salvor*. He was furious because there always seemed to be something going wrong on the Japanese ship. Leading seaman Jessy said that he thought the Japs were finding things to do, making work, as they did not know what was going to happen to them when the ship reached Hong Kong. He was probably right.

Then the quartermaster called 'Away the boat'. I, Jessy and the stoker, hurried along to the stern and clambered down into the boat. Once the engines were started, Jessy shouted for me to let go the lines, which I did. Then he steered the boat around to the ladder. The quartermaster, Frippy, piped the Captain ashore. Jessy saluted the Captain, who told him to take him ashore.

I let go the boat and leading seaman Jessy took it to the wooden jetty. Reaching it, I leapt out on to the jetty and tied it up forward. The Captain told Jessy to wait for him. I saluted him as he walked past and headed for the path which would take him across to the *King Salvor*.

I headed for the bushes. I was half sitting, half squatting in the shade when the Australian sergeant came up. I offered him a fag again, and took one myself, then gave him the packet. As we were enjoying our fag, an L.S.T. (landing ship tanks), full of what I thought were Japs, appeared. The sergeant told me that they were North Koreans, crueller even than the Japanese. I said, 'That takes some believing!'

I asked, 'Where are they going?' He pointed to a smaller

island, saying, 'They will be given a fair trial, if found guilty, they will be shot.' I said, 'Is that the shooting I can hear in the mornings?' He replied, 'Yes, they are always shot early morning. If anyone is found not guilty, which is not very often, they are put in a prison camp.'

I asked him if there had been any British prisoner of war camps. He told me that there had been over five hundred British prisoners. None had survived. The five hundred had been sent to Labuan to build an air strip, in what was mostly a swamp area. When the Japanese officer in charge of the camp was relieved after a few months, half of the prisoners were already dead. Starvation, malaria, beriberi and ill treatment being the causes. This officer disappeared and has never been traced. The remaining two hundred and fifty prisoners were sent to a camp in another part of Brunei. None of them survived either. The officer in charge of this camp, was a sergeant major Sugino. When Japan was defeated, he was found guilty of murder and taken to Rabaul in New Guinea and shot. Colonel Suga, the camp's Commander, some how managed to commit suicide. He pointed to a large army tent at the far end of the beach and said, 'There is the trial of a junior officer going on in there now, if he is found guilty, he will either go to prison or be hung.'

He offered me one of my cigarettes and suddenly jumped up, saying, 'Come with me.' I followed him along a jungle track, which eventually opened up into a large space. There were two Nissen huts. He said, 'Go and look in that one.' I went over and opened the door, the hut was full of mouldering Australian Red Cross boxes. I said, 'Is the other one the same?' He said, 'Yes, if there is anything here that you can salvage and use, you can have it.' I said, 'Are you sure?' He said, 'Yes.' I thanked him and asked him to excuse me, while I ran back to the boat.

Running out of the jungle, I shouted, 'Jess!' He poked his head out of the boat. I shouted again, 'Jess, come on!' He and the stoker jumped out of the boat and I shouted, 'Follow me.' I raced back to the huts and started rummaging around for boxes which were not too badly squashed. Jess and the stoker appeared and I said, 'The sergeant has said that we can have any of these if they are alright.' We found quite a few unharmed boxes and took them back to the boat, until the engine room was absolutely packed full. Jessy and the stoker then settled back into the boat and I went back to my shelter, puffed out, it was over ninety degrees. I thanked the sergeant, telling him, 'You have saved our lives!' The sergeant said, 'Here comes your Captain.'

I went back to the boat and waited for the Captain to come within range. I then approached him, saluted and said, 'Excuse me sir, the sergeant has shown me two Nissen huts full of rotting Australian Red Cross parcels, he said we could have some if we wished, I thanked him and we've filled the engine room – I hope that is alright sir?' He muttered something which I took to be, 'Yes.' He stepped into the boat, told Jess to take him back to the ship. On reaching the ladder, Frippy piped him on board.

When he had disappeared, the stoker handed a parcel to Jess, who was standing on the ladder platform, who passed it to me, halfway up the ladder, then I passed it to the bosun's mate. I told him to take it down into the mess deck. A few more interested characters turned up. A human chain was formed. Once all the boxes had been taken on board, Jess took the boat to the stern and I tied it up and then clambered back on board and went down to the mess deck. Some of the other crew were interested in what was going on and I explained what had happened. I told them that Jess was going to share the contents out between the mess decks.

Every box was emptied and the contents carefully sorted out.

The box I opened contained tins of fruit and tinned Christmas pudding. In other boxes, there was writing paper, envelopes, a small pencil, toilet paper, one small tin of cigarette tobacco and a packet of cigarette papers. I think there was some chocolate as well, packed tight so that it hadn't gone mouldy. Leading seaman Jessy came down into the mess and said, 'We will give each seaman's mess the same contents, it will be up to them how they share it out. If we can get some more parcels, we'll do the same for the other messes.'

Hands were being called at 0600 hours, and turned to at 0700 hours to hose down the decks, then work until about 10.30, then take it easy until 1600 hours, then hose the decks down again. It was said that someone on a ship in Manus had fried an egg on the deck – sadly we had no eggs to test it!

Few would eat the mish-mash meals, though the cook continued to do his best, he would still appear, do his cooking and then vanish. Frippy did his best too, making a Manchester tart with lard. I would stick with my cheese, biscuits and Daddies Sauce! I was never very fat, due to war-time rationing. My ribs were beginning to show as well as my skin turning more yellow.

Poor old Lightning, the mess deck dodger, had a face as red as a lobster – he was stuck down in the mess deck all day, with smelly bodies lying on lockers and all about the place. Then there were the poor engineers, working below in the terrible heat, to keep the desalinators working. We should never have left Hong Kong!

I needed a good wash, but there was no water until 1600 hours. A tin of apricots was shared between three of us, at tea time. Sometimes the tins didn't have labels on, so it was a guess as to what you got. You might find yourself sharing a tin of Christmas pudding for breakfast! Whatever it was, we were very grateful to be eating this food, intended for Australian prisoners of war.

The next day was the same. Took the Captain ashore, and as soon as he had gone on his way, the three of us dashed to the huts and started to sort out the good boxes, and take them back to the boat, loading them in, until the engine room was full.

I then went over to my shady retreat. The sergeant came over. I gave him some cigarettes and thanked him again. We sat together in the shade. I said, 'The Japs can't stretch the job out much longer.' We sat there yarning. His working party wasn't shifting much debris. Some were playing a game of what they called 'two up', which involved throwing coins up in the air. The sergeant said, 'That keeps them quiet for hours!' What that some of our P.O.s were like him! He looked down the beach and said, 'Here comes your Captain, and he doesn't look too happy!' He then rose and walked away.

I walked back to the boat, as the Captain walked past, I saluted, he answered the salute, stepped into the boat and told Jessy to take him back to the ship. Once the Captain had climbed back on board, the human chain formed again and the boxes were quickly taken down to the mess deck. After tying the boat astern, and returning to the mess deck, we sorted out the boxes and the contents were given to the other messes. I never bothered with dinner, it was too hot.

I thought that the ship was anchored in the wrong place. It was anchored in the U part of the lagoon, I think it should have been anchored outside of the lagoon. We had not seen any sampans since being here. There was not a breeze, the water in the lagoon was flat calm. There was no activity ashore. The dinner utensils were washed and cleared and a cup of tea was made, then everybody found somewhere to collapse. Even the engineers had stopped working.

It was hard to imagine what it must have been like, fighting to regain this island. At 1600 hours the water came on. The hands turned too, to hose the decks down and to do what the forecastle P.O. wanted to be done. I and Jessy went for a good wash and to do some dobeing – this never took very long to dry, so we were soon able to iron it.

The P.O.G.I. had guns' crews cleaning the guns. I was excused, so I made Jessy and Lightning a cup of tea and we had the mess deck to ourselves. At 1700 hours, the water was turned off. It was decided that the water would be turned on again at 1800 hours for one hour, to enable the hands who were finishing at 1800 hours to have a wash and do any dobeing. It was mainly only shorts and white fronts (which were optional). Each hand had a bucketful of water to wash in, and then they hosed each other off.

When clean and dry, most of them, me included, went down to the sick bay. Acting able seaman Tristram liberally painted the purple unction on to the body parts that needed it. He had found some ointment which he gave out and was alright for the nether regions! He hot-poulticed boils (very painful), cleaned and dressed various cuts, handed out aspirins and the everyday mepacrine tablets. He did very well, I must admit – we looked like a band of Sioux warriors on the warpath!

We were then back to the messes to sort out what was left in the Red Cross boxes. There may have been more in them than I have described, but that is all I can remember!

When writing letters, we had to put a sweat band around our foreheads, to stop sweat dropping down on to the paper. Brummie wrote to his newly wed wife every day. I hoped there had been a mail delivery in Hong Kong for when we got back there.

I never got much sleep that night, was glad when 0600 hours came. Hands turned to to hose down the decks. I climbed down into the boat to give it a good clean, then sat in the cabin until I heard the call 'Motor boat crew, man your boat'. The same routine was followed, the Captain was piped on to the boat by Knocker White and we took him to the wooden jetty. Once again, as soon as the Captain had gone, we (Jessy, the stoker and me) made our way to the huts to see if we could find any more decent boxes. There were hundreds of boxes there. They must have been there since the first prisoners arrived.

When the engine room was full, I made my way to my shady spot. The sergeant joined me. His men were still playing the money game. I gave him some cigarettes, which later he shared out with his men. Then we sat and yarned. I asked, 'What verdict did the Jap officer who was being tried, receive?' He replied, 'He has been found guilty. His crimes will now be studied. If he is found guilty of cruelty, he will be jailed. If guilty of murder, he will be jailed for a long time, or hung.'

As we sat there talking, and looking out at the lagoon, I said, 'Look, there is a large ship approaching.' He patted me on the shoulder and said, 'I am going home!' It was the troop-carrying ship, the *Empire Fowey*. She dropped her anchor outside of the lagoon. Instead of life boats, there were small landing craft in their place, with troops climbing down into them. I looked hard, said to the sergeant, 'They are Indian troops.' He said, 'They are from the fourth Indian division. They are taking over from us.' He then told me that the Japanese had used Indian P.O.W.s for live shooting and bayonet practice. I wondered what they would think of Admiral Lord Mountbatten's orders – would they even be able to speak English well enough to understand the orders? I decided that the Japs were going to have a hard time.

We both stood up, I shook hands with this tough, battle-hardened soldier, saying, 'Thank you again for the food parcels, everyone on board the ship really appreciates you letting us have them; thanks also for sharing my shelter, I've really enjoyed your company.' He said, 'Me too, and thanks for the Tailor Mades.'

We stood, watching the landing craft approach. As soon as they hit the beach, the ramps came down and the troops poured out, with all their gear. The Aussie soldiers signalled to the Japanese P.O.W.s to go down and give the Indians a hand, knowing full well what would happen. The Indians angrily waved them away, they did not want the Japanese contaminating their gear. The sergeant slapped me on the shoulder, and looking up at the sky, said, 'There is bad weather about', then he strode over to sort things out. I never spoke to him again.

I sat back down in my shelter, the temperature was up around a hundred degrees. I decided that the South China Sea is not the best place to be when bad weather is about. After a short time, the Captain appeared. He must have wondered what was going on, what with the landing craft, Indian troops, Aussie troops and Japanese P.O.W.s all over the place. The sergeant saluted him and the Captain returned his salute, they conversed for a while, then saluted each other again, before the Captain strode towards the boat. More salutes were exchanged, the Captain stepped into the boat, the leading seaman told me to let go the lines, which I did, before stepping into the boat myself. I looked around and gave the sergeant a wave, he waved back, then we were on our way back to the ship for the last time.

Once beside the ship, the Captain soon vanished and the boxes were handed out to the ready crew members, who took them down to the mess deck. The leading seaman took the boat around to the stern and I tied her up. We all climbed out of the boat and headed down to the mess deck, where Jessy and others sorted out what was now the last of the boxes.

The quartermaster piped through the tannoy 'the ship will leave at 0900 hours tomorrow, hands to dinner.' I did not fancy any dinner, I had corned beef and biscuits with Daddies Sauce then opened a tin of apricots, which I shared with leading seaman Jessy. At 1600 hours, the hands turned too, the motor boat was brought around, hoisted up and lashed down. Everything that could be lashed down was, including the sea boat. We were all ready to leave.

It was tea time, but what tea? A tin of Christmas cake, sliced into three, with a tin of apricots, also for three – but it was better than corned beef and biscuits again! The water came on at 1800 hours, a bucket of water each. I had a flannel down, then went off to the sick bay with the others to get some treatment. I decided to sleep up on deck – took my hammock mattress and found a parking place, under the motor boat – had quite a decent sleep.

The tannoy roused us at 0600 hours, in the distance we could hear the sound of gun fire, more Japanese or Koreans going to meet their ancestors – better to be shot than being tortured to death. I had another bucket wash. We all now had to be dressed in white fronts, white shorts, long black socks, black shoes and white caps. At 0900 hours, hands lined the ship; once we were all in place, the anchor was weighed, the ship slowly went astern up the lagoon, stopped, then slowly went ahead. The Aussie soldiers waved.

I was glad that the tough sergeant and his squad were going home. They will have sad memories of Labuan and the comrades they left behind though. The Japanese soldiers had been so savage and cruel.

Chapter Twenty-Four

H.M.S. Whitesand Bay –
Labuan to Hong Kong

Fig 6. The Labuan War Cemetery

We turned right out of the lagoon, passed the *Empire Fowey*, who dipped her red ensign flag in salute – the *Whitesand Bay* returned the salute by dipping and then raising her white ensign, the *Empire*

Fowey then raised her red ensign. We turned left around her stern, then proceeded towards the South China Sea – so leaving this dot on the map, this sad, cruel little island. Leaving behind the graves of the young Australian soldiers, who had died in the retaking of the island, and the remains of the hundreds of British soldiers who also died here. Murdered, tortured, dying of malaria, beriberi, dysentery, starvation and ill treatment. Not helped by the fact that the Royal Navy and allied navies had put a blockade on the islands – ensuring that the Japanese fed themselves before any P.O.W. Two handfuls of uncooked rice a day was all they were given, this they had to cook themselves. Leaving behind also what must be one of the worst war crimes ever committed: the deliberate infecting of the women and girls with syphilis. A notice had gone up on board the ship, telling the company of this terrible act.

The sergeant was right about the bad weather ahead. We were to steam into the worst weather the ship had seen. The cook had appeared, but could not do any cooking, as the sea was too rough, huge waves were crashing over the bow and breaking over the bridge, sea snakes and all! It was little help that the Captain was always sea sick in rough weather. He would retire to his sea cabin, which was behind the wheelhouse. All the ports were closed, so no fresh air could get in to freshen up the mess decks.

Previously when rough weather had occurred, the Captain would go to his sea cabin, and the fine R.N.V.R. lieutenant would take over, and there was no problem. However, he had left the ship, so we would have to see what the arrogant, new, No. 1 officer could do. The Captain of the *King Salvor* was doing a wonderful job, towing his crane ship – it was a strange-looking craft – oval shaped, with a large crane fixed to the deck, between amidships and right forward; her speed was two knots, just enough to potter around a harbour to do any work required.

The Captain of the *King Salvor* was probably a R.N.R. Master Mariner, called back from the Reserve, like Dad was during the First World War. Should the tow break, there would be no hope of saving the crane ship, it would be swept away.

The clouds and the sea, seemed joined. We lost sight of the *King Salvor*. Frippy was on the wheel, he was a proper sailor, he said that these seas were as rough as he had ever seen. At one time, the wheel was over as far as it would go to starboard, but the ship was still being pushed to port by the waves. It was too much for the new No. 1 to handle. The Captain had to be roused out of his sea cabin to take over the ship. He and the sub-lieutenant shared a sick bucket! The ship had to be carefully edged, little by little, into a large circle, until it came around parallel with the *King Salvor*, it was a nightmare.

The storm or whatever it was, typhoon maybe, was certainly slowing us down. The Captain did a fine job bringing the ship almost parallel with the *King Salvor*. He then retired, once more, back to his sea cabin.

We were back on four hours' water. The Red Cross parcels were finished. The bad weather abated, but we were to hit more before making it to Hong Kong.

Chapter Twenty-Five

H.M.S. Whitesand Bay –
Hong Kong to Thursday Island

As soon as we reached Hong Kong, the ship made straight for the water tanker. Once the tanks were full, we were off to the usual anchorage. A signal was sent to the hospital ship, asking it to send a cutter. The quartermaster then piped all men wishing to visit the hospital ship to muster on the quarterdeck. And so it was that a cutter full of us 'unclean' headed for the hospital ship, where the nurses tended to our ailments. Now that we had plenty of water for our bucket baths and to thoroughly rinse our dobeing, we would soon be clean again.

The ship's company were absolutely delighted that, at last, it was realised that the ship and the ship's company were clapped out! The ship was to go down to Auckland, New Zealand for a six-week refit. How the E.R.A.'s (engine room artificers) had managed to keep the desalinators going was a wonder, bearing in mind the very hot conditions. If Admiral King had liked us a bit more, the Americans might have given us replacements – it seems though, that we will have to wait until the ship gets to Auckland, however long that will take.

I had gone back to being a quartermaster. Frippy had taken

my place in the motor boat. The side party had tied up astern. I was on watch. The coxswain told me to report to the divisional officer, R.N. Lieutenant Bullock, he was a fine officer. The crew all agreed that he should have been made first lieutenant, instead of the arrogant individual we ended up with. He treated the H.O.s in the same way as the proper sailors.

I reported to Lieutenant Bullock, he said that I had been in the Navy three years on the 29th April 1945 and, as such, was entitled to my first good-conduct badge, which he produced. It was dull red in colour. He said, 'Sew this on to the left arm of your uniform. You will be entitled to a further sixpence a day.' The badge was the same shape as a lance corporal in the Army. I thought to myself, 'I know all the knots, I can splice any rope, box the compass, steer a ship, work the guns, heave the lead. I can scrub decks, paint bulkheads, and do something that none of my present shipmates have done, that is to help coal ship. I have coxwained a motor boat and have now been granted my first good conduct stripe, but I am still only an acting able seaman.' I wonder if the Navy doesn't intend to make H.O.s full able seamen? The sixpence made my pay four and ninepence a day. I still paid Mum five shillings a week allowance. She was worth every penny.

The postman went ashore, taking mail with him to post home, and brought back a nice heavy bundle of mail. Brummie had quite a few letters. Getting post cheered everyone up. I had several letters, they were practically the same, nothing very exciting had happened in Wallisdown. Everyone was alright. Dad had found himself a job washing up in a hotel in Bournemouth. Mum said he called it 'pearl diving'. She said she couldn't keep him indoors – what is the matter with the man? Still don't know if Jock has been called up. Reg was still looking after the garden and working in the market garden. Mum still had her pet chickens. There was no news from Mum about what Ron was doing, still working and going out with his mates I expect. I'm afraid there wasn't much to do in Wallisdown. Mum still didn't seem to be very happy, I got the feeling she would love to go back to Portsmouth. In my letters back to Mum, I told her about the thousands of houses that had been destroyed and the many shops that had been wrecked – Portsmouth was a disaster area, it would take years to rebuild. She would have to resign herself to living in Wallisdown.

The ship was getting ready to leave Hong Kong. Everybody was looking forward to ten days' leave in Auckland. The E.R.A.s had patched up the desalinators, but would they last until we got to Auckland? How the side party were settled for their good works, I do not know. They were a nice little family – lucky to have survived the Japs.

The ship still didn't have a trained medical officer or sick bay attendant, but the coxswain made sure that the sick bay had been supplied with everything required. Acting able seaman Tristram was still in charge, treating the various rashes etc. None of the crew had had to be installed in the hospital ship.

There was leave for both watches. The Geordies behaved themselves.

The depot ship the *Berry Head* was formerly a maintenance ship, so there were still engineers and stores aboard her. Our E.R.A.s had boarded her via the motor boat. There must have been a bit of skulduggery, regarding the acquisition of the bits and pieces needed to keep the desalinators going!

At last the ship was ready to leave. Stores had come on board, we would have to wait and see what food we would have. Tinned stuff I expected, real potatoes for a while and fresh bread (the *Berry Head* had a bakery on board). The Captain had gone ashore in the motor boat, but was back before long. Once back on board, he ordered leading seaman Jessy to take the motor boat round to the falls, where it was hoisted aboard. He spoke to the first lieutenant, who spoke to the forecastle P.O. The ship had full water and fuel tanks and so without pomp or ceremony, the forecastle party weighed anchor and the ship slowly steamed out of the harbour.

Knocker White, who was a proper sailor, having two good-conduct stripes, denoting he had been over seven years in the Navy, and myself, a one-badge acting able seaman H.O., were to take the ship nonstop down to Australia. The coxswain took the ship out of the harbour, and once clear, I took over the wheel. We sailed the South China Sea, passed Manila, into the Sulu Sea, down past Mindanao, into the Celebes Sea, then through the Moluccas Sea, into the Banda Sea. Passing Timor, we sailed into the Arafura Sea.

The ship came down from Hong Kong in the company of another frigate, H.M.S. *Veryan Bay*. The passage down was without incident. The ports were open, hot air passed through the ship. It was around one hundred degrees. Most of the crew were still sleeping up on the deck at night. The water situation was a little better, the desalinators were holding up quite well. Everyone was still being careful with the water though. Bucket baths were still the order of the day. I wondered if the showers on the *Veryan Bay* had been locked! There didn't seem to be a lot of activity on her.

The fresh food, bread and potatoes were soon finished. Frozen beef had been brought on board and cottage pies were made whilst the potatoes lasted. No one fancied roasts or pot mess, it was too hot. There were tinned beans, tomatoes and custard powder. I couldn't see why there wasn't dried egg, like they had during my buffet car days with Frederick Hotels – they must have chickens in Australia? An omelette would have made a nice change! There were plenty of dehydrated potatoes, carrots and cabbage. The cook was very happy to be away from the Japanese, and was once again doing his best with the rubbish he had to cook with, but I knew that a lot of us would rather go hungry than eat it!

When in the Banda Sea, the desalinators had started to give up the ghost again. The Captain decided to make for Thursday Island for repairs. The ship parted company with the *Veryan Bay* and headed for the Torres Straight. The *Whitesand Bay* reached Thursday Island in the Torres Straight, near Cape York, and anchored in the harbour. Hands were piped to dinner. I made do with biscuits, corned beef and Daddies Sauce.

The ship was declared an 'open ship', meaning that anyone could go ashore. The motor boat and sea boat were lowered. Leave was granted from 13.30 until 1900 hours, apparently it gets dark very early in this part of the world. I changed my dress, deciding to go ashore at once, although it was blazing hot. Brummie decided to come as well. We mustered on the quarterdeck. No money was given to us, we were still using Malayan Straits money from Hong Kong.

As there were not that many of us going ashore early, we only needed the motor boat. Down the ladder and into the boat we went. We didn't have far to go and were soon tying up to a wooden jetty. Frippy jumped out of the boat, on to the jetty and soon had her tied up. I and the others jumped out of the boat and we made our way into the shade of the coconut trees. It was good to get off the ship.

Of my companions, I can only remember Brummie and a thin, lanky Scots lad who was always grinning and was as daft as a brush! We wandered along until we found a nice open space, where we sank down to the ground and enjoyed the peace and quiet, it was like being in another world. We didn't know if there were any snakes on Thursday Island, but as we were not far from Australia, and we knew there were snakes there, we hopped up and decided it was time to move on.

Going further through the coconut trees, we came to a wide track and had to decide whether to turn left or right. Brummie said, 'Right', so off we went. Jock, or Haggis as he was better known, was some way ahead of us. He waited for us to catch him up, then told us that there was an open gate around the corner. We found the gate and slowly walking through, keeping an eye out, we spotted an American sailor. He was walking towards us across an open space. He wore his cap 'flat-a-back' and was smoking a cigarette. He waved for us to come forward, which we did – only to stop, dumbfounded at what we saw. It was like a mirage. There in front of us was a stall, similar to the type you see selling fish and chips on the beach in Southend-on-Sea. Attending the stall were two middle-aged white ladies, dressed in green coats, white aprons and wearing green pancake hats. They were as surprised to see us as we were to see them.

They said, 'British sailors? Can't remember seeing British sailors before! What would you like? Coffee and doughnuts or a Coke?' The American sailor arrived and asked for a Coke. One of the ladies handed it to him and off he sauntered, Coke in one hand and fag in the other. Brummie looked at Haggis and me as if to say, 'We joined the wrong Navy!' We seemed to have stumbled across a small American base, though there was no stars-and-stripes flag flying. We settled for coffee and doughnuts. Bliss! 'Another coffee and doughnut please!' 'Certainly,' came the reply.

Thursday Island was inhabited, I supposed by Australians. I had read about the group of islands in the Torres Strait, trading in dried coconut flesh. I think it was called Copra. I've learned since that the population had also been pearl fisherman. The open space must have been the back end of the American base, I expect the stars and stripes was flying at the other end.

There were some locals climbing the coconut trees on the other side of the open space; once up the tree, they were knocking down coconuts. Haggis, who, as I mentioned, was as daft as a brush, now proved it. Watching the locals, he said, 'If they can do it, so can I!' He made for the nearest tree and started to climb. He got about a third of the way up and got stuck. He shouted, 'I can't go any further.' I shouted back, 'Climb back down, very carefully!' He started to climb down and was doing quite well, until, about ten feet from the ground, he slipped and slid the rest of the way down. He was wearing white shorts, which were no protection from the barbed trunk of the coconut tree. By the time he got to the ground, the insides of both his thighs were skinned.

Brummie said, 'We had better get him back to the ship.' Thanking the ladies for their coffee, doughnuts and hospitality, for which they said we were very welcome, we made our way back to the jetty. Once we got there, we started to wave at the ship, hoping that Knocker White would see us. We kept pointing to Haggis' thighs (which must have looked strange!) and waving like mad. I said, 'I reckon if he doesn't get his legs looked at quickly, they will soon start going septic.'

I imagined that the officer of the watch would be reluctant to send the motor boat back so soon, he'd prefer to stick to the stated time, which would have been two hours later. Finally, though, Knocker White got the message and the boat could be seen leaving the ship and making its way to the jetty. Haggis' thighs were beginning to weep, that coconut bark is dangerous! We all got into the motor boat and leading seaman Jessy soon had us back to the ship. Haggis struggled up the ladder, saluted the quartermaster and hobbled off to the sick bay. Brummie explained what had happened to our friend, the sub-lieutenant.

I descended into the mess deck and told them what they had missed. A few shoes came flying my way, which I dodged, saying, 'If Haggis hadn't tried to be Tarzan, me and Brummie would still be there, drinking coffee and eating doughnuts!' I told them about the American sailor, cap 'a flat back', fag in one hand and tin of Coke in the other. Imagine doing that at Whale Island!

Brummie came down into the mess deck and repeated what I had said. It was a very nice, enjoyable afternoon (not so much for Haggis!). The one American sailor that we saw was the only one. I wondered what sort of American base it was, no flag flying? There seemed to be American bases everywhere. Little wonder Admiral King didn't want the Royal Navy out here.

Not wanting any tea, I sat down, like a few others, to write letters. I knew there would not be any mail at Townsville (where we were due to stop), we would have to wait until we got to Sydney. The E.R.A.s had finished the repairs, the ship would leave in the morning. Leading seaman Jessy made a mess kettle of tea. He was a very good leading seaman, he was eventually made up to petty officer.

After a cup of tea, I took my mattress up on deck and found some space under the motor boat, which had been brought back on board. The water had been turned off, so, not being able to wash, I decided to get my head down. The tannoy woke me at 0600 hours. I rolled up my mattress and hurried down to borrow a bucket and have a good wash and sponge down. Biscuits, jam, a fag and a cup of tea, for breakfast.

Chapter Twenty-Six

H.M.S. Whitesand Bay – Thursday Island to Townsville, Australia

At 0900 hours the cable party fell in, and the anchor was carefully hoisted and weighed. The ship slowly left this lovely little island, where I and a few others enjoyed a few hours of civilisation (Haggis may not agree!). The ship turned into the Torres Strait, around Cape York, into the Great Barrier Reef, making its way down to Townsville, where, to our annoyance, because of Australian quarantine laws, the ship was told that it could not tie up alongside the jetty, but had to anchor three to four hundred yards away, meaning that there was no shore leave, unless the motor boat and sea boat were lowered and hoisted back up in the morning.

It was decided to lower the boats. Liberty was given from 1800 hours until 22.55. Leave was given to the port watch first. Those wanting to go ashore mustered on the quarterdeck at 1800 hours, station cards were handed in. First, the motor boat was loaded with liberty men, then the sea boat. This was manned by two able seaman, proper sailors. A tow was passed from the whaler (sea boat) to the motor boat. Leading seaman Jessy secured it to the stern, then carefully pulled away and headed for the jetty. He approached the jetty at an angle, slipping the tow rope, which was quickly pulled in by the bowman in the whaler. The coxswain of the whaler skilfully brought it alongside the jetty. There was an Australian sailor on the jetty, who took the lines of the whaler and secured them. Leading seaman Jessy then took the motor boat around in a circle, coming in alongside the jetty, in front of the whaler. The Aussie sailor secured the motor boat's lines also.

I stepped on to the jetty with Brummie, Yarker, and a lad from Leicester. On the jetty, there was a table and chair. Fixed to the table, there was a pole about eight feet high, at the top, a light bulb had been fitted, which was switched on. The Aussie sailor sat at the table doing paperwork.

We four strode off into the town. What a sight it was! Bright lights, saloon bars with hitching rails outside, like cowboys use for tying up their horses. There was one wide road that went the whole length of the town. In the centre of the town, there was a wide zebra crossing, going diagonally from one side of the road to the other. This was the only place to cross. Apparently, some of the lads did not use the crossing, and got an earful from the local policeman!

We found a café and all went in. I ordered a pint of milk, and drank it straight down. I then ordered steak, eggs and bread and butter, slowly savouring each mouthful. The others were doing the same. Next we had a cup of tea, then sat back, very contented. Eventually, Brummie said, 'Let's go.' We paid our bill using sterling, said, 'Thanks and goodbye' – leaving a good tip.

We strolled out into a very warm evening. It was barely 1900 hours but it was already dark. We went for a walk, enjoying the feel of terra firma under our feet. We found a saloon bar and soon discovered that there were no pint glasses. The Aussies use schooners, so four schooners of beer were ordered. There were several tough, sun-burned Aussies in the bar, they wore bush hats, they were friendly. Brummie pulled out a packet of Senior Service and they immediately asked if they could have a Tailor Made. Brummie held out the pack, and they all took one.

Aussies seem to like rolling their own cigarettes, but unfortunately, although there was tobacco to be had, there was a shortage of cigarette papers. In future, I would have to remember to go into the gents to get my cigarettes out, otherwise I'd be surrounded by Aussies all the time! Surely they have Tailor Mades in Australia?

Our new Aussie friends were very friendly, one of them asked, 'Where are you going?' The lad from Leicester said, 'Auckland.' 'You'll like it there,' came the reply. 'It's very old fashioned.' I wondered if the Aussies and Kiwis were very friendly with each other.

Yarker said, 'One more schooner then we'll move on to another bar.' We drank up, and then saying 'goodbye' to everyone in the bar we moved on up the road. We didn't see a single woman in the town. Walking almost out of the town, we came across another saloon bar, no women in there either! Some of our lads were in there having a good time with the Aussies.

We never saw a car or any other form of transport, it seemed like a real cowboy town. I said, 'We better make a move.' We walked back the length of the road and through the town, then turned into the road that led down to the jetty. Lying in the middle of the road was a young jock. Usually, a nice quiet lad. He was as drunk as a skunk! Too much of the golden amber! A couple of us hoicked him up on to Brummies broad shoulders, who carted him down to the jetty and laid him on the table. Fortunately, the sailor had gone.

The wind was rising, as was the sea. It gave me a strange feeling to see the ship anchored up in the Great Barrier Reef. The nearest land being the Solomon Islands. The liberty men started to gather on the jetty. We watched the boat and the whaler leave the ship. The sea was now rather choppy. Some of us were going to get wet. The whaler came alongside the jetty. The motor boat turned in a circle and tied up in front of the whaler. One or two liberty men needed assistance getting into the boats, including jock, who was still out for the count. Once all aboard, leading seaman Jessy waited a few more minutes for any latecomers. A couple of sailors came sprinting down the jetty and just made it. A few more were too late.

The motor boat left the jetty and straight away the whaler was taking in water over the bows. I was in the whaler, getting soaking wet. Jessy took the motor boat as close as he could to the ship's side, then let go the tow. The bowman quickly pulled in the tow rope. Lines had been thrown down from the stern of the ship and the whaler was quickly secured.

The rise and fall of the ship was about six feet, we could almost see the keel. There was a rope ladder, 'never had the pleasure of the ship's ladder.' Liberty men had to wait until the whaler rose with the waves, then jump up on to the ladder. Willing hands then pulled them over the side, on to the deck. Once all liberty men were safely on board, soaking wet, the whaler was carefully brought around to the stern, and very strongly secured. The bowman and coxswain had the job of bailing her out, then had the job of climbing up over the stern and inboard.

It was now the motor boat's turn to disembark. Somebody mentioned sharks, that cheered them up on the motor boat! Little jock, still under the influence, had to be hauled aboard. Two strong seaman stood either side of the rope ladder, then two liberty men at the stern of the motor boat, grabbed jock and at the top of a wave heaved him up, and he was caught by the seaman aboard the ship and hauled on board, then taken down to the mess deck. Everyone else got back on board without incident.

The Captain insisted on the motor boat being hoisted on board. The whaler could stay tied up astern. Leading seaman Jessy and Frippy brought the motor boat around to the starboard side of the ship and it was hoisted aboard. All this rigmarole caused by Australian rules!

The next morning, the whaler was hoisted aboard and the anchor was weighed. The Captain took the ship alongside the jetty – whether he asked permission or not, I do not know. The crew all thought he should have taken the ship alongside the jetty the day before.

The crew who had been left behind the day before, were soon on board. If they had had the sense to go to the local police station and report that they had missed the ship, and would the kind policeman please give them a note showing the time that they had arrived at the police station to report their dilemma, they would not get it in the neck as much as those who had simply waited for the ship to come and get them. I expected that they would get a 10A, extra work would be found for them, there would be loss of pay, loss of rum and loss of leave when the ship reached Sydney. Little jock, nursing a fat head and feeling sick, thanked all who helped him, said he would never touch another drink!

Then the tannoy shouted 'hands to stations for leaving harbour'. The port watch didn't get any leave. There may have been differences of opinion between the Captain and the Harbour Board after the previous night's difficulties and danger of losing a liberty man overboard. Anyway, the ship's lines were let go, and we proceeded into the Great Barrier Reef, where the ship started to pitch high out of the water. I realised that the Great Barrier Reef was much different to what I thought it was.

Chapter Twenty-Seven

H.M.S. Whitesand Bay –
Townsville to Sydney, Australia

The coxswain took the ship out of the harbour and indicated for Knocker White to take over the wheel – his was the forenoon watch. The ship was pitching differently now that we were away from land and out in the open sea. One minute we were walking uphill, then next minute walking downhill.

Hands were piped to dinner. We were still having the dehydrated veg. I took over the wheel, having the afternoon watch, 1200 noon until 1600 hours. The ship was lifting so high out of the water, then coming down with such a crash that the whole ship shuddered. The Asdic probe had been lowered and for some reason could not now be raised. The waves must have bent it. The Captain was in his sea cabin, a few of the crew were not feeling too good. Jock wished he could die!

Chits were going around the mess decks, asking what each man wished to do with his ten days' leave when in Auckland. He could have ten days on a farm, or with a family, or please yourself what he did. Being a town boy, I decided I would love to see what life was like on a farm.

The ship was quite difficult to handle, first being pushed

263

to starboard, then over to port. I had not seen seas like it, worse even than when we left Labuan. I had my work cut out, moving the wheel to starboard, then quickly back to port. After a couple of hours, my shoulders began to ache. I hoped that the steering motor, positioned in the after-steering room, didn't pack up, it was getting a fair amount of work. The ship had increased speed. I'd be glad when my relief turned up. How long will this weather last? It was definitely getting cooler.

We had at last, stopped taking the mepacrine. I was still a yellowish-brown colour, with yellow eyes, the same as the rest of the seamen. It was said that Lady Astor proposed, in the House of Commons, that all servicemen and women who had served abroad should wear a badge to denote that fact. If she did propose such a thing, she did not win.

My relief turned up at 1600 hours, he said in the voice pipe tube that the quartermaster of the dog watches had taken over. He could not tell what course he was to be steering, as the ship was all over the place. I said, 'Cheerio, I'll see you in four hours' and made my way down to the mess, where the sick, lame and lazy were beginning to stir. I ate ship's biscuits with Daddies Sauce. I hoped that when the ship finally got to Sydney, the stores manager would have a list as long as his arm.

I thought that it would be coming into spring in Australia. So the crew would have to turn into blue uniforms. I got my head down, as did the bosun's mate, for a couple of hours. At 2000 hours I made my way back to the wheelhouse and reported to the bridge that the quartermaster of the first watch had taken over the wheel. The ship was much steadier now. I could not really understand why I, an H.O., had been made quartermaster. I did not mind though, better than scrubbing bulkheads!

The weather was slowly getting better. At 2200 hours, the

Fig 7. H.M.S. Whitesand Bay

bosun's mate went and made mugs of kye (cocoa), which was very welcome. Having increased speed, the ship would soon be in Sydney.

The rest of the voyage was without incident. Nothing had changed with the ship, water was still restricted due to the problems with the desalinators, and we still had to make it down to Auckland. Admiral King had certainly made life difficult for us!

At last the ship reached Sydney. Dressed in our blue uniforms, we lined the ship. The coxswain had taken the wheel. I did not know it, but I had steered the ship for the last time. Entering harbour, the ship tied up alongside the *Veryan Bay*. Leave was given until 22.50. At 1800 hours a few liberty men appeared. On the way down to Sydney, everybody had been given their pay in sterling. The liberty men made their way into Sydney. There was to be another liberty boat at 1900 hours. Port watch were off-duty, starboard watch were on-duty. I had the first watch of 2000 hours until midnight.

At 22.30 the first liberty men started to return to the ship. As they returned their station cards, they were asked what they thought of Sydney. Apparently, the pubs shut at 1800 hours, they were not very happy! It was called the six o'clock swill or something like that. The pubs lined their bars with full schooners. As soon as the workers knocked off, they raced into the pubs and drank as much beer as they could, before the pubs closed. There were quite a few drunks around as a result – best to keep out of their way!

Hotels didn't have the same rules, you could go in and order scrambled egg on toast and a cup of tea, sit back quietly and then order a schooner of beer – no problems, you could stay all evening. They were pleased to have your company, especially if there were three or four of you.

Whether we would be able to enjoy this hospitality, would of course, depend on how long the ship was to stay in Sydney. The E.R.A.s were bodging up the desalinators again, for the last time, they hoped!

I was relieved at midnight, I slept on the lockers until woken up to go and take the morning watch, 0400 hours to 0800 hours. I would then have twenty-four hours off – time to catch up with my dobeing. A small water tanker had come alongside, the water tanks were filled up, so there was plenty of water now to have a good bucket wash down and do your dobeing all at the same time. I had the washroom to myself.

All hands had turned to. Able seaman Derek Booth was cook of the mess. No stores had come aboard yet, so we still had to put up with the dehydrated rubbish. Derek said that now it was much cooler, he would make a pot mess, I said, 'Good luck!' I decided to sit down and write a letter, telling them at home that the ship had reached Sydney and that I was looking forward to my ten days' leave on a farm in Auckland. I said that I hoped they were all well, and for Dad to give my best to Paddy and Mr. Habgood – I hoped to see them all in the not too distant future.

'Stand easy' was piped. The hands clattered down the ladder into the mess. Derek had the tea made. We only had ten minutes – just time for a cup of tea and a smoke, before 'out pipes'. It reminded me of when I was training at Collingwood – the class were doing foot drill, I had been suffering from toothache for some days. The class was marching, the P.O.G.I. called the class to halt. I was shaking with pain, not marching properly. The P.O.G.I. said, 'What's the matter with you?' I told him that I had toothache. He said, 'At stand easy, report to the sick bay. Tell them you have to be back by out pipes.' We then continued marching. At last 'stand easy' was piped. I raced toward the sick bay, my rifle in one hand, pulling my webbing equipment off with the other. Racing into the sick bay I said to the sick bay attendant, 'I have terrible toothache and I have to be back on parade by out pipes!'

He went into the surgery and explained the situation to the doctor, who told me to come in and sit in the chair. He quickly examined my mouth, and found the offending tooth. He gave me an injection, waited about a minute, then pulled it out. A quick rinse, then the S.B.A. helped me back into my webbing equipment. I grabbed my rifle and raced back to my class, just as 'out pipes' was sounded. The class continued marching, and I continued spitting out blood. It's amazing what can be accomplished in ten minutes – it seems that Navy doctors can also pull teeth!

After 'out pipes' I finished writing my letter home. It was Saturday, starboard watch were off-duty. Derek had done quite a good job with the pot mess and had also managed to make a Manchester tart. Not a bad meal. Stores were coming aboard the next day, Sunday.

Liberty boats were at 13.00 and 13.30. I decided to go ashore, and at 13.30 handed in my station card, which was examined by the sub-lieutenant. Then off I went, with my yellow-brown tan and yellow eyes, to see the sights of Sydney.

It was like a hot summer's day in England, the shops were very busy, the streets were full of people. The girls (called Sheilas by the Australian youth) were in their summer dresses, women were pushing prams along the pavements. The pubs were quite full, cars motoring along the roads. I thought again, how great it was to be back in civilisation!

I found my way to the nearest bar, ordered a schooner and sat down in the corner, quietly enjoying watching the world go by. I went to the toilet and lit a cigarette, came out and ordered another schooner. I decided I would drink up and then go and find somewhere to eat.

Finishing my beer, I said, 'Cheerio' and left the pub. I was walking down the street, when a large black car pulled up alongside me, the window opened and a voice shouted from within, 'Have you got any cigarettes for sale?' I answered, 'Sorry, no.' The voice shouted back 'pommy b★★★★★d!' then drove off. I was quite taken aback! Thought to myself, 'That wasn't very civil!' I carried on walking, slightly shaken. Knocker White had been down to Australia before the war, in a cruiser. I remembered that he had warned us that we might be called pommy b★★★★★ds. Brummie had asked him where the pommy had come from. Knocker had explained that it might be from when prisoners came over from England as they were known as 'Prisoners of Mother England' (POME), but he wasn't certain.

Brummie said, 'That sounds wrong, we should be calling them pommy b★★★★★ds!' Knocker replied, 'They have always, and will always, call us pommy b★★★★★ds! If they call you it in a funny way, fair enough, but if they are nasty about it, punch them!' With those wise words echoing in my head, I carried on walking. We all had plenty of cigarettes, but no one was prepared to take a chance on selling them, not like on the *Alresford*!

It was strange to see Wrens walking about the streets, looking in the shops as if they were at home. What a lovely draft to have, to be sent down to Sydney, must feel like a holiday, though there must have been extra work to do, especially since the Royal Navy did not have the co-operation of Admiral King.

It was time to find somewhere to eat. I eventually found a nice-looking hotel, went in and found a table. I ordered a steak with egg and bread and butter, which was lovely. I stayed in the hotel until the six o'clock swill was well over. If I hadn't, I guessed there would be a good chance of being called a pommy b★★★★★d again. After such a big meal and with a contented stomach, I was in no state for fisticuffs!

It was getting dark, I thought that if it was a clear night, I should be able to see the Southern Cross. The shops were closed, so were the pubs. I decided to stay for another hour or so. The owners were nice, asking where I came from and telling me that they had relations in the UK. They were glad that the war was over and that their relatives had made it through safe and sound.

I paid my bill, left a tip (the meal was worth it!), shook hands with the owners, and said my goodbyes. They were too polite to comment on my yellow eyes and yellow-brown skin. I kept forgetting how strange we must look to people, especially those of us seamen who had been exposed to the sun.

I walked out into a pleasantly warm evening and made my way back to the ship. The Southern Cross was high in the sky. Making my way into the dockyard , I crossed the *Veryan Bay* on to the *Whitesand Bay*, where I picked up my station card and went down into the mess deck.

Knocker was playing cards with three shipmates. I said, 'Knocker, you were right, I did get called a pommy b★★★★★d!' Knocker said, 'What did you do?' I replied, 'Nothing, they were in a car, wanted cigarettes, but I didn't have any, so they shouted pommy b★★★★★d at me and drove off!' 'Well, I did warn you,' he said, 'Brits will always be pommy b★★★★★★s to some Aussies!' I said, 'Well, apart from that, I had a very nice afternoon and evening, although I haven't got any pay left.' With that, I fetched and slung my hammock, went for a good wash, said goodnight to Brummie, and fell into a contented sleep.

At 0600 hours, 'hands to rise and shine' was piped. Plenty of mutters and moans. We were still waiting for a proper meal on board ship. Although, we were lucky that there was plenty of water. I had the afternoon watch, so had no need to hurry. I went for a good bucket bath, had breakfast (jam and biscuits), then went up on deck to do my dobeing. I made a washing line, and hung my clothes on it. They would not take long to dry and would soon be ready to iron.

I was sitting in the mess, when the forecastle P.O. came down and told me to report to the divisional officer, lieutenant Bullock. Putting on my cap, I hurried along to the division office. There were five other seamen in there, I can only remember one of them. His name was Mills. He looked like a film star called Cesar Romero. He was tall, with dark wavy hair, like a Spaniard. His nickname was Cesar.

The D.O. said, 'You six will be leaving the ship tomorrow, as your demobilisation numbers have been received. Other numbers have been received also, but the ship can only allow six members to leave. You six must have all your gear on the jetty at

1400 hours tomorrow. A lorry will come to fetch your gear, then a coach will take you to a naval establishment called H.M.S. *Golden Hind*. You will wait there for transport back to the U.K.'

We stood there, stunned. I knew that Brummie would be disappointed, as would all the other H.O.s, not to be going home also. I trooped back to the mess deck and down the ladder, with my dobeing in hand. In the mess were Lightning, the mess deck dodger, Yarker, the bosun's mate, and the cooks of the mess. I didn't know how I felt really. Glad to be going home, but sad to be leaving so many of my fellow H.O. shipmates behind. It would be hard for Cesar and me to tell the other H.O.s that we were leaving, when it seemed that they had to stay.

I had the afternoon watch, so had a quick wash, and changed into my number three blue suit. 'Hands to dinner' was piped early, but I disregarded the call, knowing that stores would be coming the next day. I ran up the ladder, and took over the afternoon watch. News had spread. I felt awful. The thought that Brummie and all the other H.O.s would have to go back to Hong Kong, once their six weeks in Auckland and ten days' leave per watch, was over, seemed unfair.

Cesar approached the sub-lieutenant to ask if we could go down to Auckland for our leave, then leave the ship when it came back up to Sydney. He said to speak to the first lieutenant about it, but we knew what the answer would be. If we wanted to go down to Auckland, we would not be able to leave the ship when it returned to Sydney, we would have to go to Hong Kong. So that was a 'no' for us.

If the ship's Captain had been the Captain from the *Alresford*, I may have asked about becoming a proper sailor, but sadly our commanding officers had knocked any idea of staying in the Royal Navy out of my mind. I would rather join the Merchant Navy, or

271

Mercantile Marine, as Dad insisted it was called and thus so did I!

I said to Yarker, the bosun's mate and an H.O., 'I do not know what to say, it's really taken me aback – being demobbed is the last thing I expected!' He replied, 'It's taken all the H.O.s by surprise, but someone had to be the first, you Cesar and the others must have the lowest demob numbers.' I said, 'Yes, that must be it.' No more was said about it during the watch.

At 1600 hours, hands were dismissed, all the seamen made their way back to their messes, prior to having a wash before tea. I turned over the watch to Derek Booth, I wasn't sure if he was a proper sailor or a H.O., I did not stay long enough to start a conversation.

I went down into the mess, removing my collar and jumper, ready to go for a wash. I looked around at Brummie and the others in the mess, said, 'Well, I did not expect that, I knew it had to happen sometime, but I didn't think I'd be one of the first.' Brummie replied, 'Someone had to be first, your luck was in. I would have liked to come with you!' I said, 'I wish you were coming too, sorry that you're not. Anyway, I'm off for a wash.' Brummie said, 'So am I', so we grabbed our washing gear and made our way to the washroom. We didn't speak. That's the way things were in the Navy, you never knew when you were likely to be drafted. I know this was different, because I was going home, not being drafted to another ship, but just the same – I would not see any of them again. Eventually, all the other H.O.s would be demobbed. Of course, the proper sailors had no option, they would be staying with the ship, but they too could be drafted somewhere else at any time.

With all of this running through my mind, I had a good wash and went to find something to eat. I decided to get my head down for an hour or so, before going on my last 2000 hours to midnight watch. Waking after a couple of hours, I washed my face and dressed ready for what I thought would be my last watch in the Royal Navy.

I had a talk with leading seaman Jessy, who although having kept a still tongue in a wise head during all of our trials and tribulations aboard the *Whitesand Bay*, did tell me that the Captain and first lieutenant were the worst he had ever served under and that the P.O.G.I. was of the same opinion (the coxswain was like the invisible man!). I said, 'I'm glad I'm a H.O. and can leave the ship!'

Leading seaman Jessy went to make a cup of tea. When he brought it back, I thanked him and said, 'It has been a pleasure to serve with you. This could have been a happy ship, but I think the Captain would have preferred the war to continue, so that he could get his D.S.C. with a crew of proper sailors, not H.O.s, I reckon the first lieutenant thinks the same. I'm sorry that you have to go back to Hong Kong with them.' Jessy replied, 'I'm working on becoming a petty officer and move on.' I am pleased to say, that I found out many years later that he did indeed become a P.O.

I said, 'I cannot understand why I am still an H.O. I was made a quartermaster, but not a full able seaman!' He replied, 'Well Fred, I think you are above the average able seaman, that's why!' I laughed and said, 'I have had to help coal ship, I don't suppose there are many on here that have had to do that!' He replied, 'None I expect, I certainly haven't!' With that I went up on the deck to take over the first watch.

It was a clear, warm night, the sky was full of stars, I don't think I had ever seen so many. Yarker was rather quiet. He didn't comment on the stars. I said, 'Now that the Navy is starting to send H.O.s home, it shouldn't be long before all are demobbed.' He said, 'I hope so.' Yarker was a very good footballer. I think he was on Preston North End's books. I was glad when the liberty men started to come back on board, somewhat 'happy' – laughing and joking as they collected their station cards and went off to their messes.

The officer of the watch was my 'friend' the sub-lieutenant. I kept away from him. He did not know how to treat men. I found out years later that when he got back to England, he held a senior position in a famous cathedral – strange, bearing in mind his lack of respect and any kindness toward the men on the ship. He was only a part-time sailor himself, always seasick – why he thought he was above us, I do not know. The liberty men coming back on board, soon shut up when they saw him. What a difference between him and the old navigating officer on board the *Alresford* – he was never happier than when he was talking about the stars and navigation to anyone who would listen, the more the merrier. I learned such a lot from him.

Midnight came and I turned the watch over to my relief. I went down to the mess, had a quick wash, grabbed my pillow and laid on the lockers, not bothering with my hammock. I did not think I was going to get much sleep, as I was back on watch at 0400 hours. At 03.45 the duty-bosun's mate gave Yarker and I a shake and we got ready to go on watch. I took over from the duty quartermaster. There was nothing to report. Yarker took over the quarterdeck, in case the officer of the watch appeared, whilst I, with torch in hand walked around the ship, checking the mooring ropes and checking the wheelhouse. There was no requirement to check the water/air temperature like on the *Alresford*. After completing the inspection of the ship, I went back to the quarterdeck to make an entry in the night-duty book that everything was secure, including the mooring lines. The officer of the watch did not appear.

At 0600 hours, the tannoy sounded 'hands to rise and shine'. The officer of the watch appeared. At 0800 hours my relief appeared and I and Yarker made our way down to the mess. I quickly undressed and went for a good bucket bath, dressed in my number three blues, had some breakfast, biscuits, cheese and Daddies Sauce. I wondered how much cheese and Daddies Sauce I had eaten in the last three years or more. However much it was, this should be my last breakfast of it.

I tipped out my kitbag to sort things out, then started to repack it. I had some ironing to do first, I wanted everything to be clean and smart. My ditty box went into my kitbag. I packed my brown case with a change of underwear and toilet gear, plus plenty of cigarettes.

At 12 midday, 'hands to dinner' was piped. Frippy was the duty quartermaster. An H.O. called Ernie Mosely had made a steak pie, with pussers peas (which had been soaked overnight), mashed carrots and potatoes. There was Chinese wedding cake for afters. Ernie came from Birmingham, you could not wish for a nicer chap. He was much older than me or Cesar. I thought that he should have been demobbed before either of us. It was a quiet dinner.

A few minutes before 'all hands to fall in on the quarterdeck' was piped, all the hands in the first part of the starboard watch (the second part were amidships) came and shook mine and Cesar's hand and wished us all the best. Then the tannoy called the hands to fall in immediately, followed by a call for the six ratings leaving the ship to report to the divisional office.

I put my cap on, and made my way to the office. Lieutenant Bullock gave me what pay I was entitled to, he told me that my service papers would be forwarded on to H.M.S. *Golden Hind*. I said, 'Thank you', not to my surprise, he held his hand out and we shook hands. I then made my way back to the mess deck to check that I had packed everything. I had already lashed my hammock.

At 13.45, Brummie came down to the mess deck to help me with my gear. Being Brummie, he took my kitbag. I had my hammock and brown case. Once on the quarterdeck, I shook hands with Frippy and Brummie, then carried my gear across the *Veryan Bay* to the jetty, to wait for the lorry. The other five H.O.s were doing the same. I shook hands again with Brummie, we had become good friends. He made his way back across the *Veryan Bay*, I never saw him again.

Chapter Twenty-Eight

H.M.S. Golden Hind –
Sydney to Portsmouth and Home

We had a long wait on the jetty for the lorry to collect our gear, but it eventually came and we loaded up. While we waited for the coach to pick us up, we heard the familiar 'hands to stations for leaving harbour, hands to line ship'. Then the *Whitesand Bay* slowly went astern, passed the *Veryan Bay*, and steamed sedately out of Sydney Harbour. I and the others stood to attention and saluted as she passed by – seeing all our shipmates for the last time. I thought what a shame it was that she had not been a happier ship.

The coach appeared and we all climbed on board. The first thing Cesar did was ask the driver if there were any pubs on the way to the *Golden Hind*. The driver said, 'No, but there is a hotel, though I'm not sure that you will be able to go in. I'll stop there and ask.'

After about ten miles, the hotel appeared and true to his word, the driver stopped, parked on the forecourt and went in to ask if we could go in for a drink. He came out saying, 'Yes, you can go in.' Cesar led us into a very posh lounge area, where astonished, very well-dressed men and women, who had never seen British sailors before, welcomed us. The men were wearing bow ties and white evening jackets, with very well-creased black trousers and highly polished shoes. The women were in very fashionable dresses and high heels.

We must have appeared a very strange species to them, but they made us very welcome. Cesar was in his element. They asked us which ship we had been on and where had we been. Cesar told them that the ship had been on escort duty and anti-pirate patrol in the South China Sea. When the word 'pirate' was mentioned, Cesar found himself surrounded by women, wanting to know more. For the next hour he told them how, apparently, the ship had chased pirates all over the South China Sea and beyond.

The men were interested in where we came from in the U.K. and what it had been like during the air raids. They told us that they had been rationed in some things, for example cigarette papers were in short supply at the moment. They enjoyed the Senior Service which we offered them. Did Cesar give all his cigarettes away to the ladies, I wonder?

The driver was getting agitated, he was keen to get going. The ladies wanted us to stay, but common sense eventually prevailed and we said our 'goodbyes'. If we had stayed much longer, I think Cesar would have been married! We climbed on board the coach, the ladies and blokes (as men were called in Australia) were waving, the ladies blowing kisses to Cesar, and he blowing them back. He was a real ladies' man!

It did not take long to travel the other eight miles to H.M.S. *Golden Hind*. The gates were open when the coach arrived, no sentries to be seen. The driver drove through and stopped. We all stepped off the coach, which drove off, leaving us stranded.

We wandered around until a face appeared in a window – the window opened and Cesar told the face that we had just come from H.M.S. *Whitesand Bay* – the information did not appear to register with the face, but he did say that he thought a lorry had taken some kitbags and hammocks to hut 23. He pointed us in the right direction and told us to go and have a look – everything else could be sorted out tomorrow, then the face vanished.

H.M.S. *Golden Hind* was no more than a lot of huts, running vertically and horizontally across the camp. Those running vertically were administrative huts and stores etc. Those running horizontally were for the troops. We wandered around, everybody must have had their heads down, as there was no one to be seen. We finally found hut 23. The face was right, our gear was there. Inside the hut consisted of a long table with bench stools along either side. There were hammock rails to sling our hammocks. Nothing comfortable about the place at all. We sat either side of the table, looking at each other. How long were we to be here?

We decided to go for a walk around to find where the mess hall, ablutions and canteen and regulatory office etc. were. As we wandered around, the tannoy sounded 'hands to tea'. A few figures appeared, we followed them into the mess hall where bread and jam or marmalade, a nice cake and mugs of tea were available. The bread was new and crusty, we all thoroughly enjoyed it. Afterwards we went back to the hut. I picked a place and hung my hammock, then took my collar and jumper off, grabbed my toilet gear and a towel and with the others wandered over to the ablutions. When we got there, low and behold there were showers! I had a good wash, promised myself a shower the next day.

We all returned to the hut, put our collars and jumpers back on and went out to find the canteen. It turned out to be a pretty good canteen, with barmaids serving the beer and a few bar snacks available, which I couldn't remember having in any Naafi before. We found a table, and had a couple of schooners. There were quite a few inmates enjoying their beer; where they had been all day, I have no idea.

There was a variety show on that night, but we decided to give it a miss and made our way back to hut 23. When we got back, we found three more ratings inside, they were all smoking and drinking beer, which is a crime in the Navy (the drinking beer, not the smoking). Suddenly into the hut strode an officer, a chief petty officer and an escort. The three drinking beer were handcuffed and taken away. The officer then came up to us and asked who the leading seaman was. Cesar said there was no leading seaman. He looked at us all, then back at me, because I still had my jumper on. He said, 'You with the badge, what's going on?' I said, 'We have just arrived today, off the frigate H.M.S. *Whitesand Bay*, which is on her way to Auckland.' He replied, 'I don't believe you', and with that, the C.P.O. handcuffed me and I was led away, protesting that we really had only just arrived that day. Apparently, officer rounds had not been carried out for weeks, but someone had snitched on the three ratings drinking beer.

I was taken to the guard room, my handcuffs were taken off and I was shoved into a cell. The door clanged behind me. I told them that all they had to do was phone the harbour authorities, who would confirm that the ship had left today, but it was no good, they were not listening, so all I could do was stretch out on the wooden bunk, with my cap as a pillow and go to sleep.

The door clanged open in the morning, and I was told that I could go. I put on my cap and marched out of the guard room, turned left and marched out. I suddenly realised that I had marched out of the camp and was heading for Sydney! I quickly turned around and hurried back into the camp. When I got back to Hut 23, I was met by some very relieved shipmates. Cesar said, 'I don't fancy the chances of those three that were taken away!' We all agreed that they were for the high jump.

It was still early, so I went for a wash then waited for the call to breakfast. Breakfast consisted of porridge, bread and jam or marmalade. No chance of cheese or Daddies Sauce. After breakfast, we made our way to the regulating office, to report we had left the *Whitesand Bay* yesterday, and to do our joining routine. The C.P.O. told us that there was no evening leave, or leave of any sort, so no station cards needed.

Golden Hind, such a posh name for such a crummy bunch of huts, was eighteen miles from Sydney. There was no way of getting there. The camp was surrounded by countryside, it was built on an old racecourse. The C.P.O. asked for our names and numbers and told us that we were in the port watch. He told us that hands are called to rise and shine at 0600 hours, breakfast at 0700, fall in on parade at 0800 hours, where names will be called and answered. Names called would be given work, those not called would be dismissed. Dinner at midday. We should fall in on parade again at 1300 hours. Those names called for work and answered, would resume work. Everybody would be dismissed at 1600 hours, except the duty watch, tea would be at 1700 hours, the duty watch may, on occasion, have a late tea. He then said, 'Go back to your huts and clean them. Everything you need will be in a locker, now push off!' So off we went!

The Navy had invented a new breed of rating, called 'leading patrolman'. They wore a badge like a crown on their right sleeve. They seemed to think that they were the cat's whiskers! Seeing some coming our way, we turned around and went the other way – out of sight, out of mind, as the old saying goes.

We made a detour back to the hut and changed into our boiler suits. 'Stand easy' was called. There was nothing to eat or drink, so we had a smoke. 'Out pipes' sounded, we stayed where we were, so that was it for the morning. Midday came and 'hands to dinner' was called. I was looking forward to this. There was nothing like the Navy's soup. I don't know whose recipe it was, but as I have mentioned before, every naval establishment had the same wonderful soup! Dinner was great, steak pie, mashed potato, cabbage and peas, then fruit and custard. Never had a dinner like it – three courses!

We made our way back to the hut to wait for the rum bosun to fetch the rum. One of the shipmates, can't remember his name, made his way to the rum store. When he came back, the mess kettle was almost half full. Cesar said, 'Where did you get that lot from?' The shipmate said, 'I asked for hut 23's rum and this is what I was issued with!' Cesar said, 'Pour out our tots, the rest must belong to those who have done a runner!' I said, 'I am going to have my tot and no more, I'm not going to muck up any chance of going home!' The others agreed. It would break the hearts of many old sailors to see rum being poured away, even if it was two of water and one of rum!

At 1300 hours, the tannoy told us to fall in on parade. Our names were called and answered. The chosen few were to go back to their jobs. The rest were dismissed back to their huts, with nothing to do. We learned that Australia had to be cleared of all servicemen and women. They also wanted to find and expel any deserters. A bounty of £20 would be paid to anybody turning in a deserter. It was a great opportunity for any young lady who had been 'let down' by a deserter, to get her own back and claim the £20! We all dreaded the thought of being called to report to the regulating office, to be told that we had to go off to Darwin, or some other place in Australia, to bring back a deserter. You could be gone for days!

Deserters were being brought in every day. Some were

dressed ordinary, some were dressed like barons!! If any became stroppy, the leading patrolman would take them into the prisoner's baggage store – a hammock mattress would be tied around them, then three or four of our gallant patrolman would punch their lights out; punches being to the body, via the hammock mattress, which meant that there would be no marks. The face was never touched, only the body. The deserter would be left on the floor. The leading patrolman ruled the roost!

We were told during our joining routine, that sometimes the duty watch may have a late tea. If we, the port watch, were on-duty and at 1600 hours, when the parade was usually dismissed, were told to 'stand fast – duty watch'. All would groan', the reason being that a master-at-arms (MAA), would appear from behind the guard house, behind him would be a line of handcuffed deserters. When they had all been brought out, the first deserter would be called in front of the M.A.A., who would read a warrant, that was as long as your arm, full of 'dos' and don'ts', then he would state, ninety days in prison to be served in Colombo, the deserter would be taken away and the next would be brought before the M.A.A. The same warrant would be read and the deserter would be given, say, sixty days to be served in Colombo, and so it went on, deserter after deserter brought before the M.A.A., all having the same warrant read to them and given sixty or ninety days, all to be served in Colombo. It wasn't until the last deserter had received his prison length that we were dismissed to go and have some tea.

The deserters would have to wait for transport to Colombo, which could take any length of time – they then had the trip to Colombo, however long that may take, before starting to serve their prison sentence.

So the days went by, doing nothing, not even told to sweep

up fag ends. It was getting much warmer. Deserters were brought in from time to time. Where they were kept I don't know, there must have been other cells somewhere else. There were so many of the poor devils waiting to be transported to Colombo. Was it worth deserting? I decided not!

One morning, on parade, we were told we would be going home on H.M.S. *Indefatigable*, a fleet air-craft carrier. She was being turned into a floating hospital. All hospital buildings were being emptied of sick military personnel and would be moved to the *Indefatigable*. I presumed that the flight deck would have to have all beds bolted to the deck, and patients strapped into their beds. Accommodation would also be needed for nurses and wrens.

I and all the others who had been loafing about in hut 23 were quite happy doing nothing other than falling in and falling out, having dinner, then our tot of rum and getting our heads down – 'What's wrong with that?' 'Nothing,' we thought!

Sadly our peaceful and comfortable life was shattered. We all fell in one morning on parade. After having our names called and answered we were told to have all our gear outside the hut at 1000 hours. All of us were waiting for passage home, as passengers. Passengers? Passengers? That was a joke, the Navy doesn't have ratings as passengers!

After loading all our gear into lorries, we boarded the coaches which had arrived to take us back to Sydney. Arriving in Sydney, we were taken to the dockyard and H.M.S. *Indefatigable*, where we told that we were to be a 'working party' – what a surprise!

The aircraft carrier was a monster compared to the *Whitesand Bay*. A space had been made for us and leaving our hammocks on the jetty, we lugged our kitbags up along the gang plank and dropped them there, then went back for our hammocks and little brown cases. There were ratings loafing about, I guessed that they must be ship's company. We were there to do the work.

The petty officer in charge said, 'You are in time for dinner, after which you will fall in on the jetty in your working gear.' He then shouted at one of the ratings to get off his backside and show us where the heads and washrooms were. I thought, 'That's a nice way to begin friendly relations!' The rating could not have been an H.O. or he would have been home by now. After showing us where the heads and washrooms were, he took us to the mess deck, as 'hands to dinner' had been piped. He told us where to sit, then said to grab a tray and get behind the queue.

We watched those in front of us sliding their trays along the counter and did the same. Soup, dinner and seconds all on the same tray. I said to Cesar, 'They have been eating like this, while we have been eating dehydrated rubbish!' Cesar said, 'Yeah, but I would sooner serve on a smaller ship.' I can't remember whether I agreed with him. Did I take my tray back? I can't remember that either!

Going back to the mess, I changed into my boiler suit, then fell in on the jetty. The P.O. said, 'There must be a shortage of sugar and melon and lemon jam.' Melon and lemon jam? I had never heard of it! The P.O. then said, 'There is a landing net over there, place four bags in the net, hook it on to the crane's hook, then the net will be hoisted up and over to the flight deck.' The bags were two hundred pounds each. Laying out the net, we humped four bags over and put them on the net, then hooked the net to the crane, and it was hoisted up and over on to the flight deck.

This continued until 1600 hours, when we packed up for the day. The P.O. said, 'All the melon and lemon has been loaded, the sugar will be finished tomorrow. The sugar has to be guarded, so you, Beedie, will finish the dog watches, then do the middle watch, then lucky you, you can have the rest of the day off. Now, you can go and get washed and changed into your number threes. After tea, get yourself up on the flight deck and guard that sugar!' He then added, 'Although I would like to see the joker who can nick a two-hundred-pound bag of sugar!' He then gave the 2000 hours to midnight, and the morning 400 hours to 0800 hours watch, to one of the other four – who would also be given the rest of the day off.

Cesar offered his sympathy, but didn't offer to take my place though. I washed, changed and had my tea, then made my way up to the flight deck and squatted, cheesed off, on one of the sugar bags. It soon began to get dark. I thought, 'The 1800 hours swill will soon be over, some of the crew will be on shore leave enjoying the fun, bless 'em!' I had the lights of Sydney to keep me company and a brilliant starry night.

I was relieved, in due course, by one of the four. He told me that nearly all the patients were on board, including some with mental conditions, who were accommodated in a caged-off area in the middle of the flight deck. Apparently there were also some old couples, taking passage home. By all accounts, the ship's fuel tanks were full to the brink, as she would be sailing nonstop to Portsmouth.

Before I left him, I told him I'd see him at midnight. I went below via the mess room in the hope of getting a cup of tea. No chance! So I went to the mess, where Cesar and the three others were playing cards, they were quite happy, having no watch to keep. I took off my collar, found a space on one of the lockers and using my cap as a pillow, got my head down. I would have to rely on instinct to wake up. I fell asleep straight away and woke at about 23.30, went for a quick wash and on my way back called into the mess room, in the hope of getting a cup of tea. There was a kitchen attached to the mess, in there were a few of the ship's company, smoking and having a yarn. They looked at me when I walked in and I said, 'Any chance of a cup of tea? I have the middle watch.' One of them said, 'No tea yet, only kye. Make yourself a corned beef sandwich if you wish.' I certainly did! Made myself a real doorstep of a sandwich with the crusty bread and lots of butter. Grabbing my cup of kye and my sandwich I made my way back to the mess, where I tidied myself up, slowly drinking the kye until I'd finished it.

It was time to go on watch, so munching my sandwich, I made my way to the flight deck and the pile of sugar sacks and a cheesed-off crew mate. I told him about the kitchen, but he said he was going to go straight down and get some sleep. He'd see me at 0400 hours – then he was gone.

It was going to be a long four hours, there was nothing to do and smoking was not allowed. I walked around the sacks to keep myself awake. At around 02.00 I sat on a sack, my cap was on the back of my head. Out of the gloom, two figures appeared, shining their torches in my face as they approached. One snapped, 'Who are you?' I answered, 'Sugar sentry.' Then I saw that he was a lieutenant and his companion was a P.O. He snapped, 'Stand up, stand to attention, put your cap on straight. I suppose you are one of those shore-based loafers!' I said, 'No, I have just left a seagoing frigate.' He replied, 'Well, the sooner you get big-ship bullshit in your head, the better for you! Take his name P.O.' I saluted him and he answered, then he and the P.O. departed and I thought 'Here we go again!' It turned out, that he was the so-called 'passenger officer' – OUCH!

I was relieved at 0400 hours, went below, undressed and had a shower. It was the first shower I had ever had in my life – it was great. I dried myself and put on clean underwear. I decided I would get some sleep, then after breakfast, I would do some dobeing – but where to dry it? I was hoping that a ship this size would have a laundry.

I turned in and soon fell asleep. I was woken by a thumping on my hammock, by a P.O. He said, 'Is your name Beedie?' Looking over the edge of my hammock, I replied, 'Yes.' He said, 'The passenger officer has made a list of names for various jobs. He has put you down as lookout, so turn out, get dressed, lash your hammock – then get yourself and your kit over into the watch-keeper's mess. I will show you. I will be back in half an hour, so get going!' I said, 'Yes P.O.' Although I didn't say it, I thought, 'The so-called passenger officer, the unprintable creep, has got me!'

I turned out quickly, got dressed, lashed my hammock, made sure all my kit was packed and my little brown case ready. The P.O. turned up, grabbed my hammock, saying, 'Follow me.' I humped my kitbag and brown case, following him through passage after passage, up a flight of ladders, into a quiet mess room. I was puffing and blowing. The P.O. said, 'You are not very fit are you!' I could not answer him. There were one or two asleep in hammocks and a couple more loafing about on lockers. The P.O. said, 'This is Fred Beedie, he is here as lookout, three more to come.' There were a few nods. I thought, 'I am here to do your job!'

'Hands to dinner' was piped, I followed the crowd. Another three-course dinner – unbelievable! After dinner I made my way back to the mess and said to one of the ratings, 'Is there a laundry?' He replied, 'Yes.' I said, 'I would rather do my own.' He said, 'I'll show you where you can do that, there is also a drying room, but make sure all your gear is heavily marked, or it will walk!'

I spent the afternoon catching up with my dobeing and drying it. The rating who had shown me where the drying room was had said that I could borrow the mess room iron, so I was able to do my ironing as well. When I had finished, I took my clean, ironed clothes back to the mess. There I found three new faces.

After tea, I and the other three had to decide who was going to be the starboard watch and who was going to be the port watch. There was a cribbage board with a pack of cards in the mess, so the cards were cut and dealt – the two highest would be starboard watch, the two lowest the port watch. I had a low card, so was in port watch. It was decided to cut the cards again, to see who would have first watch. Starboard watch got the honours! My opposite was a nice chap, all three were H.O.s, the others were proper sailors. The four of us were all badge men. I also had a gunners badge, the others also had badges of some sort, so there was no hassle.

The rating who said I could use the iron, said, 'I will show you the Air Defence Position (A.D.P.), it's the highest point on the ship. Up and up we all went, it was some height! We could see for miles. All we needed to know now was when would we sail? All the sugar and melon and lemon jam was loaded. All the patients were aboard and in their beds, lashed in. The weather was not very good. The tannoy then announced that we would leave at 1100 hours the next day.

The next morning, the ship was ready to leave Sydney for its non-stop journey to Portsmouth. Hands were to line ship. My oppo, as I will call him, said, 'Where do we go?' I said, 'I don't know.' The others said, 'Anywhere.' So we picked a spot and stood looking at all the waving Sydney-ites. I guessed that there would be a lot of tears being shed, as partnerships were broken up. Small boats were keeping up with us, waving and cheering and hooting.

Of course, we were not allowed to wave back – so we stood there, until she had left Sydney Harbour. We were then dismissed.

The ship sailed between the Sydney Heights and out into the Tasman Sea. Down into the mess we went. The P.O. came in and said, 'After dinner, the afternoon watchman will take the watch. That was the starboard watch. I and my oppo would not go on watch until noon the next day.

The ship could not go at full speed, that would use up too much fuel, so an economical speed was found, ensuring that the fuel would last the voyage. I settled down in the mess, knowing I was going to get a good night's sleep.

The weather was not improving. It was getting worse. By the time I went on watch at noon the next day, it was turning into a full gale. I thought that perhaps the Captain would take the ship down into the lower latitudes, where it was calmer than in the Great Australian Bight, which was one of the most treacherous seas in the world.

Then, life became a bore. All I and my oppo did was go on and off watch for twenty-four hours. There was nothing to do but get your head down. I would eat, do my dobeing and get ready to go on watch. On watch, all I could see was sea. The ship had now left the lower latitudes and was into the Indian Ocean. You can't imagine how big these seas are. Day after day, the same course. I was up in the A.D.P. getting roasted. I wondered how the patients were doing, it must be insufferable down there.

The ship was miles away from the shipping lanes, never saw a whale or a dolphin or a albatross. Nothing but empty sea. There was a tremendous amount of rain clouds, all of different sizes and shapes, just drifting across the ocean. I did not mind getting a drenching, when the ship sailed through one.

The ship must be getting near to Aden. At night we could

see lights far ahead. We sailed into the Gulf of Aden, there was more shipping around now. Then we sailed into the Red Sea. I kept reporting dhows on the port and starboard side. Although the ship's radar would also be picking them up, I had to keep a sharp eye out, or I would get a rollicking from the bridge.

The ship entered the Gulf of Suez and the Suez Canal, slowly passing the large lake on the left and the large army camp where Stripy was conned into thinking he was going home, but got drafted to a cruiser instead. I wondered how he was getting on. I hoped he was at home, tending to his roses. What a grand old sailor he was! We saw soldiers moving about and plenty of camels attended by Arabs. I had at last lost my yellow tan and my eyes were clear. I hadn't seen another sailor aboard with yellow skin and eyes, apart from Cesar, wherever he was.

The ship left the Suez Canal, passed Port Said, entering the Mediterranean Sea. What a bore! Once the ship had entered the Indian Ocean, the weather had improved. So far, it had been a fair sailing, although the Med can get nasty if it wants to. It must have been a relief to the patients that the sailing had been fair. There had not been any sea burials. Perhaps we had been lucky. Although I knew that the ship had facilities for burials at sea if needed.

We all wondered if the ship would stop at Malta to refuel, but no, she sailed on by. We passed Gibraltar and rounded into the Bay of Biscay, it was summer time, August 1946, and the weather in the bay was fair. We steamed up the English Channel, through the Solent. It was night time. I had the middle watch and reported quite a number of ships. We steamed through Portsmouth Harbour – it was about 0200 hours. I looked across at Portsmouth, thinking that it was just five years ago that I stood as a boy, with Dad and Mr. Stribley, and watched Portsmouth burn.

The ship tied up alongside the jetty, under the signal tower. I came off watch, without anybody telling me. I said to my oppo, 'I am going to have a wash and get my head down.' He said, 'So am I', which we did. Rise and shine at 0600 hours. The showers were in use, so I had to put up with a good wash, then went back to the mess to wait for breakfast. Then it would be a case of waiting to see what would happen.

The patients had been taken off the ship as soon as she docked. There were not that many H.O.s aboard. 'Stand easy' came and went. At about 1100 hours, the tannoy stated, 'All ratings for demobilisation to have all gear ready at the gang plank at 1400 hours.' 'Hands to dinner' was piped and I had my last three-course dinner. Lovely soup, minced beef with vegetables, rice with jam on the top.

At about 13.30 we four H.O.s started to help each other lug our gear down to the gangway. At 14.00, I and all the others, including Cesar, carried our gear down the gangplank onto the jetty. There were fifteen of us in total, all H.O.s A lorry came, we loaded all our gear, and it left for Stamshaw Camp. I thought, 'Here we go, another camp!' A coach arrived, and once we were all on board, took off through Portsmouth, past Whale Island, and after another mile, turned left into Stamshaw Camp – unfortunately another pit!

Our kitbags etc. had been dumped outside a hut. A P.O. told us we would have to stay overnight. We would be demobbed in the morning. Lugging our gear into the hut, I chose a bunk, sorted my gear out and thought, 'Tonight is my last night in the Navy!' Cesar was in great form, he could not get home quick enough to Coventry, to woo the ladies with his salty tales!

'Hands to tea' was piped. Once again it was bread, butter, jam or marmalade, followed by cake and tea. There was a canteen, so Cesar, myself and the other four decided to have a last drink together. There was only one Cesar! He had helped to keep our spirits up. The ship would be less happy without him. Frippy had been a natural comedian too, and being a proper sailor, had had no option but to take life as it came. I said, 'Well, there is one thing I will miss, and that is the soup!' They laughed and all agreed. With that, we all trooped back to the hut, where we cheered our last night in the Navy, then turned in.

As usual, rise and shine was at 0600 hours. Breakfast consisted of porridge and a cup of tea, then back to the hut to wait. There were only about a dozen of us left. A P.O. came into the hut, he said, 'You will leave your hammocks, that will be one less thing to carry. Your demob suit will be in a large oblong box. I suggest you should lash it with cod line to enable you to carry it over your shoulder.' We all agreed that that was a good idea. Cesar commented, 'Blimey a decent P.O.!' The P.O. produced a coil of cod line, which was cut into lengths. He gave each of us a piece, then said, 'You will fall in at 1000 hours.'

This we did, and were marched to the paymaster's office, where we formed a queue. The P.O. said goodbye, and was gone. When it was my turn, I marched into the office, a lieutenant commander was sat at a desk. I walked up, halted, saluted, he did not answer, just asked, 'Name and number.' I told him, he then said, 'You have one month's leave. I will give you one month's ration tokens, plus a railway warrant. Also, here is your gratuity booklet to the sum of £87. There are instructions on how to use it on the front. Your service papers[6] will be sent on to you. You will now receive all pay due to you, plus payment up to the day of your release, which will be the 24th September 1946. He passed the money across to me, and I picked it up and saluted. He made a gesture in return. I got the impression that he was a bit fed up!

I marched out of the office and picked up my kitbag, demob box and brown case, which was lashed to the side with a loop. The P.O. said, 'You can go.' I walked out of the gate. There were touts offering £5 for my demob box. I waved them away, deciding to wait for Cesar. When he came through, he politely told the touts to 'Get lost!' Then with our kitbags on our left shoulders and our demob box and brown cases over our right shoulders, we trudged off to where the others were also gathering.

We had to stop twice on our way to the train station, to get our breath and rearrange our gear on our shoulders; it was further than we thought. The trams run on the main roads in Portsmouth and there were no buses. We bought our railway tickets with our warrant cards, and when the London train arrived, we all piled on board, it would go down to Southampton before going on to London. On arrival in Southampton, I humped my kit on to the platform with the help of Cesar and there were hand shakes all round. It was almost tearful to say goodbye to Cesar, he had been a very good shipmate and friend. We knew we would never see each other again. We slapped each other on the shoulder and he climbed back on the train, waving, as it slowly pulled away and disappeared from sight. Another good friend gone.

I humped my gear over to the platform for the Bournemouth train. I had my one-way ticket ready. The train arrived and I humped my gear on board, and into an empty carriage. I sat there, dwelling on what had happened over the last sixteen months. The train pulled out and made its way to Bournemouth Central Station.

When we reached Bournemouth, I humped my gear off the train and made my way out to the road to hail a taxi. I soon had a ride, and the driver helped me to load my gear into the boot. Getting into the taxi, he said, 'Where to?' I said, '99 Bryant

Road, Wallisdown, please.' The taxi took off and the driver said, 'You look as if you have been in the sun.' I replied, 'Yes, I have.' I told him about the ship I had been on, and how we had been out in the Far East, telling him the names of a few places we had been. He said, 'Sounds like a Cook's tour!' I said, 'Yes, it does.'

Arriving outside number 99, he said, 'Have this ride on me.' I replied, 'Well, thank you, but at least have a drink on me.' I gave him a pound, and he helped me to hump my gear out of the boot. He said, 'Cheerio mate.' I answered, 'Cheerio', then I opened the gate that I had shut sixteen months earlier, walked down the path and around to the back door. I walked in, put my gear on the kitchen floor and shouted, 'Hello Mum, I'm home!'

Endnotes

1 Anderson Shelter – Designed in 1938 to help Britain prepare for German air raids. Named after Sir John Anderson. Could shelter up to six people. Constructed mainly of six sheets of corrugated steel, bent in an arch shape (like a small Nissen hut) with corrugated steel end panels, one of which contained the door. Families were supplied with the materials and constructed their own shelters, using the instructions provided.

2 Morrison Shelter (or table shelter) – Designed by John Baker and named after the Minister of Home Security, Herbert Morrison. Mainly consisted of a steel table-like top and mesh sides, one of which could be lifted open to act as a door. Could be used as a table during the day and slept in at night. Came in kit form for families to assemble in the home.

3 H.M.S. *Alresford* – H.M.S. *Alresford*, was sold to Belgium for mercantile use on 13th March 1947.

4 Wallisdown Football Club – Albert Franklin, the landlord of the Kings Arms in Wallisdown, got his football team in the end. Farmer Vine allowed them to use the field that we used to use when training with Captain Pusey's stalwarts. I believe that Wallisdown Football Club were still playing until quite recently. Here are a few names of those who started Wallisdown F.C. – Peter and Pat Vine (the farmer's sons). R. Woods, Army. S. Light, Royal Marines. D. Wade, Navy. W. Blakeley, R.A.F. B. Pounds, Navy. D. Claxton, Army – he served in the fourteenth army in Burma, he was a bricklayer. I heard that he fell from some scaffolding, and broke his back, I don't know if he survived the accident, I certainly hope he did.

5   The H.M.S. Whitesand Bay Association – Many years later, my wife and I were attending an annual reunion of H.M.S. *Whitesand Bay*'s Association, at the Union Jack Club in London. The Association consisted of shipmates from all the commissions up to 1955, when H.M.S. *Whitesand Bay* was scrapped. During the evening, a shipmate approached me, he had a gentleman with him. He said, 'This is Wiggy's brother, he would like to know what happened to him.'

Wiggy's brother did not want to shake hands or have a drink, so I got on and told him everything that I knew had happened. I explained that a cutter had come alongside with a chaplain and a Navy doctor on board; how they were looking for another ship, but that the doctor had agreed to look at Wiggy when told that our Maltese doctor, who had left the ship, had been treating him for flu, but he wasn't getting any better. As I was telling the story, Wiggy's brother's face was hardening and his fists were clenched. I told him how the doctor was only gone five minutes and when he came back, told us that Wiggy was very ill and that we needed to call for a hospital boat right away, which we did.

I explained how Wiggy's shipmates had wrapped him in a blanket, and carefully brought him down to the quarterdeck and onto the hospital boat, which took him to a hospital ship. I went on to tell him that the *Whitesand Bay* had then set sail for French Indo-China and that three days later we got the news that Wiggy had died. The brother's face had turned white, his face was a hard mask, his fists still clenched. He gave me one last look, turned on his heels and walked out of the club.

I returned to my table – there was Frippy, Mosely, Smy, Booth, Brighton, Reed and Lacey, with our wives of course. No Brummie or Cesar. I told them about Wiggy's brother and how he had been white with fury when he heard what had happened, but had not said a word, had just walked out. Frippy said that he thought the brother had every right to be angry. We all agreed.

Lieutenant Benson, R.N.V.R. attended the reunion one or two times, the sub-lieutenant and the Captain attended once. The midshipman was at every reunion, he had completely changed.

The Association has been finished many years now. I am the only one left from my commission, all the others have 'crossed the bar'.

6   My service papers – About two weeks later, I received an 'On His Majesty's Service' letter, informing me that my service with the Royal Navy would cease on the 24th September 1946. Also enclosed, were my service papers. I had been released under Class A. The letter informed me that in the event of future enemy conflict, I would be called back into the service under Class A.

Photographs

Fig 1.   Malta, with Brummie, Leicester and Yarker.

Fig 2.   Port Said. Given to me by a shipmate at the H.M.S. Whitesand Bay
Association reunion.

Fig 3.   Me and the P.O.G.I. aboard the *Whitesand Bay*. Given to me by a
shipmate at the H.M.S. Whitesand Bay Association reunion.

Fig 4.   Temples at Port of Cam Pha. Given to me by a shipmate at the
H.M.S. Whitesand Bay Association reunion.

Fig 5.   Escorting the B.Y.M.S. Given to me by a shipmate at the H.M.S.
Whitesand Bay Association reunion.

Fig 6.   The Labuan War Cemetery. Given to me by the tough Australian
Sergeant, as a reminder of the horrors that had occurred there.

Fig 7.   H.M.S. *Whitesand Bay*, taken by a photographer in Sydney.

Lightning Source UK Ltd.
Milton Keynes UK
UKHW011149230320
360766UK00002B/798